SIXTH EDITION

INTERACTIONS
Reading

1

Elaine Kirn

Pamela Hartmann

Lawrence J. Zwier
Contributor, Focus on Testing

McGraw Hill

Interactions 1 Reading, Sixth Edition

Published by McGraw-Hill ESL/ELT, a business unit of The McGraw-Hill Companies, Inc.,
1221 Avenue of the Americas, New York, NY 10020. Copyright © 2014 by The McGraw-Hill
Companies, Inc. All rights reserved. Printed in the United States of America. Previous editions
© 2007, 2001, and 1995. No part of this publication may be reproduced or distributed in any
form or by any means, or stored in a database or retrieval system, without the prior written
consent of The McGraw-Hill Companies, Inc., including, but not limited to, in any network
or other electronic storage or transmission, or broadcast for distance learning.

Some ancillaries, including electronic and print components, may not be available to customers
outside the United States.

This book is printed on acid-free paper.

3 4 5 6 7 8 9 0 DOW/DOW 1 0 9 8 7 6 5 4

ISBN: 978-0-07-759507-4
MHID: 0-07-759507-6

Senior Vice President, Products & Markets: Kurt L. Strand
Vice President, General Manager, Products & Markets: Michael J. Ryan
Vice President, Content Production & Technology Services: Kimberly Meriwether David
Director of Development: Valerie Kelemen
Marketing Manager: Cambridge University Press
Lead Project Manager: Rick Hecker
Senior Buyer: Michael R. McCormick
Designer: Page2, LLC
Cover/Interior Designer: Page2, LLC
Senior Content Licensing Specialist: Keri Johnson
Manager, Digital Production: Janean A. Utley
Compositor: Page2, LLC
Printer: RR Donnelley

Cover photo: Matej Kastelic/Shutterstock.com

All credits appearing on page iv or at the end of the book are considered to be an extension
of the copyright page.

The Internet addresses listed in the text were accurate at the time of publication. The
inclusion of a website does not indicate an endorsement by the authors or McGraw-Hill, and
McGraw-Hill does not guarantee the accuracy of the information presented at these sites.

www.mhhe.com

www.elt.mcgraw-hill.com

A Special Thank You

The Interactions/Mosaic 6th edition team wishes to thank our extended team: teachers, students, administrators, and teacher trainers, all of whom contributed invaluably to the making of this edition.

Maiko Berger, **Ritsumeikan Asia Pacific University**, Oita, Japan • Aaron Martinson, **Sejong Cyber University**, Seoul, Korea • Aisha Osman, Egypt • Amy Stotts, **Chubu University**, Aichi, Japan • Charles Copeland, **Dankook University**, Yongin City, Korea • Christen Savage, **University of Houston**, Texas, USA • Daniel Fitzgerald, **Metropolitan Community College**, Kansas, USA • Deborah Bollinger, **Aoyama Gakuin University**, Tokyo, Japan • Duane Fitzhugh, **Northern Virginia Community College**, Virginia, USA • Gregory Strong, **Aoyama Gakuin University**, Tokyo, Japan • James Blackwell, **Ritsumeikan Asia Pacific University**, Oita, Japan • Janet Harclerode, **Santa Monica College**, California, USA • Jinyoung Hong, **Sogang University**, Seoul, Korea • Lakkana Chaisaklert, **Rajamangala University of Technology Krung Thep**, Bangkok, Thailand • Lee Wonhee, **Sogang University**, Seoul, Korea • Matthew Gross, **Konkuk University**, Seoul, Korea • Matthew Stivener, **Santa Monica College**, California, USA • Pawadee Srisang, **Burapha University**, Chantaburi, Thailand • Steven M. Rashba, **University of Bridgeport**, Connecticut, USA • Sudatip Prapunta, **Prince of Songkla University**, Trang, Thailand • Tony Carnerie, **University of California San Diego**, California, USA

Photo Credits

Table of Contents

A 21st-Century Course for the Modern Student

Interactions/Mosaic prepares students for university classes by fully integrating every aspect of student life. Based on 28 years of classroom-tested best practices, the new and revised content, fresh modern look, and new online component make this the perfect series for contemporary classrooms.

Proven Instruction that Ensures Academic Success

Modern Content:
From social networking to gender issues and from academic honesty to discussions of Skype, *Interactions/Mosaic* keeps students connected to learning by selecting topics that are interesting and relevant to modern students.

Digital Component:
The fully integrated online course offers a rich environment that expands students' learning and supports teachers' teaching with automatically graded practice, assessment, classroom presentation tools, online community, and more.

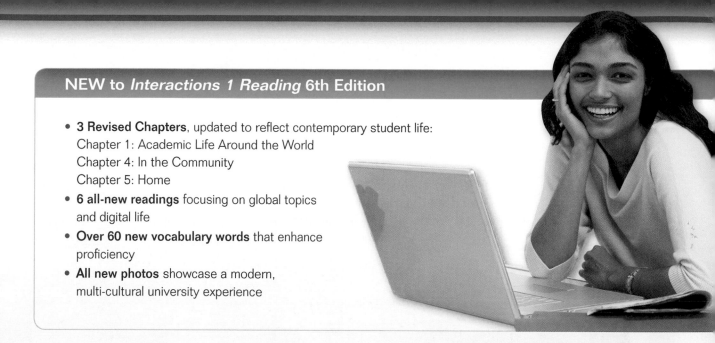

NEW to *Interactions 1 Reading* 6th Edition

- **3 Revised Chapters**, updated to reflect contemporary student life:
  Chapter 1: Academic Life Around the World
  Chapter 4: In the Community
  Chapter 5: Home
- **6 all-new readings** focusing on global topics and digital life
- **Over 60 new vocabulary words** that enhance proficiency
- **All new photos** showcase a modern, multi-cultural university experience

Emphasis on Vocabulary:

Each chapter teaches vocabulary intensively and comprehensively. This focus on learning new words is informed by more than 28 years of classroom testing and provides students with the exact language they need to communicate confidently and fluently.

Practical Critical Thinking:

Students develop their ability to synthesize, analyze, and apply information from different sources in a variety of contexts: from comparing academic articles to negotiating informal conversations.

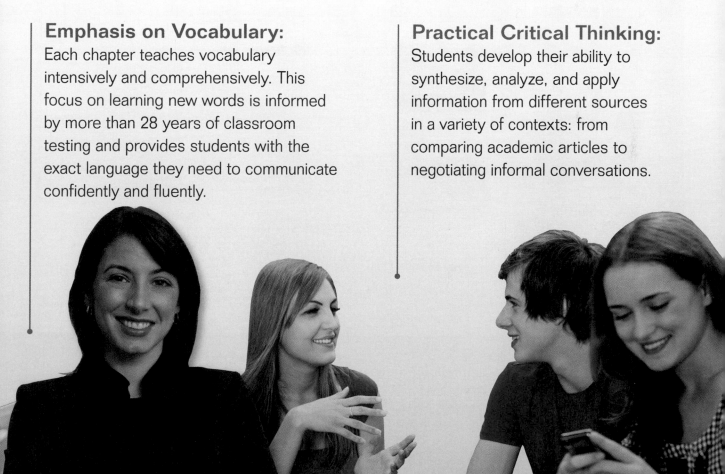

Highlights of *Interactions 1 Reading* 6th Edition

Part 1: Reading Skills and Strategies
Each chapter begins with a text on an engaging, academic topic that teaches students the skills that they need to be successful.

Communication for the Modern Student
A focus on real-life and academic communication based on engaging readings prepares students for success in school and in life.

Part 2: Main Ideas and Details Students are challenged by a second text and learn crucial reading skills like skimming for main ideas and finding supporting details.

---

2. Do you live at home with your family, in an apartment with others your age, in a dormitory or residence hall, in a private home, or in another living situation? Give details for your answer.

3. Do you feel comfortable in living situations with unfamiliar strangers? Why or why not? What are the advantages (good features) and disadvantages (possible problems) of living with people who are not relatives?

4. How can strangers become upset with each other? How can they become close friends?

PART 2 Main Ideas and Details

Reasons *Not* to Live in Shared Housing Situations

Before You Read

1 Previewing Vocabulary Read the vocabulary items below from the second reading. Then listen to the words and phrases. Put a check mark (✓) next to the words you don't know Don't use a dictionary.

Nouns		Adjectives	
academics	opportunities	crowded	valuable
comfort	safety	homesick	well-paying
debt		insecure	
decision	**Verbs**	lonely	**Adverb**
excuses	care	miserable	academically
expense	harm	terrible	
harm	miss	unsafe	
luxury	take chances		
	waste		

FOCUS

Recognizing Topics, Main Ideas, and Supporting Details in a Paragraph
• The word *topic* means "the subject of speech or writing." A paragraph usually tells about one topic. The paragraph heading gives information about its topic.
• The *main idea* tells the most important point, or idea, about the topic. Sometimes one or two sentences of a paragraph tell the main idea.
• *Supporting details* give examples or more information about the main idea.

Example

Don't Live in a Campus Dorm!

A dormitory or residence hall is the worst kind of shared housing on a college or university campus. That's because you have to live closely with strangers. These people probably have unpleasant personalities, bad habits, and negative values. The building may be crowded, noisy, dirty, and uncomfortable. The food can be terrible. You can't stay healthy, study, or succeed in higher learning if you live with others.

Topic: In the example above, the title is the topic. It's the advice "Don't Live in a Campus Dorm!"

Main Idea: The first and last sentences are underlined. The first gives the main point of the whole topic. The last summarizes the most important idea.

Supporting Details: Other sentences give *reasons* for the negative advice: possible personalities and habits or values of residents, features of the building, bad food, and effects on you if you choose dorm life.

Read

FOCUS

Reasons Why *Not*...
Sometimes reasons *not* to do something help in important decision-making. Here is some negative advice on housing situations, leaving home, academic study, and decision making. They are different people's *opinions*, of course. As you read, you can consider how their reasoning makes you feel. Does it help you think or does it make thinking more difficult? Can you think of reasons that are the *opposite* of these writers' views?

2 Recognizing the Topics and Main Ideas of Paragraphs Read the following article. Then answer these questions about the article.

1. What is the title and topic of the whole article?

2. What is the topic of each paragraph? (Hint: Look at the paragraph heading.)

A. _____

B. _____

C. _____

D. _____

3. What is the main idea of each paragraph? Underline one or two sentences and then read them aloud. Remember: the main idea is not always the first sentence. As an example, a possible summary and a main-point sentence have been underlined in Paragraph A.

Topics for the Modern Student
Engaging social and academic topics draw the student in, making learning more engaging and more efficient.

Part 3: Vocabulary and Language-Learning Skills This section helps students become independent readers, teaching them how to get meaning from context and infer word definitions.

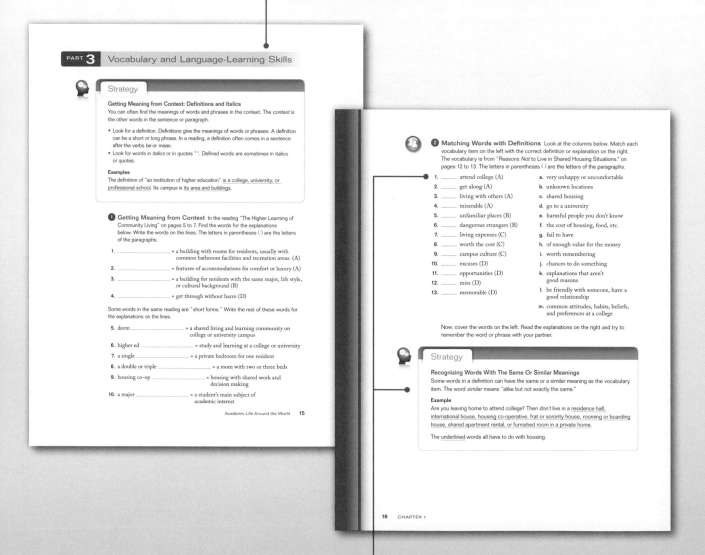

PART 3 Vocabulary and Language-Learning Skills

Strategy

Getting Meaning from Context: Definitions and Italics
You can often find the meanings of words and phrases in the context. The *context* is the other words in the sentence or paragraph.

- Look for a definition. Definitions give the meanings of words or phrases. A definition can be a short or long phrase. In a reading, a definition often comes in a sentence after the verbs *be* or *mean*.
- Look for words in *italics* or in quotes " ". Defined words are sometimes in italics or quotes.

Examples
The definition of "an institution of higher education" <u>is a college, university, or professional school</u>. Its *campus* <u>is its area and buildings</u>.

1 **Getting Meaning from Context** In the reading "The Higher Learning of Community Living" on pages 5 to 7. Find the words for the explanations below. Write the words on the lines. The letters in parentheses ( ) are the letters of the paragraphs.

1. _____ = a building with rooms for residents, usually with common bathroom facilities and recreation areas. (A)

2. _____ = features of accommodations for comfort or luxury (A)

3. _____ = a building for residents with the same major, life style, or cultural background (B)

4. _____ = get through without harm (D)

Some words in the same reading are "short forms." Write the rest of these words for the explanations on the lines.

5. dorm _____ = a shared living and learning community on college or university campus

6. higher ed _____ = study and learning at a college or university

7. a single _____ = a private bedroom for one resident

8. a double or triple _____ = a room with two or three beds

9. housing co-op _____ = housing with shared work and decision making

10. a major _____ = a student's main subject of academic interest

Academic Life Around the World **15**

2 **Matching Words with Definitions** Look at the columns below. Match each vocabulary item on the left with the correct definition or explanation on the right. The vocabulary is from "Reasons *Not* to Live in Shared Housing Situations." on pages 12 to 13. The letters in parentheses ( ) are the letters of the paragraphs.

1. _____ attend college (A)   a. very unhappy or uncomfortable
2. _____ get along (A)   b. unknown locations
3. _____ living with others (A)   c. shared housing
4. _____ miserable (A)   d. go to a university
5. _____ unfamiliar places (B)   e. harmful people you don't know
6. _____ dangerous strangers (B)   f. the cost of housing, food, etc.
7. _____ living expenses (C)   g. fail to have
8. _____ worth the cost (C)   h. of enough value for the money
9. _____ campus culture (C)   i. worth remembering
10. _____ excuses (D)   j. chances to do something
11. _____ opportunities (D)   k. explanations that aren't good reasons
12. _____ miss (D)   l. be friendly with someone, have a good relationship
13. _____ memorable (D)   m. common attitudes, habits, beliefs, and preferences at a college

Now, cover the words on the left. Read the explanations on the right and try to remember the word or phrase with your partner.

Strategy

Recognizing Words With The Same Or Similar Meanings
Some words in a definition can have the same or a similar meaning as the vocabulary item. The word *similar* means "alike but not exactly the same."

Example
Are you leaving home to attend college? Then *don't* live in a <u>residence hall, international house, housing co-operative, frat or sorority house, rooming or boarding house, shared apartment rental, or furnished room in a private home</u>.

The <u>underlined</u> words all have to do with housing.

16 CHAPTER 1

Emphasis on Vocabulary Each chapter presents, practices, and carefully recycles vocabulary-learning strategies and vocabulary words essential to the modern student.

x

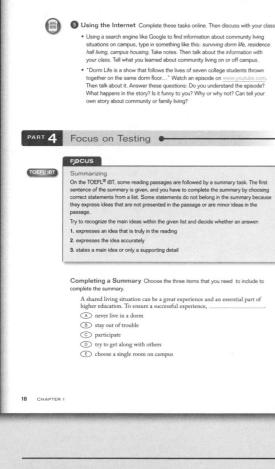

5 **Using the Internet** Complete these tasks online. Then discuss with your class.

- Using a search engine like Google to find information about community living situations on campus, type in something like this: *surviving dorm life, residence hall living, campus housing.* Take notes. Then talk about the information with your class. Tell what you learned about community living on or off campus.

- "Dorm Life is a show that follows the lives of seven college students thrown together on the same dorm floor…" Watch an episode on www.youtube.com. Then talk about it. Answer these questions: Do you understand the episode? What happens in the story? Is it funny to you? Why or why not? Can tell your own story about community or family living?

PART 4 Focus on Testing

FOCUS

TOEFL® iBT

Summarizing

On the TOEFL® iBT, some reading passages are followed by a summary task. The first sentence of the summary is given, and you have to complete the summary by choosing correct statements from a list. Some statements do not belong in the summary because they express ideas that are not presented in the passage or are minor ideas in the passage.

Try to recognize the main ideas within the given list and decide whether an answer:

1. expresses an idea that is truly in the reading

2. expresses the idea accurately

3. states a main idea or only a supporting detail

Completing a Summary Choose the three items that you need to include to complete the summary.

A shared living situation can be a great experience and an essential part of higher education. To ensure a successful experience, _____

- (A) never live in a dorm
- (B) stay out of trouble
- (C) participate
- (D) try to get along with others
- (E) choose a single room on campus

18   CHAPTER 1

Part 4: Focus on Testing Students learn how to prepare for both typical college exams and international assessments.

Results for Students A carefully structured program presents and practices academic skills and strategies purposefully, leading to strong student results and more independent learners.

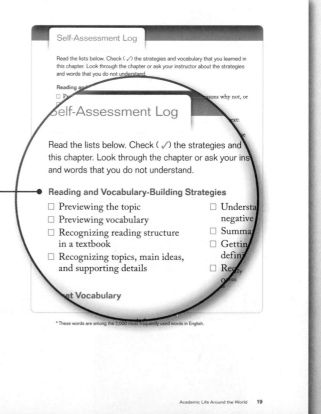

Self-Assessment Log

Read the lists below. Check (✓) the strategies and vocabulary that you learned in this chapter. Look through the chapter or ask your instructor about the strategies and words that you do not understand.

Reading and
☐ Pr   asons why not, or

                                                                        xt:

Self-Assessment Log

Read the lists below. Check (✓) the strategies and this chapter. Look through the chapter or ask your ins and words that you do not understand.

Reading and Vocabulary-Building Strategies
☐ Previewing the topic   ☐ Understa
☐ Previewing vocabulary   negative
☐ Recognizing reading structure   ☐ Summa
   in a textbook   ☐ Gettin
☐ Recognizing topics, main ideas,   defini
   and supporting details   ☐ Re

et Vocabulary

* These words are among the 2,000 most frequently used words in English.

Academic Life Around the World   **19**

xi

Scope and Sequence

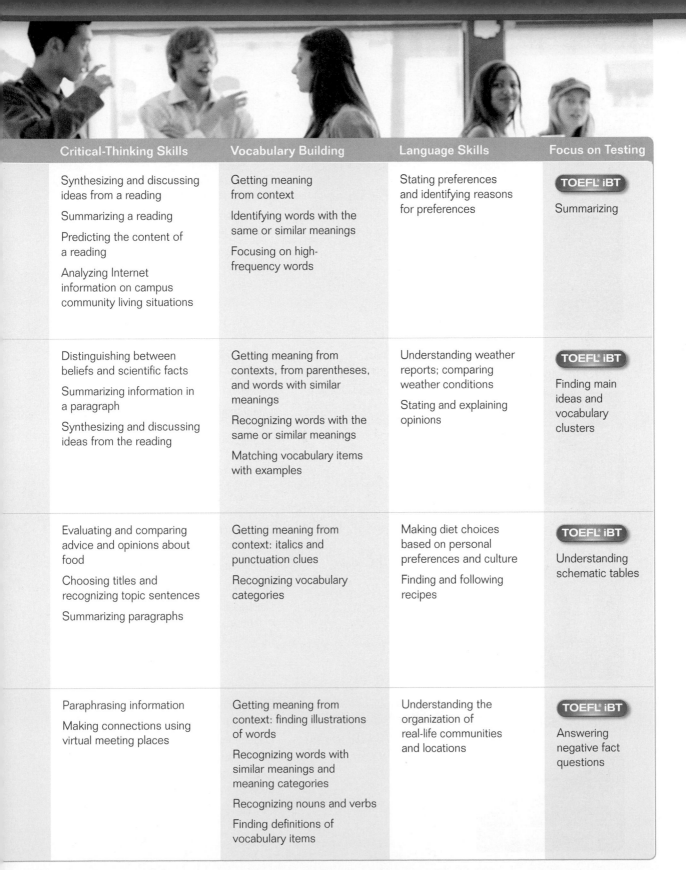

Critical-Thinking Skills	Vocabulary Building	Language Skills	Focus on Testing
Synthesizing and discussing ideas from a reading Summarizing a reading Predicting the content of a reading Analyzing Internet information on campus community living situations	Getting meaning from context Identifying words with the same or similar meanings Focusing on high-frequency words	Stating preferences and identifying reasons for preferences	**TOEFL® iBT** Summarizing
Distinguishing between beliefs and scientific facts Summarizing information in a paragraph Synthesizing and discussing ideas from the reading	Getting meaning from contexts, from parentheses, and words with similar meanings Recognizing words with the same or similar meanings Matching vocabulary items with examples	Understanding weather reports; comparing weather conditions Stating and explaining opinions	**TOEFL® iBT** Finding main ideas and vocabulary clusters
Evaluating and comparing advice and opinions about food Choosing titles and recognizing topic sentences Summarizing paragraphs	Getting meaning from context: italics and punctuation clues Recognizing vocabulary categories	Making diet choices based on personal preferences and culture Finding and following recipes	**TOEFL® iBT** Understanding schematic tables
Paraphrasing information Making connections using virtual meeting places	Getting meaning from context: finding illustrations of words Recognizing words with similar meanings and meaning categories Recognizing nouns and verbs Finding definitions of vocabulary items	Understanding the organization of real-life communities and locations	**TOEFL® iBT** Answering negative fact questions

Scope and Sequence

Critical-Thinking Skills	Vocabulary Building	Language Skills	Focus on Testing
Summarizing historical information and ideas Researching and evaluating historical information online	Getting meaning from context: punctuation and phrase clues Recognizing words with similar and opposite meanings Recognizing nouns and adjectives	Researching and discussing family housing in different cultures	**TOEFL iBT** Understanding definitions and explanations
Interpreting and discussing anecdotes Summarizing an anecdote	Understanding new vocabulary in context Recognizing nouns, verbs, and adjectives Understanding adverbs of manner	Recognizing and discussing cultural attitudes and customs Researching and reporting on unfamiliar cultures	**TOEFL iBT** Practicing vocabulary questions
Choosing information to complete a mind map Summarizing using a mind map	Figuring out new or difficult vocabulary Identifying synonyms Identifying parts of speech from suffixes Choosing word forms with suffixes	Giving advice about health Evaluating and agreeing or disagreeing with health tips	**TOEFL iBT** Practicing for timed readings
Completing an outline with reading material Evaluating the advantages and disadvantages of the media Classifying different types of stories Summarizing a story	Understanding suffixes (nouns, adverbs, adjectives) Understanding word families	Retelling a story plot Discussing and justifying media choices Persuading others to watch a particular show	**TOEFL iBT** Focusing on comparison and contrast

Scope and Sequence

Critical-Thinking Skills	Vocabulary Building	Language Skills	Focus on Testing
Summarizing stories by identifying pros and cons Interpreting proverbs	Understanding negative prefixes Figuring out vocabulary from prefixes and suffixes Recognizing words with similar meanings	Discussing and comparing proverbs Researching poems, quotes, and proverbs	**TOEFL iBT** Understanding inferences and points of view in readings
Comparing and contrasting the ancient and modern Olympics Classifying supporting details Recognizing point of view Distinguishing opinion from fact Summarizing opinions	Understanding and working with prefixes, stems, and suffixes Identifying antonyms	Researching and supporting points of view on competitive sports Convincing others to understand a point of view	**TOEFL iBT** Taking notes and recognizing contrasts in reading passages

1 Academic Life Around the World

> We learn more by looking for the answer to a question and not finding it than we do from learning the answer itself.

Lloyd Alexander
American author

In Part 1, you will read about different living arrangements for students and other college-aged adults. In the rest of the chapter, you will read about, discuss and explore pros and cons of different types of housing.

 Connecting to the Topic

1. The people in this photo live in this building. What do these people do?

2. Describe the kind of housing these women live in. Would you like to live in this kind of building?

3. What are some advantages and disadvantages of living on a university campus?

The Higher Learning of Community Living

Before You Read

1 **Previewing the Topic** Look at the descriptions of the photos. Next to each description, write the number of the matching photo.

_____ Relaxing in a messy room

_____ At home relaxing with friends

_____ At home studying

_____ In a dorm room studying

▲ Photo 1

▲ Photo 3

▲ Photo 2

▲ Photo 4

In small groups, look at the photos and discuss these questions.

1. What is each place? Who are the people? (Examples: family, friends, college students, roommates/housemates) What are they doing?

2. Imagine the conversation in each picture. What do you think the people are saying or texting to one another?

3. How is each situation like your own? How is it different?

2 Predicting Work in groups of three. Think and talk about possible answers to these questions. Write them down.

1. What are some kinds of living accommodations on college campuses or in the community? Describe them.

2. How might residents of shared housing be similar? How might they be different?

3. What are some possible challenges (problems) in sharing living situations with strangers (not family)? List three.

4. What is some good advice for occupants of the same room or apartment? Give your group one suggestion.

3 Previewing Vocabulary Read the vocabulary words from the first reading. Then listen to the words and phrases. Put a check mark (✓) next to the words you don't know. Don't use a dictionary.

Nouns		Verbs	Adjectives
▩ advice	▩ lifestyle	▩ attend	▩ common
▩ attitudes	▩ major (area	▩ get along	▩ considerate
▩ challenges	of study)	▩ get through	▩ private
▩ community	▩ personalities	▩ relate	▩ shared
▩ cultural	▩ privacy	▩ stay out of	▩ similar
background	▩ rules	▩ survive	
▩ features	▩ security		**Adverb**
▩ habits	▩ strangers		▩ away from home
▩ interests	▩ variety		

Read

4 Reading an Article Read the following article. Then do the activities that follow.

The Higher Learning of Community Living

Introduction and Definitions

A   Before college, most young people around the world live in a family home. Their first living experience **away from home** may be in a dormitory or residence hall at an "institution of higher ed (education)." One definition of *dorm* is "a building with rooms for residents, usually with **common** bathroom facilities and recreation areas." In many ways, college dormitories are like other kinds of **shared** housing, like co-ops (co-operatives), international houses, apartment rentals, or **private** homes. Both on campus and in the larger **community**, shared living accommodations vary in size, number of occupants, cost, facilities, amenities, and other **features**. Residents without

5

their own (bed)rooms may have to share space in doubles or triples with one or 10
two roommates. But even occupants with private single rooms have to **relate**
to people of various **lifestyles** and **habits** in the same building or area. In fact,
some institutions define *dormitory* as "a shared living and learning community
on a college or university campus." That's because the main advantage of any
kind of communal living is the "higher learning" of **getting along** with others. 15

The Residents of Campus Housing

B   The occupants of residence halls or other kinds of shared living
accommodations can differ greatly. On some campuses, first-year students
have to live in dormitories, so most dorm residents are of **similar** ages. In
"special interest housing," building residents may have the same **major** (area
of study), lifestyle, or **cultural background**. Even so, they will have a **variety** 20
of **interests**, experiences, habits, **personalities**, **attitudes**, and preferences.
Survival means "getting through the experience without harm." So what is
most important for survival in shared living situations? It's good relationships!
For "higher learning" at colleges or universities, or in the larger community, not
only students but also other adults need to relate to one or more roommates, 25
residents on the same floor, or occupants of the same building or area.

Some Challenges of Communal Living

C   What are some possible challenges of living with others? What if there's
not enough space, **privacy**, quiet, cleanliness, healthy living, or **security**? What
about bad relationships with roommates or housemates, different lifestyles, or
unwanted company? Without solutions, such differences can grow to big 30
problems for young people away from home and family for the first time. They
may be happy about their new independence, but the challenges of transition
to community living with **strangers** can be difficult.

How to Survive Living with Others

D   Shared living situations can be one of the best (or worst) parts of adult life.
How can we **get through** this transitional time of life without harm? People 35
with experience in living with others give this **advice**. 1. It's most important
to get along with the other residents of the same room, floor, building, or area.
Be **considerate** and pleasant. You may not become close friends, but don't be
enemies! 2. Next in importance to surviving communal living situations is
to **stay out of** trouble. Be direct and honest (not shy) about your own needs 40
and values. Do you want to stay healthy? To stay out of harmful situations?
To study and learn well? 3. And finally, participate in shared living! Create
house **rules** and follow them. **Attend** meetings and other educational events.
Stay informed, and get to know good people! If you're true to your own values,
you'll "**survive**" nearly any kind of new living experience. And it may even 45
become one of the best memories of your life!

Conclusion and Summary

E   For some people, their first experience away from home and family is
in a shared living situation at a college or university. Other adults may need
or want to live communally later in life. People are different, of course, so

it's very important to get along with roommates, housemates, and others 50
in the same area or community. Following rules, staying out of trouble,
and participating are good ways to meet the possible **challenges** of
residential living.

After You Read

5 **Getting the Main Ideas** Read the following main ideas for the five
paragraphs in the reading "The Higher Learning of Community Living." Match
each main idea with its related paragraph. Write the letter of the paragraph
on the line after the number.

1. _____ Especially for young people away from home for the first time, some
features of shared living situations can make college life difficult.

2. _____ Even if the occupants of a residence hall and other communal living
accommodations are very different from one another, they need
positive relationships.

3. _____ Many students' first living experience away from home and family is in
a dorm or shared living community with unfamiliar strangers.

4. _____ Probably, the best ways to "survive" a college or other shared living
experience are to get along with others, to stay out of trouble, and to
take part in educational events.

5. _____ In conclusion, difficult or challenging residential living situations with
others can become positive, memorable experiences if people follow
good advice.

Strategy

Recognizing Supporting Details in Paragraphs
The information in each paragraph of a reading selection tells more than the main
idea. It also gives details about the main idea. *Details* are "single or specific pieces of
information." Some kinds of details are definitions, examples, reasons, and advice.

6 **Recognizing Supporting Details** Read the five main idea questions about the reading "The Higher Learning of Community Living." Three details correctly answer each question. Cross out the untrue, unrelated detail. The first item is an example.

1. What are the meanings of some words related to shared living situations in higher ed?
   a. A *dorm*, or *dormitory*, is a *residence hall* on a college or university *campus*.
   b. ~~Occupants is another word for cultural facilities, recreation areas, amenities, and other features of academic life.~~
   c. *Singles*, *doubles*, and *triples*, are kinds of bedrooms in residential buildings. They have different numbers of *occupants:* one, two, and three.
   d. Other than *dorms*, some kinds of buildings where unrelated adults may live together are *international houses*, *cooperatives*, apartment rentals, and even private homes

2. What is usually true about the occupants of a campus residence hall or other shared or community housing?
   a. Young people away from home for the first time don't need housing because their new independence brings them higher learning.
   b. On college campuses and in the community, people other than first-year students can choose from different kinds of shared living accommodations
   c. Even students or other adults with the same area of study, cultural backgrounds, or life styles can have different interests, habits, and personalities.
   d. Occupants of the same room, floor, or building have to relate to one another. Good relationships will probably make their living experience more pleasant.

3. What are some potential problems or challenges of life in on-campus dormitories or other kinds of shared housing?
   a. There may not be enough space, privacy, or quiet. Residents may feel uncomfortable with crowding, noise, or the company of strangers. It may be impossible to study or stay healthy.
   b. Roommates or other occupants may be from unfamiliar places or cultural backgrounds. They may have different lifestyles. They may use harmful substances.
   c. Young people away from home and family for the first time may find it difficult to "transition" to independence in their academic life. So may other adults in other life situations.
   d. The building appearance, location, cost, and amenities can be the best possible. The food is probably the best in the world. There can be too much comfort and luxury.

4. How might students and others meet the challenges of community living in academic or other life situations?
   a. They can have considerate and pleasant attitudes toward roommates and other people in the house or residence hall.
   b. They can get into trouble from shyness about their health, use of substances, and success in their studies.
   c. They can be direct and honest about their own needs and values. They can stay away from harmful or dangerous situations.
   d. They can make and follow rules, attend meetings and events, stay informed, and get to know good people.

5. What are the main points of the reading selection "The Higher Learning of Community Living?"

a. Some young people transition to independence from family in shared housing situations on a college and university campus. Others do so later in life in the larger community.

b. For the first time, they live closely with strangers. They have to get along with people with different backgrounds, personalities, attitudes, preferences, and values.

c. For a successful, positive, and memorable college or later life experience, it's important to follow rules, stay out of trouble, and participate in helpful events and activities.

d. Shared housing experiences are always negative and dangerous. Stay at home with your family. And don't live in a quad!

Now go back to Activity 2 on page 5 and look at the questions again. Look at the answers you wrote down before you read the article. Change them if necessary.

- Give definitions or explanations in your answer to Question 1.
- Tell similarities and differences in your answers to Question 2.
- Describe situations in your answers to Question 3.
- Give advice in your answer to Question 4.

FOCUS

Recognizing Reading Structure In A Textbook

Most reading material has reading *structure*. The word structure means "organization or form." This book, *Interactions 1 Reading*, has a structure. It has a title, chapters, two readings in each chapter, paragraphs, and a heading for each paragraph.

7 **Recognizing Reading Structure in *Interactions I Reading*** Read the information below about the structure of this book and answer the questions.

1. A *title* is the name of something to read. What is the title of this book?

2. *Interactions I Reading* has 10 chapters. *Chapters* are the largest divisions of the book. What is the title of Chapter 1?

3. Each chapter of this book has two *readings*. What is the title of the first reading in Chapter 1?

4. The information of most reading selections is in paragraphs. A *paragraph* is a division (part) about one idea or one kind of information. How many paragraphs are in the reading "The Higher Learning of Community Living?"

5. Each paragraph has a heading. The *heading* of the first paragraph is "Introductions and Definitions." What is the heading of Paragraph C?

8 **Discussing the Reading** Talk about your answers to the following questions.

1. On the subject of shared living, what are some important new vocabulary items you learned? (Some possible examples are *dormitory*, *residence*, *residents*, *facilities*, *amenities*, etc.) What are some definitions of these words and phrases?

2. Do you live at home with your family, in an apartment with others your age, in a dormitory or residence hall, in a private home, or in another living situation? Give details for your answer.

3. Do you feel comfortable in living situations with unfamiliar strangers? Why or why not? What are the advantages (good features) and disadvantages (possible problems) of living with people who are not relatives?

4. How can strangers become upset with each other? How can they become close friends?

Reasons *Not* to Live in Shared Housing Situations

Before You Read

1 **Previewing Vocabulary** Read the vocabulary items below from the second reading. Then listen to the words and phrases. Put a check mark (✓) next to the words you don't know Don't use a dictionary.

Nouns
- academics
- comfort
- debt
- decision
- excuses
- expense
- harm
- luxury
- opportunities
- safety

Verbs
- care
- harm
- miss
- take chances
- waste

Adjectives
- crowded
- homesick
- insecure
- lonely
- miserable
- terrible
- unsafe
- valuable
- well-paying

Adverb
- academically

F⊙CUS

Recognizing Topics, Main Ideas, and Supporting Details in a Paragraph
- The word *topic* means "the subject of speech or writing." A paragraph usually tells about one topic. The paragraph heading gives information about its topic.
- The *main idea* tells the most important point, or idea, about the topic. Sometimes one or two sentences of a paragraph tell the main idea.
- *Supporting details* give examples or more information about the main idea.

Don't Live in a Campus Dorm!

A dormitory or residence hall is the worst kind of shared housing on a college or university campus. That's because you have to live closely with strangers. These people probably have unpleasant personalities, bad habits, and negative values. The building may be crowded, noisy, dirty, and uncomfortable. The food can be terrible. You can't stay healthy, study, or succeed in higher learning if you live with others.

Topic: In the example above, the title is the topic. It's the advice "Don't Live in a Campus Dorm!"

Main Idea: The first and last sentences are underlined. The first gives the main point of the whole topic. The last summarizes the most important idea.

Supporting Details: Other sentences give *reasons* for the negative advice: possible personalities and habits or values of residents, features of the building, bad food, and effects on you if you choose dorm life.

Read

FOCUS

Reasons Why *Not*...

Sometimes reasons *not* to do something help in important decision-making. Here is some negative advice on housing situations, leaving home, academic study, and decision making. They are different people's *opinions*, of course. As you read, you can consider how their reasoning makes you feel. Does it help you think or does it make thinking more difficult? Can you think of reasons that are the *opposite* of these writers' views?

2 Recognizing the Topics and Main Ideas of Paragraphs Read the following article. Then answer these questions about the article.

1. What is the title and topic of the whole article?

2. What is the topic of each paragraph? (Hint: Look at the paragraph heading.)

   A. _____

   B. _____

   C. _____

   D. _____

3. What is the main idea of each paragraph? Underline one or two sentences and then read them aloud. Remember: the main idea is not always the first sentence. As an example, a possible summary and a main-point sentence have been underlined in Paragraph A.

Reasons *Not* to Live in Shared Housing Situations

A   Are you leaving home to attend college? <u>Then *don't* live in a residence hall, international house, housing co-operative, frat or sorority house, rooming or boarding house, shared apartment rental, or furnished room in a private home.</u> That's because living with others can make life **miserable**. Why is it difficult to get along with roommates, housemates, or other strangers in the same building? They will come from different places and different cultural backgrounds. They will probably have unpleasant personalities, unhealthy habits, and negative values. They make the house **crowded**, messy, and noisy. They may get you into trouble or **harm** you in other ways. Then you won't study. You'll fail **academically**. <u>You will have a **terrible** educational and life experience if you live in shared housing.</u>   5   10

Reasons *Not* to Go Away to School in Another Town, City, or Country

B   The most important features of the higher education experience are **safety** (security), health, **comfort**, and **luxury**. So why *isn't* it a good idea to leave home, family, and friends for academic study on a college or university campus? One reason is that you'll have to live in an unfamiliar place with dangerous strangers. These people probably won't share your interests, attitudes, and values. They may not like or care about you! Won't you feel **lonely**, **homesick**, **insecure**, **unsafe**, or miserable with new kinds of people from different cultural or language backgrounds? And how can you stay healthy in noisy, messy, crowded houses or buildings with bad food and harmful substances? How can you exercise, relax, study, and sleep? Living and studying in towns, cities, states, provinces, or countries not your own can never be a comfortable, happy, or positive experience.   15   20

Reasons *Not* to Continue Academic Study after High School

C   College is expensive, especially if you live away from home. Many students go into great **debt** to pay for academic education and living **expenses**. And years of "higher learning" aren't worth the cost. Not all students learn enough from their studies for a good life after college. Few get **well-paying** jobs or make a lot of money in their areas of study or private business. Some people are not good at or interested in **academics**, so they **waste** their time on campus. They're not working, so they lose money during that time. They might even learn bad or dangerous habits from "campus culture." **Valuable** experience comes from *the real world*, not the classroom. There's no reason to go to college. And there are many negative reasons not to.   25   30

Reasons *Not* to Use Negative Reasons in Decision Making

D   Often, reasons "why not" are just bad **excuses**. People may be afraid to

leave their homes and families, to meet strangers in unfamiliar places, or to 35
take chances. Maybe they don't want to try new ways of thinking, living, or experiencing life. They might not like to feel alone, shy, or uncomfortable. But perhaps the specific "reasons" aren't important. Negative thinking can cause people to **miss** the best **opportunities** in life. Isn't life-changing experience worth more than security, comfort, or even money? Probably, it's better to 40 think out each important **decision** in academic life and living. Consider both the advantages and disadvantages of each choice. Learn valuable things about yourself and the world. Stay true to your values. Become a better person. And have fun. Especially in new places with different kinds of people, your college years can be the best and most memorable time of your life. 45

After You Read

Strategy

Summarizing

How can you show your understanding of reading material? You can summarize it. Here is some information about summaries:

- A summary is a short statement of the main points and important information of reading material.
- A summary has some words from the reading and some not from the reading.
- A summary of a paragraph or short article has only a few sentences. It is much shorter than the original.
- A good summary tells the main idea and supporting details in your own words

Example

Summary of Paragraph A from the reading "Reasons *Not* to Live in Shared Housing Situations:"

For academic, physical, relationship, or personal reasons, living with strangers in a residence hall or other shared campus housing can mess up your higher education experience. Do you want a difficult educational or life experience? If not, don't live in communal housing with unrelated strangers!

3 Summarizing a Paragraph Work in groups of three. Each person chooses one of the other Paragraphs B, C, or D from the reading "Reasons *Not* to Live in Shared Housing Situations." Read your selection carefully. Summarize it in writing. Begin with a sentence about the topic or title. Add the important information. Write no more than three sentences. Then read your summary to your group.

4 **Discussing the Reading** Discuss the following questions with your group.

1. Do you agree with the negative advice on shared housing on college campuses in Paragraph A? Why or why not? What might be the opposite of that advice?

2. What do you think of Paragraph B's reasons *not* to go away to school? Can you think of other negative advice? What are some possible reasons for the opposite decisions?

3. What kinds of people might the advice against higher education in Paragraph C help? Which seem better for *your* situation—the negative reasons or their opposites?

4. Which helps you more in making choices in your academic life—negative or positive advice? Or do you make important life decisions in another way? If so, what is it?

5 **Talking It Over** What are you preferences? For each boxed topic below, check (✓) one or two topics important to you. In groups, tell the reasons for your choices. Compare your ways of thinking with those of your classmates.

Housing	Housing Features
☐ Home with Family	☐ Appearance of the Accommodations
☐ Dormitory/Residence Hall	☐ Location on Campus or Near School
☐ "Special Interest" Housing	☐ Amount of Space or Privacy
☐ Fraternity or Sorority House	☐ Number of Roommates
☐ Co-operative Housing	or Housemates
☐ Boarding or Rooming House	☐ Common Areas or Kitchen
☐ Living with Host Family	☐ Bathroom Facilities
☐ Sharing an Apartment Off Campus	☐ Amenities (for Comfort or Luxury)
☐ Living with Friends or Relatives	☐ Food Quality
☐ Living with Strangers	☐ Cost
☐ Living Alone	☐ Noise vs. Quiet
☐ Other	☐ Safety and Security
	☐ Other

Location of School	Studies After High School
☐ Home Town or City	☐ No More Formal Education
☐ Different Place in Home Country	☐ Adult School
☐ Different Country	☐ Vocational or Private School
☐ Different Continent	☐ Courses on College Campus
☐ Online Only (Distance Learning)	☐ Online Courses
☐ Real World Only (Experience)	☐ Certificate Program
	☐ Degree Program
	☐ Graduate School
	☐ Other

PART 3

Vocabulary and Language-Learning Skills

Strategy

Getting Meaning from Context: Definitions and Italics

You can often find the meanings of words and phrases in the context. The *context* is the other words in the sentence or paragraph.

- Look for a definition. Definitions give the meanings of words or phrases. A definition can be a short or long phrase. In a reading, a definition often comes in a sentence after the verbs *be* or *mean*.
- Look for words in *italics* or in quotes " ". Defined words are sometimes in italics or quotes.

Examples

The definition of "an institution of higher education" is a college, university, or professional school. Its *campus* is its area and buildings.

1 **Getting Meaning from Context** In the reading "The Higher Learning of Community Living" on pages 5 to 7. Find the words for the explanations below. Write the words on the lines. The letters in parentheses ( ) are the letters of the paragraphs.

1. _____ = a building with rooms for residents, usually with common bathroom facilities and recreation areas. (A)

2. _____ = features of accommodations for comfort or luxury (A)

3. _____ = a building for residents with the same major, life style, or cultural background (B)

4. _____ = get through without harm (D)

Some words in the same reading are "short forms." Write the rest of these words for the explanations on the lines.

5. dorm _____ = a shared living and learning community on college or university campus

6. higher ed _____ = study and learning at a college or university

7. a single _____ = a private bedroom for one resident

8. a double or triple _____ = a room with two or three beds

9. housing co-op _____ = housing with shared work and decision making

10. a major _____ = a student's main subject of academic interest

2 Matching Words with Definitions Look at the columns below. Match each vocabulary item on the left with the correct definition or explanation on the right. The vocabulary is from "Reasons *Not* to Live in Shared Housing Situations." on pages 12 to 13. The letters in parentheses ( ) are the letters of the paragraphs.

1. _____ attend college (A)
2. _____ get along (A)
3. _____ living with others (A)
4. _____ miserable (A)
5. _____ unfamiliar places (B)
6. _____ dangerous strangers (B)
7. _____ living expenses (C)
8. _____ worth the cost (C)
9. _____ campus culture (C)
10. _____ excuses (D)
11. _____ opportunities (D)
12. _____ miss (D)
13. _____ memorable (D)

a. very unhappy or uncomfortable
b. unknown locations
c. shared housing
d. go to a university
e. harmful people you don't know
f. the cost of housing, food, etc.
g. fail to have
h. of enough value for the money
i. worth remembering
j. chances to do something
k. explanations that aren't good reasons
l. be friendly with someone, have a good relationship
m. common attitudes, habits, beliefs, and preferences at a college

Now, cover the words on the left. Read the explanations on the right and try to remember the word or phrase with your partner.

Strategy

Recognizing Words With The Same Or Similar Meanings
Some words in a definition can have the same or a similar meaning as the vocabulary item. The word *similar* means "alike but not exactly the same."

Example
Are you leaving home to attend college? Then *don't* live in a residence hall, international house, housing co-operative, frat or sorority house, rooming or boarding house, shared apartment rental, or furnished room in a private home.

The underlined words all have to do with housing.

3 **Recognizing Words with Similar Meanings** In each group of vocabulary items from Chapter 1, find the three words with similar or related meanings. Which word doesn't belong? Cross it out, as in the example. For each group of words, explain how they are similar in one sentence.

1. dormitory ~~recreational facilities~~ residence hall campus housing

   These words are similar because they are all places to live at university.

2. furnished rooms accommodations educational events places to live

3. privacy strangers unfamiliar people occupants of other buildings

4. challenges problems trouble participation

5. academically terrible unpleasant miserable

6. homesick alone valuable lonely

7. waste lose high-paying use up

8. exercise dangerous harmful unsafe

4 **Focusing on High-Frequency Words** Read the paragraph below and fill in each blank with a word from the box.

afraid	consider	opportunities	places	reasons
cause	decision	person	Probably	values

Often, reasons "why not" are just bad excuses. People may be _____ to leave their homes and families, to meet strangers in unfamiliar _____, or to take chances. But perhaps the specific _____ aren't important. Negative thinking can _____ people to miss the best _____ in life. Isn't life-changing experience worth more than security, comfort, or even money? _____, it's better to think out each important _____ in academic life. Then you can _____ both the advantages and disadvantages of each choice. Stay true to your _____. Become a better _____. And have fun.

₁ ₂ ₃ ₄ ₅ ₆ ₇ ₈ ₉ ₁₀

⑤ Using the Internet Complete these tasks online. Then discuss with your class.

- Using a search engine like Google to find information about community living situations on campus, type in something like this: *surviving dorm life, residence hall living, campus housing.* Take notes. Then talk about the information with your class. Tell what you learned about community living on or off campus.

- "Dorm Life is a show that follows the lives of seven college students thrown together on the same dorm floor…" Watch an episode on www.youtube.com. Then talk about it. Answer these questions: Do you understand the episode? What happens in the story? Is it funny to you? Why or why not? Can tell your own story about community or family living?

PART 4 Focus on Testing

F◉CUS

Summarizing

On the TOEFL® iBT, some reading passages are followed by a summary task. The first sentence of the summary is given, and you have to complete the summary by choosing correct statements from a list. Some statements do not belong in the summary because they express ideas that are not presented in the passage or are minor ideas in the passage.

Try to recognize the main ideas within the given list and decide whether an answer:

1. expresses an idea that is truly in the reading

2. expresses the idea accurately

3. states a main idea or only a supporting detail

Completing a Summary Choose the three items that you need to include to complete the summary.

A shared living situation can be a great experience and an essential part of higher education. To ensure a successful experience, _____.

- Ⓐ never live in a dorm
- Ⓑ stay out of trouble
- Ⓒ participate
- Ⓓ try to get along with others
- Ⓔ choose a single room on campus

Self-Assessment Log

Read the lists below. Check (✓) the strategies and vocabulary that you learned in this chapter. Look through the chapter or ask your instructor about the strategies and words that you do not understand.

Reading and Vocabulary-Building Strategies

- ☐ Previewing the topic
- ☐ Previewing vocabulary
- ☐ Recognizing reading structure in a textbook
- ☐ Recognizing topics, main ideas, and supporting details
- ☐ Understanding reasons why not, or negative advice
- ☐ Summarizing
- ☐ Getting meaning from context: definitions and italics
- ☐ Recognizing words with the same or similar meanings

Target Vocabulary

Nouns

- academics
- advice*
- attitudes*
- challenges*
- comfort
- community
- cultural background
- debt*
- decision*
- excuses
- expenses
- features
- habits
- harm
- interests*

- lifestyles
- luxury
- major (area of study)
- opportunities*
- personalities
- privacy
- rules*
- safety*
- security*
- strangers
- variety

Verbs

- attend*
- care*

- get along
- get through
- harm
- miss*
- stay out
- relate
- rent
- survive
- take chances
- waste

Adjectives

- common*
- considerate
- crowded
- furnished
- homesick

- impossible*
- insecure
- lonely
- miserable
- private*
- shared*
- similar*
- terrible*
- unsafe
- valuable
- well-paying

Adverbs

- academically
- away from home

* These words are among the 2,000 most frequently used words in English.

2 Experiencing Nature

A change in the
weather is sufficient
to re-create the world
and ourselves."

Marcel Proust
French novelist

In this CHAPTER

In Part 1, you will read about how weather influences our lives. In the rest of this chapter, you will read about, explore, and discuss climate and climate change, and the causes and effects of various kinds of weather.

Connecting to the Topic

1. Look at the photo. Where do you think these people are? What are they doing?

2. How do you feel in warm weather? What about in cold weather?

3. Describe a hike or a walk you have experienced in nature. How was the weather? How did you feel?

The Powerful Influence of Weather

Before You Read

1 **Previewing the Topic** Look at the photos and discuss the questions in your groups.

1. Describe the people and their actions. What are they doing? What are they wearing? How do you think they are feeling? Why?

2. Describe the kinds of weather in the photos. Which kinds do you like? Which do you dislike? Why?

3. Make comparisons. How is the weather in the photos like the weather in your area? How is it different?

▼ Rainy weather

▼ Hot weather

Snowy weather ▶

▲ Windy weather

2 Predicting Think about and discuss possible answers to these questions with your group. Write down your answers. If you don't know the answers, make predictions. You can look for the answers when you read "The Powerful Influence of Weather."

1. What are the meanings of the following words related to weather? What are *biometeorologists*? What is the *atmosphere*? What is the *weather*?
2. How can some kinds of wind affect people's health?
3. In what ways might other weather conditions influence human health?
4. What effects might the weather have on people's moods and emotions?

3 Previewing Vocabulary Read the vocabulary items below from the first reading. Then listen to the words and phrases. Put a check mark (✓) next to the words you don't know. Don't use a dictionary.

Nouns		Verbs	Adjectives
▓ asthma	▓ humidity	▓ affect	▓ depressed
▓ atmosphere	▓ moods	▓ cause	▓ depressing
▓ biometeorologists	▓ pneumonia	▓ increase	▓ forceful
▓ blood pressure	▓ scientists	▓ influence	▓ humid
▓ diseases	▓ strokes		▓ irritable
▓ disorder	▓ temperature		▓ moody
▓ effects	▓ weather		▓ nervous
▓ flu (influenza)			▓ physical
▓ headaches			▓ powerful
▓ heart attacks			▓ sudden
			▓ warm

Read

4 Reading an Article Read the following article. Then do the activities that follow.

The Powerful Influence of Weather

Biometeorologists and Their Research

A   **Weather** has a **powerful** impact on the physical world. It also **affects** people's personalities. How do we know about the **effects** of weather on people? We know from **biometeorologists**. These **scientists** study weather. They study how atmospheric conditions affect human health and emotions. The word **atmosphere** means "the air around the earth." "Atmospheric conditions at a time or place" is a definition of the word *weather*. Some examples of these conditions are sun, wind, rain, snow, **humidity** (the amount of moisture in the air), and air pressure (the force of air). 5

The weather conditions of the atmosphere greatly influence (or affect) people's health, thinking, and feelings.

How Wind Can Affect Health

B   All over the world, researchers have studied how wind affects human health. Strong winds may result in a change in air pressure and temperature which can be harmful to people. According to biometeorologists in Russia, powerful winds are known to **increase** the number of people who have **strokes** (blood vessel attacks in the brain). Also, Italian researchers have found that during times of strong winds, Italians have more **heart attacks** (sudden stopping of the heart). And Japanese weather scientists say **forceful** winds often cause an **increase** in the number of **asthma** attacks. (Asthma is a lung **disorder**. It causes breathing problems.) Although wind doesn't always lead to such serious health problems, people everywhere have experienced bad **headaches** because of powerful winds.

Possible Effects of Other Kinds of Weather

C   Do other kinds of weather influence physical health? Sudden **temperature** changes in winter are often associated with a cold or the flu. (The *flu*, or

▲ Colds and flu are common in winter.

influenza, is a viral **disease**.) However, colds and flu probably increase because people are in close contact (near one another) indoors in cold weather. Colds and flu may even lead to **pneumonia** (another lung disease). Other illnesses also increase during long periods (times) of cold weather. In most places, diseases of the blood and heart attacks are more common in winter. But in some very hot and humid (wet) regions, there are more heart attacks in summer. Many people have high blood pressure (a health condition). In three out of four people, blood pressure falls (goes down) in warm weather. But some people have lower blood pressure in the cool or cold times of the year.

Weather and Mood

D   These forces of nature greatly affect people's **moods** (emotional conditions and feelings) too. For many people, winter in the northern regions is very depressing. They eat and sleep a lot, but they usually feel tired. They are **nervous** and can't work well. They are irritable (not very nice to other people). Biometeorologists even have a name for this condition. The name is Seasonal Affective Disorder (SAD). Scientists think the cause of this mood disorder is the long periods of darkness. Even during the day, it is often cloudy or gray. What can people with SAD do about their moods? Naturally, they need more light! On bright days they feel better. But people don't work very well on sunny, hot, and humid days. The best weather for good work and thinking is cool and clear.

Conclusion and Summary

E   Are the people around you becoming sick more often? Are they getting more colds or the flu or even pneumonia? Are they having more health problems like headaches or asthma attacks or heart disease? Or are *you* becoming **moody**? Are you getting more tired or **depressed** (low in mood) or sad? Remember—according to biometeorologists and other weather scientists—the cause may be the atmosphere! 50

After You Read

Strategy

Using a Diagram to Show Cause and Effect

To clearly organize your ideas on why things happen, you can use a diagram. Write notes on the *causes* of your topic on the left side and include details on its *effects* on the right side. See the example below:

Hurricanes (Causes)	→	Dangers to People (Effects)
lots of rain in a short period of time	→	flooding, damage to homes
strong winds	→	falling trees, injuries, damage to homes, blocking roads

5 Identifying Cause and Effect This diagram shows the effects of different kinds of weather on people's health and emotions. Complete the chart by filling in the five blank lines in the boxes.

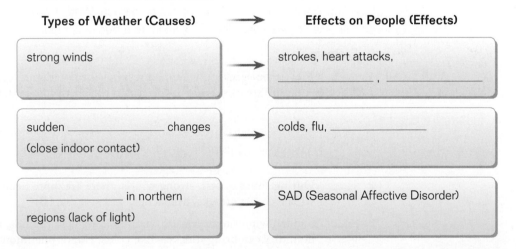

Types of Weather (Causes)	→	Effects on People (Effects)
strong winds	→	strokes, heart attacks, _____ , _____
sudden _____ changes (close indoor contact)	→	colds, flu, _____
_____ in northern regions (lack of light)	→	SAD (Seasonal Affective Disorder)

Recognizing Reading Structure: Titles and Paragraph Topics
Usually, a reading selection is about one general subject or topic. The information
in each paragraph is about a different topic within the subject of the whole reading.
Remember: Titles and paragraph headings often tell topics in a general way.

**6 Recognizing Reading Structure: Titles and Paragraph
Topics** Match the questions on the left with the answers on the right. Write the
correct letter on the line.

1. __f__ What is the title of Chapter 2 of
    Interactions I Reading?

2. _____ What is the title of the first reading
    selection in Chapter 2?

3. _____ What is the heading of Paragraph A?

4. _____ What is the topic of Paragraph B?

5. _____ What is Paragraph C about?

6. _____ Which paragraph tells about the
    effects of weather on people's moods?

7. _____ Which paragraph summarizes
    the information in the other four
    paragraphs?

8. _____ What general subject is the whole
    reading about?

a. "How Wind Can Affect
    Health"

b. "The Powerful Influence
    of Weather"

c. Paragraph E

d. Paragraph D

e. "Biometeorologists and
    Their Research"

f. "Experiencing Nature"

g. possible effects of some
    kinds of weather other
    than wind

h. ways weather can influence
    people's physical and
    emotional health

7 Recognizing the Main Ideas Read the possible statements about the main
ideas of the paragraphs in the reading "The Powerful Influence of Weather." The
letters in parentheses ( ) refer to paragraphs in the reading. Read each one and
determine if it is the main idea of that paragraph. Write *T* (true) or *F* (false) on each
line. Then change each false statement to a true statement.

Example

1. __F__ *Biometeorologists* study human responses to academic lectures.
    A definition of *weather* is "places on the earth like mountains, countries,
    and communities." (A)

    *Biometeorologists are "researchers of human responses to weather."
    A definition of weather is "atmosphere conditions like sun, wind, and
    temperature."*

2. _____ During times of fast, strong winds, there are more health problems like
    strokes, heart attacks, headaches, and asthma. (B)

3. _____ Sudden winter temperature changes, long cold periods, or heat and
    humidity can bring illnesses like colds, flu, or pneumonia. (C)

4. _____ The atmosphere and weather don't affect people's moods. People in the northern regions just like to eat and sleep a lot, work badly, are tired, and feel depressed all the time. (D)

5. _____ According to scientists, the cause of health problems and sad moods may be higher education around the world! (E)

8 **Recognizing Supporting Details** Read the five main-idea questions that follow about the information in the reading. Three details correctly answer each question. Cross out the untrue, unrelated detail. The first item is an example.

1. What are the meanings of some words and phrases related to the topic of weather?

   a. A definition of *biometeorologists* is "researchers with interest in human responses to the weather."

   b. The word *atmosphere* means "the air around the earth."

   c. *Atmospheric conditions* is another phrase for weather.

   d. ~~Sun, wind, temperature, air pressure, and the amount of moisture in the atmosphere have no effect on human health and emotions.~~

2. How can some kinds of winds affect people's health?

   a. Strong, fast winds can cause a number of disorders, including asthma.

   b. Most biometeorologists are in the developing nations of Latin America, Asia, and Africa.

   c. Bad headaches and asthma attacks are some other possible examples of the effects of the winds.

   d. Maybe there are more strokes and heart attacks during windy weather of this kind.

3. In what ways might other kinds of weather influence human health?

   a. Biometeorologists are always sad or depressed or moody. Weather isn't important to them.

   b. Sudden winter temperature changes might bring colds, flu, or pneumonia.

   c. During long cold periods, people have more blood diseases and heart attacks.

   d. Air temperature affects people's blood pressure in different ways.

4. What effects might the weather have on people's moods and emotions?

   a. In northern areas of the earth, the long periods of darkness influence many people's moods.

   b. No one likes cool, clear weather because it makes it hard to work or think well.

   c. Bright, hot days with high humidity can also affect human emotions.

   d. People with SAD (Seasonal Affective Disorder) may feel hungry, tired, nervous, and depressed.

5. What is the conclusion of the reading selection about the influence of weather on people's physical and mental health?

   a. Foreign students don't do well in countries without changes in atmospheric conditions.

   b. Weather conditions in the atmosphere can greatly influence people's health, thinking, and feelings.

   c. Some kinds of illnesses and health problems increase with some kinds of weather or weather changes.

   d. The weather affects people's moods and emotions, too.

Now, go back to Activity 2 in the Before You Read section on page 23. Look at the answers you wrote down before you read the article. Change them if necessary.

- Give definitions in your answer to Question 1.
- Give examples in your answers to Questions 2, 3, and 4.

9 Discussing the Reading In small groups, talk about your answers to the following questions.

1. Is the study of the effects of weather on people useful research? Why or why not?

2. Do some kinds of weather conditions (wind, sun, temperature, humidity, rain, snow, air pressure, and other conditions) affect your health, feelings, or mood? In what ways?

3. In your opinion, do atmospheric conditions influence world events in important ways? Give reasons for your opinion.

PART 2   Main Ideas and Details

Global Climate Changes

Before You Read

1 Previewing Vocabulary Read the vocabulary items on page 29 from the next reading. Then listen to the words and phrases. Put a check mark (✓) next to the words you don't know. Don't use a dictionary.

Nouns		Adjectives	Adverbs
▪ blizzards	▪ hurricanes	▪ average	▪ generally
▪ carbon dioxide	▪ meteorologists	▪ common	▪ slowly
(CO_2)	▪ plants	▪ extreme	
▪ climate	▪ storms	▪ global	**Phrases**
▪ damage	▪ temperature	▪ major	▪ at least
▪ desert	▪ tornadoes	▪ natural	▪ from season to
▪ droughts	▪ tropical rain	▪ typical	season
▪ floods	forests	▪ worse	▪ in contrast
▪ gases		▪ yearly	▪ more and more
▪ global warming	**Verbs**		
▪ the globe	▪ cut down		
	▪ follow		
	▪ vary		

FOCUS

Getting The Topic From Titles and Headings

The title of a reading selection often gives the general subject or topic of the whole reading. Each paragraph of the reading is about a more specific (narrower) topic within the general (wide) subject. For example, below are four paragraph headings for the next reading selection "Global Climate Changes." The headings tell the paragraph topics in phrases, not full sentences. The important words begin with capital letters.

2 **Recognizing Topics and Main Ideas** Quickly read each paragraph of the article below. Then choose the best heading from the list below and write it above the paragraph. Then underline the main idea in each paragraph.

- General Changes in the Nature of Weather
- The Powerful Effect of People on Nature
- ~~Climate in Regions of the Globe~~
- Global Warming and the "El Niño" Effect

Read

3 **Reading an Article** Read the following article. Then do the activities that follow.

Global Climate Changes

Climate in Regions of the Globe

A   The word *weather* means "the atmospheric conditions at a specific place and time." The weather can vary from day to day. In contrast to weather, *climate* is "the general or average atmospheric conditions of a region." *In different areas of the globe, the climate generally stays the same from year to year.* For example, the climate in the **desert** is usually very dry. It may be cold in winter and hot in summer, but there is very little rain or humidity.

5

▲ A storm

In contrast, in tropical rain forests, there is very high humidity. In most other areas of the world, the weather is cool or cold and wet or dry in the winter season. It is warm or hot and dry or humid in the summer months.

B   According to some **meteorologists** (weather researchers), the earth's 10 climate is changing **slowly**. In most places on the earth, the weather varies from season to season or even from day to day. In contrast, the **typical** climate is similar every year. Even so, there may be global climate changes from one long time period to another. What are these changes? Some scientists believe the weather is becoming more **extreme**. There are longer periods of very cold 15 and very hot **temperatures**. There are more and more powerful **hurricanes** and tornadoes (**storms** with strong, fast winds) and **blizzards** (heavy snowstorms). **Floods** (large amounts of water on dry land) and long droughts (times without enough **rain**) are causing greater and greater physical **damage** to the human communities on Earth. These extreme forces of nature will get 20 even **worse** in the future, say some people. And every change in climate in one part of the globe will bring more extreme changes in other areas.

C   Global warming and *El Niño* are having major effects on the earth's atmosphere, weather, and climate. At least that's the opinion of many researchers and scientists. What is global warming? It is a slow increase in 25 the average yearly temperature of the planet. The cause is an increase of gases in the atmosphere. What is *El Niño*? The Spanish phrase means "The Little Boy" or "The Christ Child." It names a weather condition most common in the month of December. This "seasonal weather disorder" is a change in the atmosphere of the tropical areas of the Pacific Ocean. It increases the 30 amount of rain in the Americas and can bring strong winds and hurricanes. In contrast, *El Niño* may cause drought in the southern and western Pacific

(Asia). Blizzards, snow, and long periods of low temperatures may follow in the northern regions of the globe.

D   Not all meteorologists believe there is much natural global warming. 35
According to these scientists, the *El Niño* effect is not getting stronger.
So why is the temperature of the earth going up? Why are tropical
storms like hurricanes causing more and greater flood and wind damage?
Probably, human beings are the main cause of the extreme effects of weather
and climate changes. Cars and factories are putting more and more gases like 40
carbon dioxide (CO_2) into the earth's atmosphere. Coal and oil add carbon
dioxide to the air, too. Trees and plants take in carbon dioxide, but humans
are cutting down the rain forests and putting up buildings where green
plants used to grow. The world has a lot of people now, and it will have a lot
more people in the future. 45

After You Read

Strategy

Summarizing a Paragraph

In Chapter 1, you learned that a summary is a short statement of the important information in a reading. How can you learn to summarize better? Here are some suggestions:

- In English, think about the meaning of the information.
- In your own words, begin with the most general point about the paragraph topic. Tell the main idea in your own words.
- Then give only the important supporting details (definitions, examples, facts, and reasons) for that point.
- To shorten your summary, put similar ideas in the same sentence.

Example

- Here is a possible summary of Paragraph A from the reading "Global Climate Changes."

   All over the world, the typical climate of an area is generally similar every year. It is dry in the deserts and wet in the tropics. In many places, it is colder in winter and warm or hot in summer.

4 **Summarizing a Paragraph** Work in groups of three. Have each person choose one of the remaining paragraphs from the reading "Global Climate Changes." Read it carefully. Summarize the main idea and the important supporting details. Then tell or read your summary to your group.

5 **Discussing the Reading** Work in groups of three. Read and discuss the questions below.

1. Describe the typical climate in your area of the world. Does the weather change in the various seasons? If so, how?

2. Do you think the earth's climate is changing? If so, how and why is it changing? If not, why not?

3. What are your predictions for the future of the atmosphere and nature on Earth? Give reasons for your predictions.

6 **Talking It Over** People have many different beliefs about nature and the weather. Some ideas come from scientific fact. Others come from people's experiences or culture. In your opinion, which of the following statements are true? Check (✓) the true statements and explain your opinions to a small group. Give reasons for your opinions.

☐ Meteorologists and other researchers can study the weather, but they can't know or tell about future weather.

☐ A lot of people complain about the weather. Do they have the power to change it? Of course not.

☐ If you ask for rain, don't be surprised if you get thunder and lightning.

☐ Why do people get depressed about the rain? Without rain, there would be no rainbows.

☐ Do you want sunshine today? Carry a big umbrella and wear a heavy raincoat. Then it won't rain.

☐ Is your arthritis pain increasing? This means humid (wet) weather is coming.

▼ Dry weather   ▼ Humid weather

Strategy

**Getting Meaning from Contexts, Parentheses, and from Words
with Similar Meanings**
You can often find the meanings of new vocabulary words from the context (the
other words in the sentence or paragraph).

- The meaning can be in parentheses (   ). As explained in Chapter 1, a definition
  can come after the words *be* or *mean*. Here are examples for the words
  biometeorologists and *atmosphere*.

Example
We know about the effects of weather from *biometeorologists* (weather
researchers). These scientists study human health and emotions in response to
atmospheric conditions. The word *atmosphere* means "the air around the earth."

- There might be other words with the same or similar meanings as the item in the
  sentence or paragraph. In the following example, the adjectives *powerful*, *strong*,
  and *forceful* have similar meanings.

Example
Powerful winds from the mountains of Russia may increase the number of strokes.
In times of *strong* winds in Italy, Italians have more heart attacks. People everywhere
have bad headaches during times of *forceful* winds.

1 **Getting Meaning from Context** Complete the following sentences with
words from the reading "The Powerful Influence of Weather" on pages 23–25.
Some definitions appear following *be* or *mean*; some are in parentheses. There are
also words with the same or similar meanings. The letters in parentheses (   ) refer
to the paragraphs of the reading.

1. These weather researchers study health and emotions in response to
   atmospheric conditions. They are _____biometeorologists_____. (A)

2. This word means "the air around the earth." It is the _____
   _____. (A)

3. Some examples of kinds of atmospheric conditions are sun, wind,

_____, _____,

_____, and _____. (A)

4. Another word for "atmospheric conditions at a time or place" is

_____. (A)

5. A word for "blood vessel attacks in the brain" is _____. (B)

6. A heart attack is a _____ (B)

7. A short word for "influenza, a viral disease" is _____. (C)

8. Asthma and pneumonia are disorders or diseases of the _____

_____. (B, C)

9. The meaning of the word *moods* is _____. (D)

10. The name SAD means "_____." (D)

This condition is caused by _____. (D)

2 **Recognizing Words with the Same or Similar Meanings** In each group of vocabulary items below from Chapters 1 and 2, find the three words with the same or similar meanings. Which word doesn't belong? Cross it out, as in the example.

1. region   area   ~~real life~~   place

2. dangerous   unsafe   harmful   private

3. condition   affect   influence   have an effect on

4. homesick   lonely   waste   alone

5. human emotions   feelings   moods   physical health

6. dormitory   residence hall   campus housing   rent

7. diseases   sicknesses   health disorders and problems   science

8. sad   common   depressed   moody

9. season   time of year   air pressure   three-month period

10. human beings   meteorologists   weather researchers   scientists

For more practice, compare your answers with a partner's. Give a reason for each answer.

3 **Matching Vocabulary Items with Examples** Sometimes examples can explain the meaning of a word or phrase. For example, *sun*, *rain*, and *wind* are examples of *kinds of weather*. Look at the columns below. Match each vocabulary word or phrase in the first column with the examples in the second column.

Vocabulary

1. __d__ atmospheric conditions

2. _____ kinds of extreme weather

3. _____ air temperatures

4. _____ Earth's natural materials and gases

5. _____ countries of the world

6. _____ continents (the largest areas of the globe)

7. _____ diseases or health disorders

8. _____ how people feel (adjectives)

9. _____ seasons of the year

10. _____ natural areas or regions of the earth

Examples

a. the ocean, seas, islands, deserts, forests

b. coal, oil, carbon dioxide, air, water

c. Asia, Europe, the Australia, Africa, the Americas

d. sun, rain, snow, wind, humidity

e. happy, tired, sad, depressed, nervous, moody

f. blizzards, tornadoes, hurricanes, floods, droughts

g. Japan, China, Russia, Italy, Mexico, the United States

h. winter, spring, summer, fall

i. hot, warm, cool, cold

j. stroke, asthma, influenza, pneumonia, headaches, high blood pressure, arthritis

For more practice, give more examples for the items in the vocabulary column above.

4 **Focusing on High-Frequency Words** Read the paragraph below and fill in each blank with a word from the box.

amounts	period	slowly	typical	weather
damage	rain	temperatures	varies	

General Changes in the Nature of Weather

According to some meteorologists (_____ researchers),
                                            1
the earth's climate is changing _____. In most places
                                        2
on the earth, the weather _____ from season to season
                                    3
or even from day to day. In contrast, the _____ climate is
                                                4
similar every year. Even so, there may be global climate changes from one

Mitch in 1998, for example, trained for several days over parts of Honduras. Cell after cell, swelled by moisture from the Caribbean Sea, rolled ashore and brought more than 20 inches of rain. Deadly floods and mudslides affected the areas that saw the most constant chain of storms.

1. List three words in this reading's vocabulary cluster for *thunderstorm(s)*:

_____

_____

_____

2. List three words or phrases in this reading's vocabulary cluster for *train* (or *training*):

_____

_____

_____

3. List one phrase in this reading's vocabulary cluster for *hurricane(s)*:

_____

_____

4. Which of the following best expresses the main idea of the reading as a whole?

   (A) Meteorologists call repetitive thunderstorms "training thunderstorms."

   (B) The concept of "training thunderstorms" helps scientists understand hurricanes.

   (C) Thunderstorms often train near slow-moving weather features, causing damage.

   (D) Meteorologists are developing new ways to keep thunderstorms from training.

Self-Assessment Log

Read the lists below. Check (✓) the strategies and vocabulary that you know and can use. Look through the chapter or ask your instructor about the strategies and words that you do not understand.

Reading and Vocabulary-Building Strategies

☐ Identifying cause and effect
☐ Recognizing reading structure: titles and paragraph topics
☐ Recognizing topics and main ideas
☐ Summarizing a paragraph
☐ Getting meaning from context, parentheses, and words with similar meanings
☐ Focusing on high-frequency words

Target Vocabulary

Nouns

- amounts*
- asthma
- atmosphere
- biometeorologists
- blizzards
- carbon dioxide (CO_2)
- damage*
- desert
- disease*
- disorder
- effects*
- floods
- flu (influenza)
- headaches

- heart attacks*
- humidity
- hurricanes
- increase*
- meteorologists
- moods
- period*
- pneumonia
- rain*
- scientists*
- storms
- strokes
- temperatures*
- weather*

Verbs

- affect*
- increase*
- influence*

Adjectives

- depressed
- extreme*
- forceful*
- moody
- nervous
- powerful*
- typical*
- worse

Adverb

- slowly*

* These words are among the 2,000 most frequently used words in English.

3 Living to Eat, or Eating to Live?

To read without reflecting is
like eating without digesting.

Edmund Burke
British political writer

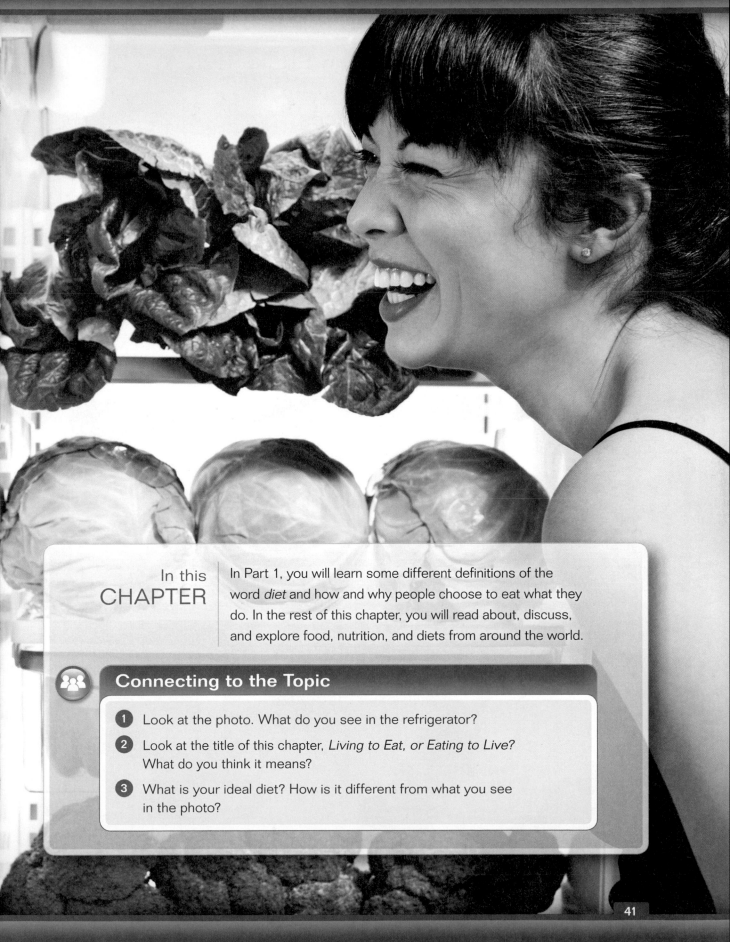

In this
CHAPTER

In Part 1, you will learn some different definitions of the word *diet* and how and why people choose to eat what they do. In the rest of this chapter, you will read about, discuss, and explore food, nutrition, and diets from around the world.

Connecting to the Topic

1. Look at the photo. What do you see in the refrigerator?

2. Look at the title of this chapter, *Living to Eat, or Eating to Live?* What do you think it means?

3. What is your ideal diet? How is it different from what you see in the photo?

Global Diet Choices

Before You Read

1 **Previewing the Topic** Look at the photos and read the questions below. Answer the questions in small groups.

1. Describe each photo. Where are the people? What are they doing? What are they saying to each other?

2. Talk about the foods in each photo. Are they packaged or prepared? Fresh, canned, or frozen? Healthy or unhealthy?

3. Make comparisons. How is the food in the photos like typical foods in your culture? How is it different?

▼ Shopping at a supermarket

▼ Dinner with friends at home

▲ Eating dinner at a restaurant

2 **Predicting** Think about these questions and write down short answers. If you don't know the answers, make predictions. Then discuss them in small groups. You can look for the answers when you read "Global Diet Choices."

1. What are some meanings of the word *diet*?

2. Are fast-food places international? What types of foods are common fast foods?

3. How do most people make decisions about food and diet?

4. What are some examples of diets based on location, history, tradition, or religion?

5. How are diet choices becoming more alike around the globe?

3 **Previewing Vocabulary** Read the vocabulary items below from the first reading. Then listen to the words and phrases. Put a check mark (✓) next to the words you don't know. Don't use a dictionary.

Nouns
- additives
- atmosphere
- breakfast
- carbohydrates (carbs)
- complex carbohydrates
- convenience
- customs
- dairy
- diabetes
- diet
- discussion
- dishes
- elements
- fast food
- fats
- habits
- insects
- low-carb diet
- minerals
- preferences
- protein
- soy products
- vitamins

Verbs
- diet
- lose (weight)
- prefer
- prohibit

Adjectives
- fried
- frozen
- healthy
- natural
- nutritious
- packaged
- permitted
- religious
- slim
- universal
- well-rounded
- worse

Adverb
- probably

Read

4 **Reading an Article** Read the following article. Then do the activities that follow.

Global Diet Choices

Meanings of the Word *Diet*

A   Most words in the English language have more than one simple basic meaning. One example is the word *diet*. The most general definition of the noun is "a person's or a group's usual food choices and **habits**." In a more specific definition, *diet* means "an eating plan with only certain kinds or amounts of food." For instance, a **diet** is often a plan to lose weight. And as a   5
verb, **diet** means "to lose weight." People can "go on a diet," meaning they are starting a program to lose weight.

International Fast Food

B   All over the world, the global diet includes **fast food** — prepared items from inexpensive restaurants, snack bars, or food stands. Some examples of typical American fast food are *hamburgers*,   10
hot dogs, *sandwiches*, and *fried chicken*. Some common international fast foods might be German *sausage* and *schnitzel*, Italian *pizza* and *pasta*, Mexican *tacos* and *burritos*, Middle Eastern *shish kebab* and *falafel*, Japanese   15
sushi and *tempura*, and Chinese *egg rolls* and *noodles*. Why is this kind of food becoming even more **universal**, or worldwide? First, fast-food restaurants usually prepare and serve the items quickly. Second, many fast-food   20
restaurants are part of fast-food chains (eating places with the same name and company owner). For instance, the biggest and most famous American fast-food chain serves hamburgers in every continent on the planet   25

▲ Fast food from around the world

except Antarctica. Its menu items may not be exactly alike in all cultures, but its 33,000 restaurants all have the same look and style. The atmosphere seems comfortable and familiar. Third, the items at fast-food places usually cost less than meals in formal restaurants or special **dishes** made at home. And finally, people usually enjoy the taste of the food, even if it is not very   30
nutritious (healthy).

How People Make Individual Food Choices

C   How do most people make their diet decisions? Individual choices are often based on former habits, cost and convenience, beliefs about health and nutrition, and ideas about physical beauty. Some people learn to like certain foods in childhood, and they don't change later in life. Many people have   35
busy lives, so they buy or prepare food and eat it as quickly as possible. Some meal-planners think only fresh and "natural" food is nutritious, so they buy vegetables, fruits, and foods without additives (chemical substances) and

prepare it in healthy ways. People with health problems — like high-blood pressure or **diabetes** (a blood-sugar disorder) — may be on special non-salt or non-sugar diets. The nutritional requirements of very young or very old people may be different from the needs of others. Some cultures prefer a slim body to a well-rounded one, so people are always trying to lose weight. They may follow popular diets, such as a **low-carb diet** — an eating system high in protein but low in refined carbohydrates.

Other Reasons for Diet Habits Around the World

D   Unlike individual food plans, the diets of whole cultures and regions come from location, history, and tradition. For example, the typical Mexican diet is a combination of foods from pre-Columbian, Spanish, and French cultures. It is rich in **complex carbohydrates** (corn, beans, rice, breads) and protein (beans, eggs, fish, meat). Fish and fish products from the seas around Japan are one of the most important parts of the traditional Japanese diet. Rich in vitamins and **minerals**, seafood is served grilled, baked, raw, dried, pickled, hot, and cold. **Soy products** (miso, tofu, and bean paste), fermented vegetables, and rice are also important in the typical Japanese diet. Religious practices may also greatly affect diet. For instance, some Jewish people *keep kosher* (follow the requirements of Jewish food preparation and eating). These laws prohibit eating pork or bacon or other meat from pigs, shellfish, snake, or **insects**. In addition, people should not eat meat and **dairy** (milk products) at the same meal. In a similar way, Muslims follow the laws of eating halal, an Islamic system of eating only permitted foods. Some foods, such as pork or insects, are not permitted. Though people can eat some meat such as beef from cows, the animals must be killed in a special way, according to ritual. Also, for religious reasons, some Christians eat fish instead of meat on Fridays. They also limit their food choices during Lent (the 40 days before Easter) in the spring.

Conclusion and Summary: The Global Diet

E   Universally, more and more meals include basic necessary food **elements** — *protein*, *carbohydrates*, and *fats*. Almost everywhere, some kind of meat, fish, dairy product, or another food with protein is part of a good **breakfast**, lunch, or dinner. There are also grains, breads, vegetables, fruit, and the like. Many dishes contain the necessary vitamins and minerals. A few families grow their own food, but most people buy food from eating places and markets in their communities. Food may be fresh, prepared, canned, **frozen**, or packaged. "Fast food" is very popular, and maybe it is becoming healthier. In some ways, diet choices are becoming more and more similar around the world. Even so, the variety of food choices is large now and is **probably** going to increase. Are cooking **customs**, eating habits, and food **preferences** all over the world becoming more or less healthy? Are they better or **worse** for human beings? These questions are interesting topics of research and **discussion**.

Recognizing Reading Structure: Main-Idea Questions for
Paragraph Topics

A well-structured paragraph has a clear topic. The material in each paragraph answers
a different main-idea question about that topic.

5 **Recognizing Reading Structure** Read each question below. Write the
correct letter on the line. Which paragraph in the reading "Global Diet Choices"
answers each main-idea question? Write the paragraph letter, A, B, C, D, or E.

1. _____ How are diet choices becoming more alike around the world?

2. _____ How do most individuals make decisions about food and diet?

3. _____ What are some diets based on location, history, tradition, or religion?

4. _____ In what ways are fast-food places international?

5. _____ What are some definitions of the word *diet*?

F☉CUS

Recognizing One- or Two-Sentence Statements of the Main Idea

You can usually find the answer to a main-idea question in the first one or two sentences
of the reading. Those sentences tell the point, or message, of the paragraph.

6 **Recognizing One- or Two-Sentence Statements of the
Main Idea** Read the main-idea statements below about each of the paragraphs
in the reading "Global Diet Choices." Write *T* (true) or *F* (false) on each line. Then
change the false sentences to true sentences to express the main idea. Next, use
them as answers to the five questions in Activity 2.

1. _____ The word *diet* has two basic definitions —"usual food choices" and
"an eating plan." (Paragraph A)

2. _____ Fast food has very little variety around the world. It is always
hamburgers, hot dogs, and fried chicken. But the atmosphere of
fast-food chains varies a lot in different countries. (Paragraph B)

3. _____ Individual choices about food and eating are more often based on
history, tradition, and culture than on habits, convenience, cost, and
beliefs about health and beauty. (Paragraph C)

4. _____ The typical Mexican and Japanese diets are based on religious law. Some
religious people choose foods according to their country's history and
location. (Paragraph D)

5. _____ Not many meals around the world include the basic necessary food
elements. Almost all families grow their own food, so the global diet
is becoming less and less varied. (Paragraph E)

7 Recognizing Supporting Details As you learned in Chapters 1 and 2, each paragraph of a reading includes not only a main idea but also details about it. These details support the point of the paragraph with specific facts, examples, or reasons. Like a well-written main-idea statement, supporting details can answer a main-idea question.

Read the five main-idea questions below from Activity 5. Which three details answer each question? Circle those and cross out the unrelated sentence.

1. What are some definitions of the word *diet*?

   a. It means "ideas or information to think about."
   b. It's a person's or a group's usual food choices or habits.
   c. A diet can be an eating plan with only certain kinds or amounts of food.
   d. It can be a way to lose weight.

2. In what ways are fast-food places international?

   a. You can find some of the same fast-food chains in different parts of the world.
   b. Quick and convenient items from America, Germany, Italy, Mexico, the Middle East, Japan, China, and other cultures are available.
   c. Formal restaurant meals can be expensive or cheap, natural or prepared, non-fat, low-carb and high-fat, and so on.
   d. Fast-food chains often have a similar look and atmosphere in every country.

3. How do most individuals make decisions about food and diet?

   a. Some adults still choose food from their childhoods because that food seems comfortable and familiar.
   b. People with busy lives may choose fast convenience foods, and people with health problems may choose "natural" foods or special diets.
   c. Age and ideas about physical beauty can influence diet decisions.
   d. A well-rounded figure is healthier than a slim body image, so Americans prohibit popular diet plans.

4. What are some diets based on location, history, tradition, or religion?

   a. The typical Mexican diet contains a combination of foods from its pre-Columbian, Spanish, and French history and traditions.
   b. Some people don't eat sugar because they are diabetic.
   c. Because of the location of the country, fish and other seafood plays a major role in the Japanese diet — along with soy products, fermented vegetables, and rice.
   d. Religious Jews may "keep kosher," Muslims may follow the laws of "halal," and devout Christians may make diet decisions for religious reasons.

5. How are diet choices becoming more similar around the world?

   a. Typical meals in many cultures are healthy because they contain the necessary food elements — protein, carbohydrates, fats, vitamins, and minerals.
   b. Fast-food restaurants are more common.
   c. Most people can buy basic, natural, fresh, prepared, canned, frozen, or packaged foods from local markets and restaurants.
   d. Health disorders like heart disease, strokes, and cancer are no longer related to food and eating.

Now, go back to Activity 2 in the Before You Read section on page 43. Look at the answers you wrote down before you read the article and answer the questions again.

- Give definitions in your answer to Question 1.
- Give examples in your answers to Questions 2, 4, and 5.
- Give reasons in your answers to Question 3.

 8 Discussing the Reading In small groups, talk about your answers to the following questions.

1. What are your opinions of fast food and of fast-food restaurants? Give reasons for your answers.

2. What are your eating habits like? When and where do you eat? What kinds of food do you usually buy from machines, food stands, snack bars, restaurants, stores, and markets? How do you prepare your food?

3. What are some reasons for your individual diet choices? Are they based on habit, your culture, religion, convenience, beliefs about health and nutrition, ideas about body image, health problems, age, popular diet plans, or something else?

4. In general, do you think eating customs and habits in various places of the world are becoming more similar or more varied? Is the global diet changing? In good ways or bad? Give reasons for your opinions.

PART 2 Main Ideas and Details

Facts About Food

Before You Read

 1 Previewing Vocabulary Read the vocabulary items below from the next reading. Then listen to the words and phrases. Put a check mark (✓) next to the words you don't know. Don't use a dictionary.

Nouns
- bugs
- caffeine
- cancer
- cholesterol
- desserts
- diabetes
- discussion
- effects
- fiber
- grains
- heart disease
- ingredients
- medicine
- memory
- nutrients
- nutritionists
- opinions
- specialists
- strokes
- substances
- whole grains

Verbs
- affect
- allow
- support

Adjectives
- available
- home-cooked
- industrialized
- opposite
- perfect
- related

Adverb
- financially

Phrases
- brain power
- in contrast

Adjectives (cont.)
- required
- spicy

Matching Paragraph Titles with Topics

Often, the title of reading material tells its topic. But a title should look or sound interesting, and it should be short. For these reasons, readers might not know the meaning of a title—at first.

2 **Matching Paragraph Titles with Topics** On the left are four examples of interesting titles on the subject of food and eating. On the right are less interesting but clearer phrases about the topic. Match the titles to the topics with lines, as in the example.

Titles	Topics
1. Food for Thought	**a.** The Effects of Amounts of Dietary Fat in Different Cultures
2. The Fat of the Land	**b.** Cooking and Eating Insect Foods for Good Nutrition
3. Food Fights	**c.** Opposite or Contrasting Opinions on the Best Eating Habits
4. Getting the Bugs Out	**d.** Brain Foods and Other Nutrients for the Mind and Memory

3 **Choosing Titles and Recognizing Topic Sentences** Read each paragraph of the article below. On the line above each paragraph, write a possible title from Activity 2. Also, underline the topic sentence in each paragraph. Remember—a topic sentence is a short statement of the main idea or point of a paragraph.

Facts About Food

Food Fights

A   Everywhere on earth there are "food specialists" with opposite (or different) opinions on the best kinds of nutrition for various purposes. A lot of people believe that the healthiest diets are high in fiber, vitamins, and minerals but low in fat, cholesterol, sugar, and salt. Some **nutritionists** say the perfect eating plan contains mostly carbohydrates without much protein.

▲ Food specialists disagree on the best kinds of nutrition.

In contrast, other scientists say people need high-protein meals with meat, chicken, fish, or milk products and only small amounts of **grains**, potatoes, breads, rice, and noodles. One famous diet plan allows only certain foods at certain times — protein with protein, carbohydrates with carbohydrates, fruits alone, and so on. Some eaters stay away from all meat and maybe even fish and milk products. They get their protein from plants, mostly beans. Others want only high-fiber food. These people may not eat white bread or white rice or even cooked vegetables. So what is the best way to eat and be healthy? The discussion of food facts will go on far into the future.

B   The necessary substances and elements for human life and health are water, protein, carbohydrates, fats, vitamins, and minerals. Most kinds of food contain some or all of the required nutrients, but these substances have different effects on people. Various ingredients and dishes affect the mind in different ways, and some kinds of nourishment have better effects on the brain than others. For instance, can broccoli increase brain power? Maybe so. Low levels of some of the B vitamins can cause a decrease in memory and thinking ability, nutritionists say, but dark green vegetables, like broccoli, contain a lot of these nutrients. Another example of a "memory helper" is lecithin — a substance from soybeans, also found in high-fiber foods like nuts and whole grains. High-protein foods influence the mind in more helpful ways than dishes high in sugar and carbohydrates. And the caffeine in coffee or tea may help thinking. Of course, its effects don't last long.

C   In many places outside big cities, food with more than four legs is part of good, healthy home cooking. Fried or grilled ants are a tasty but expensive snack in Colombia, South America. In various parts of Mexico, over 300 types of insects serve as food. In southern Africa, many people like to eat at least one kind of caterpillar or worm. They enjoy it fried, dried, or cooked in tomato sauce. In Thailand, cooks create a spicy hot pepper sauce with water bugs. In Vietnam, grasshoppers filled with peanuts are a special dish. And in some regions of China, **bugs** are not only a part of meals but an important ingredient in medicine too. Most kinds of insects have high nutritional value. They contain a lot of protein, vitamins, and minerals. Many people like their taste. They are everywhere on the planet. They add to the variety of people's diets. For several reasons, insects are an important kind of food in the global diet, and they may become a more common ingredient in the future.

D   The growing similarities in diet and eating habits around the world are influencing people of various cultures in different ways. For example, Western foods are damaging health in the industrialized island country of Japan. Instead of small meals of seafood, rice, and vegetables, the typical

Japanese diet now includes large amounts of meat, dairy products (like whole-milk ice cream), and **desserts** like tiramisu, a rich Italian dish full of chocolate, cheese, and sugar. According to Japanese health researchers, such changes in eating habits are related to a great increase in health problems 55 such as heart disease, strokes, cancer, and diabetes. On the other hand, the changing global diet is having the opposite effect on the people in the Czech Republic. The government of this European nation no longer supports meat and dairy products financially, so the cost of these foods is going up. In contrast, fresh fruits and vegetables are becoming more widely available from 60 private markets and stands. Cooks are even serving salads to schoolchildren, and families are eating healthier home-cooked meals. For these reasons, fewer Czech men are having heart attacks, the women are losing a lot of weight, and most people are living healthier lives.

After You Read

Strategy

More About Summarizing

In previous chapters, you learned some ways to summarize information. Here are some other ways to summarize a paragraph:

- First, say or write the title of the reading material. Then ask a question about the main idea that is answered in the paragraph you are summarizing.
- Begin your summary with a one-sentence general answer to your main-idea question.
- Which information and ideas (facts, examples, and reasons) from the reading support your first statement? Add those in a clear order to your summary.

Here is a possible summary of the first paragraph of the selection "Facts About Food."

What do food specialists around the world believe about nutrition? They may agree on the basics, but they can have very different opinions about the best kinds and amounts of foods for human health. For example, some people say to eat mostly carbohydrates; others believe in high-protein eating plans; still others think fiber is the most important element.

4 Summarizing Work in groups of three. Have each person choose a different paragraph (B, C, or D) from the reading "Facts About Food." Read it carefully. Begin with the title. Summarize the main idea and important supporting details. Then tell or read your summary to your group.

5 Discussing the Reading Work in groups of four. Each person gives the instruction and asks the questions in one of these items. That person takes notes on the other three people's answers. Later, he or she summarizes the discussion about that item for the class. Everyone can ask more questions and make comments.

1. Tell your ideas about good food and nutrition. Is there a "perfect" diet for health and long life? Why do you think this way?

2. Give examples of your experiences with food. In your opinion, do certain foods increase or decrease brainpower (memory and thinking ability)? If so, which ones? How do you feel when you eat them?

3. In big cities and industrialized areas of the world, people don't generally cook or choose insect dishes. What do you think about unusual foods of this kind? Why do you feel that way?

4. Tell about diet changes in your country or culture. What changes are going on? How are they affecting people? Why do you think so?

6 Talking It Over Read the statements below about food. Then write one of your own. From your knowledge and experience, which of these statements are true facts? Which are unproven opinions? Write *F* for fact or *O* for opinion on each line. Then explain your reasons to the group.

1. _____ Fresh, uncooked, natural foods are always best for the health. Cooking takes away vitamins and other nutrients.

2. _____ Hot, spicy foods damage the stomach. Chili peppers or similar ingredients don't belong in family dishes, even if they are part of the culture.

3. _____ Nuts are bad for people because they contain fat. Avocados are unhealthy for the same reason.

4. _____ Many kinds of foods are related. For instance, prunes are dried plums, and raisins are dried grapes. Tofu looks like cheese, but it really comes from soybeans.

5. _____ More coffee comes from Brazil than from any other place, and most of the world's tea comes from India.

6. _____ For various reasons (color, taste, safety, etc.), companies add natural substances from seaweed, insects, trees, flowers, and so on to packaged foods.

7. _____ With added vitamins, minerals, and nutrients, snack foods like candy, cookies, chips, and soft drinks can and will become the new "health foods."

8. _____ Even a simple, basic food like rice has many varieties — such as white, brown, black, basmati, long-grain, short-grain, and so on. There are various ways to cook and include rice in menus and meals.

9. _____ The best diets are based on religious law — usually Jewish, Muslim, or Christian.

10. _____ For good health and long life, there are a number of "perfect" foods. Some examples are vegetables like broccoli and cabbage, citrus fruits and red grapes, onions, garlic, and soybeans.

Strategy

Getting Meaning from Context: Italics and Punctuation Clues
As you have learned in other chapters, often the context of reading material contains clues to the meanings of vocabulary items.

- New or unusual words or phrases may be in *italics*. Italics are a special kind of slanted type, *like this*.
- Short definitions, similar words, explanations of the items, or examples of their meanings might come between certain kinds of punctuation marks, like quotation marks (" ") or parentheses ( ). They can also appear after a comma or a dash (—).

1 **Getting Meaning from Context: Italics and Punctuation Clues**
In the reading selection "Global Diet Choices" on pages 44–45, some vocabulary items are italicized and some have short explanations of their meaning between or after punctuation marks. For each of these definitions or group of examples below, find the words or phrases in the reading. Write the word or phrase on the line. (The letters in parentheses are the letters of the paragraphs.)

1. a person's or group's usual food choices or habits: (A) _____*diet*_____.

2. an eating plan with only certain kinds or amounts of food: (A) _____.

3. prepared items from inexpensive restaurants, snack bars, or food stands:

   (B) _____.

4. another word for *worldwide:* (B) _____.

5. types of Mexican fast food: (B) _____

   _____.

6. a blood-sugar disorder: (C) _____.

7. an eating system high in protein but low in refined carbohydrates:

   (C) _____.

8. corn, beans, rice, breads: (D) _____

   _____.

9. miso, tofu, and bean paste: (D) _____.

10. milk products: (D) _____.

Strategy

Recognizing Vocabulary Categories

Most language learners want to learn a lot of vocabulary as quickly as possible. How can they do this?

- One way is to learn several words with the same or similar meanings at the same time. For example, another word for *worldwide* is *universal*.
- Another way is to learn words in categories. A category is a class or group of items in a system of classification. For instance, the items *meat*, *dairy products*, *vegetables*, and *fruit* are "kinds of food." *Protein*, *carbohydrates*, *fats*, *vitamins*, and *minerals* belong to the category "nutrients in food."

2 **Recognizing Vocabulary Categories** Below is a list of words and phrases from Chapters 1 to 3. They belong to various categories shown in the chart on page 55. Write the words from the list under the correct category in the chart. Four vocabulary items are done for you.

asthma

~~beef and pork~~

bugs

building facilities

cancer

candy and cookies

chicken and poultry

classmates

classroom

college campus

~~college students~~

community

continents

Colombia,
    South America

The Czech Republic

dairy products

the desert

desserts

diabetes

doctors

dormitories

eating halal

emotions

flu or pneumonia

fruit

grains and breads

hamburgers

headaches

heart disease

high blood pressure

home-cooked

homesick

hunger

ice cream

insects

international

keeping kosher

meteorologists

moody

mountain areas

nutritionists

perfect health

pork or bacon

physical beauty

professors

researchers

residence hall

residents

restaurants

rice and pasta

sadness

salads

sandwiches

~~school~~

scientists

shellfish

~~sickness or illness~~

snack bars

soy products

southern Africa

specialists

strangers

a stroke

students

sushi and tempura

teachers

tiramisu

a tropical rain forest

a university

vegetables

Vietnam and Thailand

Categories			
People	Places	Possible Foods	Human Conditions
college students	school	beef and pork	sickness or illness

③ Practicing with Categories Match the vocabulary items on the left with their category on the right. Then check your answers with a partner and add one or more example to each vocabulary item on the left.

1. __d__ summer, fall (autumn),
winter, spring

    a. continents

2. _____ breakfast, lunch, dinner,
supper, snacks

    b. countries

3. _____ broccoli, corn, cabbage, beans,
potatoes, onions, green peppers

    c. subjects of college study

4. _____ business, engineering,
technology, computer science

    d. seasons of the year

5. _____ Canada, Brazil, Great Britain,
Germany, Russia, Korea

    e. weather conditions

6. _____ sun, rain, snow, ice, wind,
humidity, drought, fog, clouds

    f. eating places and food stores

7. _____ restaurants, fast-food chains,
snack bars, food stands, markets

    g. kinds of meals

8. _____ protein, carbohydrates, fats,
cholesterol, vitamins, minerals

    h. vegetables

9. _____ North America, South America,
Europe, Asia, Africa

    i. beverages

10. _____ water, coffee, tea, wine, beer,
juice, soft drinks

    j. nutrients and food elements

FOCUS

Understanding Schematic Tables

The TOEFL® iBT aims to test "global understanding" of a reading: Do you have a picture in your mind of the overall structure and meaning of a reading passage? One item that tests this kind of comprehension is the "schematic table" question. Each passage in the reading section has either a summary or a schematic table item as its last question.

A reader who sees interrelationships among ideas should be able to sort them into categories, like you did in Activity 2 on page 54. On the TOEFL® iBT, the things to be classified are more complex (reasons, events, characteristics, theories, etc.) but the idea is the same.

Practice

Based on the reading on pages 44 – 45, "Global Diet Choices," complete the chart below. Select the six appropriate phrases from the answer choices (A through H) below the chart. Write the letter under the type of diet it relates to. (Two of the answer choices will NOT be used.) Then compare your answers with those of one or two other students.

Personal Reasons for Choosing a Diet Item	Cultural Reasons for Choosing a Diet Item
▪ _____	▪ _____
▪ _____	▪ _____
▪ _____	▪ _____

A. Fast food tastes good, even though it may not be healthy.

B. German fast food includes sausage and schnitzel.

C. Some Christians eat fish instead of meat on Fridays.

D. Diabetics have to avoid foods with sugar in them.

E. Seafood can be prepared in many different ways.

F. The Mexican diet reflects pre-Columbian and European influences.

G. People who want to lose weight often choose low-carb foods.

H. Muslims avoid foods that are prohibited within the system of *halal*.

Self-Assessment Log

Read the lists below. Check (✓) the strategies and vocabulary that you learned in this chapter. Look through the chapter or ask your instructor about the strategies and words that you do not understand.

Reading and Vocabulary-Building Strategies

- ☐ Recognizing reading structure: main-idea questions for paragraph topics
- ☐ Recognizing one- or two-sentence statements of the main idea
- ☐ Recognizing supporting details
- ☐ Matching paragraph titles with topics
- ☐ Recognizing topics and main ideas
- ☐ Choosing titles and recognizing topic sentences
- ☐ Summarizing
- ☐ Getting meaning from context: italics and punctuation clues
- ☐ Recognizing vocabulary categories

Target Vocabulary

Nouns
- breakfast
- bugs
- choices*
- complex* carbohydrates
- customs
- dairy
- desserts
- diabetes
- diet
- discussion*
- dishes
- elements*
- fast food
- fats
- grains
- habits
- insects
- low-carb diet
- meals*
- minerals
- nutritionists
- preferences*
- soy products*
- variety*

Verb
- diet*

Adjectives
- frozen
- necessary*
- popular*
- product*
- universal
- worse

Adverb
- probably*

* These words are among the 2,000 most frequently used words in English.

4 In the Community

> "When I took office, only high energy physicists had ever heard of what is called the World Wide Web... Now even my cat has its own page."
>
> Former U.S. President Bill Clinton

In this **CHAPTER**

In Part 1, you will read about virtual communities and how they are different from real-life communities. In the rest of the chapter, you will read about, explore, and discuss different kinds of communities and how they operate.

Connecting to the Topic

1. Look at the people in the photograph. In how many different ways are they relating to one another? Can you name these "means of communication?"

2. Look at the title of this chapter. What kind of community do you think the people in the picture belong to? Explain your answer.

3. What are some of the advantages of virtual communities? What are some problems or challenges of virtual communities?

What Makes a (Virtual) Community?

① **Previewing the Topic** Discuss the image below in small groups. Be prepared to tell the class your ideas in answer to these questions.

The Globe From Cyberspace

1. How does the picture differ from a geographical world map? What is its main point or purpose?

2. What kinds of "regions" and other locations exist on the "virtual map?"

3. Imagine *human communities* on the map. Where do you think they are? What do you think they are doing or saying?

② **Predicting** Discuss possible answers to these questions. If you don't know the answers, make predictions. You can look for the answers when you read "What Makes a (Virtual) Community?"

1. What are some possible definitions of *human community*—in "real-life" physical locations and online in cyberspace?

2. Name some kinds of "physical-reality" vs. "virtual-reality" communities. In what kinds of "places" might their members "meet?"

3. What are some potential problems or challenges of the idea—or reality—of *community*?

3 Previewing Vocabulary Read the vocabulary items below from the first reading. Then listen to the words and phrases. Put a check mark (✓) next to the words you don't know. Don't use a dictionary.

Nouns
- applications
- comments
- content
- harassment
- level
- location
- motivation
- network
- reality
- resources
- responsibilities
- retirement
- risk

- sites
- steps

Verbs
- connect
- contribute
- exist
- interact
- keep going
- observe
- participate
- recognize
- tend (to)

Adjectives
- committed
- delayed
- geographical
- huge
- involved
- physical
- real-life
- spiritual
- virtual
- wireless

Adverbs
- forever
- however

- nowadays
- occasionally
- relatively
- therefore

Phrases
- even so
- general truth
- socially acceptable

Read

4 Reading an Article Read the following article. Then read about paragraph topics and do the activities that follow.

What Makes a (Virtual) Community?

A   The most traditional definition of a *human community* was "a group of people larger than a family that **interact**." A *community* may include people who have at least one common point of interest. In the past, community members lived **relatively** close to one another in one **geographical location**: in the same building, on the same street, in the same neighborhood or area, or in the same village, town, or city. Nowadays, however, the word *community* can mean a national, an international (worldwide), or even an online group of interacting individuals. **Therefore**, a "new" definition of *community* might be "a group of people that **recognize** that they have something in common." 5

B   A few kinds of communities share both physical location and other features. One example is a *retirement community* for people over a certain age. Another is an *intentional community* (a group with **resources**, **responsibilities**, or a common purpose, such as a social, economic, political, or **spiritual** goal). On college or university campuses, for instance, they may live in places like residence halls, fraternity or sorority houses, housing cooperatives, or special-interest housing; in other areas of life, intentional 10   15 communities can be business, school, church, or other groups that live, work, or at least meet in person. Many other interacting groups nowadays, **however**, are *virtual communities*. Their members seldom, if ever, get together physically. Instead, they **connect** from a distance over the Internet: on computers, smart phones, and other **wireless** devices. Research into these kinds of groups is relatively new. **Even so**, some of their features are similar to those of real-life communities; others are very different.

C   What kinds of meeting places exist online? Individuals might "get together" in forums, chat rooms, e-mail discussion groups, and community areas within big social networking **sites** like Facebook, Twitter, LinkedIn, and others. They may make use of blog posts and **comments**, wikis ("websites on which anyone can change **content**"), or web widgets ("small **applications** that perform a task"). And what features do these virtual locations have in common? First, they are likely to include print, audio, visual, and/or moving content about topics of interest to members. Second, participants can probably communicate with "**delayed** timing," as through e-mail or newsgroups. And third, people may connect in "real time," like through chatting, texting, or other kinds of instant messaging; their interaction is like real-life networking.

D   Just as in real-life social communities of the past and present, members of virtual communities **tend to participate** in general steps. As an illustration, individuals might first **observe** from the outside. Second, they begin to take part as "newcomers." If they participate regularly, **contribute** to community purposes, if any, and perhaps take risks, they become committed "insiders." "Full members" may turn into "leaders," who take responsibility for others; their participation is likely to help keep the community going and growing. Finally, some "retirees" leave the network for various reasons: perhaps because of new relationships in different locations, changing interests, or problems in other areas of their lives. Or they may not have enough time, energy, or other resources to continue contributing.

E   What do social researchers know about online communities? One **general truth** is that they tend to vary widely. For instance, there may be no, only a few, or a **huge** number of people **involved** in a site at any one time; they may participate for only a short time or **forever**. The **level** of commitment (caring) of full members is likely to differ greatly, too. So is the amount of time and energy they contribute: some people are doing something online virtually all the time; others take part only occasionally. Also, people are likely to be involved in different ways: for example, some only get (read or hear) content but don't add any or much information of their own. And finally, the element that connects people in a **network** can be almost anything—like any common identity, purpose, interest, problem, need, belief, experience, or another **motivation**.

F   So why do virtual communities exist? How do individuals decide to get or stay in—or keep far away from--them? According to researchers, the three most motivating elements are payback, obligation, and social acceptance. First, the advantages of membership must turn out to be worth the "cost" (like the amount of time, energy, money, or other resources contributed). Second, if people are **committed** to an interacting group, they may feel they must keep contributing. And third, people are more likely to stay in a **socially acceptable** group—or a network in which they feel accepted and valued by others. 65

G   A great advantage of online communities is that they build relationships among many different kinds of people; age, cultural **identity**, and **lifestyle** become unimportant. But what are potential challenges of virtual relating? 70 First, there may truly be risk involved, or people may feel unsafe in various ways, such as financially, physically, personally, or socially. Identity is another possible problem; individuals don't have to tell the truth about themselves online, so there can be deception involved. A third possibility is online **harassment** ("trying to harm others over the net on purpose"). 75 And finally, if there is not enough privacy (about true or false information), members can get themselves—and others—into big trouble.

H   In summary, *virtual communities* are similar to groups that exist in **physical reality** in several ways: in their definitions, purposes, steps members take to get into and out of them, reasons they **exist**, and potential 80 challenges (risks, deception, harassment, privacy). Is continuing and growing interaction online likely to improve human relationships? Or will it change the definition of *"community"* into something completely different in today's physical and virtual world?

After You Read

FOCUS

Identifying Paragraph And Whole Reading Topics

Reading material with a simple structure might begin with a general introductory paragraph. It may end with a short conclusion or summary. The several paragraphs between the first and the last are likely to give various kinds of information. These may **illustrate**, show, or otherwise relate to the reading's main ideas.

The topic, or subject, of a whole reading is more general than the specific topics of individual paragraphs. The specific topic of each paragraph should clearly relate to the general topic of the reading.

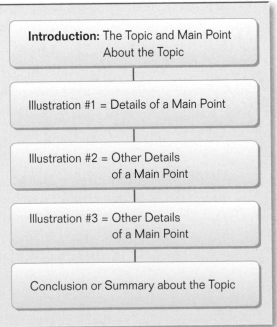

Introduction: The Topic and Main Point About the Topic

Illustration #1 = Details of a Main Point

Illustration #2 = Other Details of a Main Point

Illustration #3 = Other Details of a Main Point

Conclusion or Summary about the Topic

5 **Identifying Topics of Paragraphs** In the reading, "What Makes a (Virtual) Community?" there is a capital letter (A–H) next to each of the eight paragraphs. Choose from the phrases in the box and write the specific topic of each paragraph next to its letter.

> Examples of Kinds of Real-Life Vs. Virtual Communities
> "Participation Steps" in Interactive Communities
> Possible Definitions of *Human Community*
> Where and How Individuals "Get Together" Online
> A Concluding or Summarizing Statement and Questions
> Four General Truths about Online Communities
> People's Motivation to Interact in Cyberspace
> Some Potential Challenges in Relating to Others

A. _____ *Possible Definitions of Human Community* _____

B. _____

C. _____

D. _____

E. _____

F. _____

G. _____

H. _____

Strategy

Identifying the Main Ideas

How can readers recognize the main ideas of reading material? Here is one basic method:

- Ask and answer *one* question about the information in each paragraph.
- Then ask and answer a general question about the whole reading.
- Use your one or two-sentence answer to each question to give the main ideas.

6 **Identifying the Main Ideas of a Reading** Which phrase below best tells the subject of the whole reading "What Makes a (Virtual) Community?" Give reasons for your answer.

(A) where social, economic, political, and/or spiritual commitments are most important in human communities

(B) what virtual communities in cyberspace have in common with groups that meet in physical locations

(C) how identity deception relates to financial problems and privacy

7 Identifying the Main Idea by Asking Questions Complete the questions below about the article "What Makes a (Virtual) Community?" Use the phrases *What is/are*, *What will*, *Where do*, *What (do)*, *How do*. Each question is about a different lettered paragraph A-H from the article. The last question is about the main idea of the whole article.

A. _____*What are*_____ some possible definitions of the phrase human community?

B. _____ people meet (get together) in both physically real and virtual networks?

C. _____ the names and some features of virtual meeting places on the *web*?

D. _____ steps might members take as they get into and out of online groups?

E. _____ researchers believe to be true about interactive online communities?

F. _____ people get motivated to become members of or leave networking groups?

G. _____ one advantage—and four potential problems—of online relationships and relating?

H. _____ virtual communities have in common with "real-life" ones—and _____ happen with them in the future?

8 Changing False Statements to True Statements Read the false statements below about the main ideas of Paragraphs A-H of the reading and the main idea of the whole article. Change the underlined pieces of false information and rewrite the sentences to make them true. Then use the sentences as correct answers to the eight questions in Activity 7.

1. A *human community* can be defined as "a group of people <u>smaller</u> than a family *larger* that interact and that recognize they have <u>nothing</u> in common."

2. In <u>virtual online communities in cyberspace</u>, members get together physically in *something* a real location; <u>in real-life, intentional groups</u>, they mostly interact on computers and wireless devices from a distance.

3. Some kinds of *virtual meeting places* are <u>retirement housing, residence halls, sorority houses, cooperatives, businesses, and school buildings.</u> These are all <u>unlikely</u> to include content on topics of common interest, delayed communication, and instant messaging.

4. The steps participants in online groups take are often the same. First, they might only use web widgets and wikis to observe. Then observers become newcomers. "Full members" can take part regularly, contribute, and stay a long time—or not. Before they become committed <u>insiders</u>, they are <u>leaders</u>. <u>No one can leave at any time.</u>

5. There are general truths about online groups: <u>only a few</u> people can be involved in a site; their level of commitment <u>stays the same</u>; and <u>only one common interest</u> can bring them together.

Strategy

Learning to Paraphrase

In Chapter 3 you learned to summarize by asking questions that are answered in a paragraph. Another way to summarize is to *paraphrase* the main idea and the important supporting details. A paraphrase is a restatement using other words.

- First, be sure you understand the correct meaning of each important idea or piece of information in the reading.

- Think of words and phrases with similar meanings to express the same ideas. For example, below are phrases or ideas from "Communities in Real-Life Locations," with possible ways to paraphrase them.

  - real-life communities in the physical world   =   groups of people that interact in neighborhoods and cities
  - human needs such as housing, food, land, work, and money   =   basic necessities of life
  - informal agreements   =   understandings among neighbors and leaders
  - cities became bigger, more crowded, noisier, and more dangerous   =   urban growth caused problems
  - greater resources   =   more money

- Then put your paraphrases together with other words in a short paragraph. Make sure your paragraph tells the main points of the original material in logical order. Here is an example of a possible paraphrased summary of Paragraph A.

Community design or organization is for people that interact in neighborhoods and cities. Its main purpose is to fulfill the basic necessities of human life. At first, there were informal understandings among neighbors and leaders. Then came structured government. Urban growth caused problems, however. Residents with more money moved to suburbs. These moves decreased the sense of community.

4 Paraphrasing Work in groups of three. Each person chooses one of the other Paragraphs B, C, or D from the reading "Communities in Real-Life Locations." Read it carefully. Reread the main idea. In a few sentences, summarize the paragraph, paraphrasing the main idea and important details. Then tell or read your summary to your group.

5 Talking it Over Work in small groups. Talk about your answers to the following questions. Be prepared to tell the class some of the most important information.

1. In your opinion, has the design of villages, towns, and cities through the centuries changed for the better or the worse? (Consider the earliest communities, small-town life, city centers with suburbs, huge urban areas, and the newer "smart cities.") Give reasons for your answers.

2. As you compare the benefits and potential challenges of these pairs of environments, tell about your experiences living in or visiting them:

   a. rural vs. urban living

   b. small-town vs. large-city life

   c. organized vs. unplanned neighborhoods

   d. "smart cities" vs. places with little technology

3. What more do you want to know about "smart" or "intelligent" city design? What ideas do you have about the ideal place to live?

4. Do you have experience with "community organizing?" If so, what are your feelings about it? If not, do you think it might improve or harm human relationships and people's living situations? Give detailed reasons for your opinions.

PART 3 Vocabulary and Language-Learning Skills

Strategy

Getting Meaning from Context: Finding Illustrations (Examples) of Words
Sometimes illustrations (examples) of the meaning of a word are in another sentence or sentence part. These illustrations will all be part of the same "meaning category," a group of words that have similar meanings.

The words *for example, for instance, as an illustration, like,* and *such as* introduce an illustration. You can use the illustration as clues to the meaning of the other words.

Example
Social scientists believe that huge urban areas have negative effects on people; **for instance**, residents of large cities tend to be more depressed, irritable, and nervous than people in rural environments.

1 **Finding Illustrations of Meaning Categories** Read the vocabulary phrases below. Write illustrations (examples) of each one from the reading selection "What Makes a (Virtual) Community?" on pages 63–65. (The letters in parentheses are the letters of the paragraphs.) Some items are done as examples.

1. Possible elements or features of human communities: (B) _____*purpose*_____,

_____, _____, _____, _____

2. kinds of *intentional communities*: (B) _____social_____, _____,

   _____, _____business_____, _____

3. kinds of web meeting places, including *networking sites* and applications: (C)

   _____forums_____, _____, _____, _____,

   _____, _____, _____

4. ways to communicate with "delayed timing" or in "real time": (C)

   _____, _____, _____, _____

5. roles individuals might take in online communities: (D) _____observers_____,

   _____, _____

6. elements in the "cost" of committed group membership: (F) _____,

   _____, _____, _____

7. some potential challenges or problems of online relating: (G)

   _____, _____, _____, _____

8. ways contributors might feel "at risk" (unsafe) on the Internet: (G)

   _____, _____, _____, _____

 2 Naming the Meaning Category Think of a word that you can illustrate with four examples. Write them in the chart. Tell your group the examples. Can they name the word you are thinking about?

Word	Illustrations/Examples
smart phone	iphone, Android, Samsung, Blackberry

 ## Strategy

Recognizing Words with Similar Meanings and Meaning Categories

To improve your vocabulary quickly, you can learn new words at the same time. They should have something in common (be part of a meaning category: alike in some way). Here are two good ways to do this:

- Look at the words and phrases with the same or similar meanings together—like *human community*, *neighborhood residents*, *interacting individuals*, and *group members*.
- Learn items in categories. For example, the words *villages*, *towns*, *cities*, *suburbs*, and *urban areas* are all places where people live and may interact.

With both methods, the words and phrases in each grouping should be the same *part of speech*, such as *nouns*, *verbs*, *adjectives*, or *adverbs*.

3 **Identifying Similar Meanings and Meaning Categories** All the words and phrases in each of the groups below are the same part of speech. How do the items belong together? If they have the same or similar meanings, write S on the line. Or are the vocabulary items members of the same meaning category? Then write C for category on the line. Name the possible category.

1. __S__ virtual/non-physical/existing in cyberspace/not real-life/online
2. __C__ purposes/beliefs/resources/preferences/needs/risks/interests
3. _____ meet/interact/get together/connect/communicate/network
4. _____ smart/intelligent/well-structured/quick/technologically ahead
5. _____ small/compact/full of people/crowded/close/not big/little
6. _____ kids/children/sons/daughters/descendents
7. _____ financially/socially/personally/physically/culturally /economically
8. _____ housing/food/land/work/money/transportation/space/privacy
9. _____ sensors/monitors/computers/smart phones/wireless devices/wikis
10. _____ schools/workplaces/parks/open land/green spaces/shopping areas

Strategy

Recognizing Nouns and Verbs

A very useful vocabulary-learning method is to recognize parts of speech. Some words can be more than one part of speech. As examples, in the first sentence below, the words *sense*, *design*, and *need* are nouns; in the second sentence, *senses*, *need*, and *design* are verbs.

Examples

In many *senses*, the *design* of a community should relate to the *needs* of its occupants. A social scientist *senses* their importance; that's why city planners *need* to *design* places in certain ways.

Some words in noun and verb pairs, however, have different forms or endings. Here are some examples of related words from Chapter 4.

Noun	Verb
arrangement	arrange
connections	connect
decision	decide
definition	define
government	govern
interaction	interact
location	locate
organizers	organize
residents	reside
transportation	transport

4 **Recognizing Nouns and Verbs** Here are some sentences with noun/verb pairs. In each blank, write the missing word—the noun related to the underlined verb or the verb related to the underlined noun.

1. We can <u>define</u> the word *community* as "a group of people that interact." Another _____ is "a group that recognizes they have something in common."

2. Social <u>interaction</u> is considered a basic human need. Communities should be organized so that people can _____ with one another.

3. Can you <u>locate</u> information on a Google map? Or do you need a map that shows its physical _____?

4. As cities grew, they needed organization to <u>govern</u> the large numbers of people in them. This was the beginning of city _____.

5. How do city planners <u>arrange</u> structures, streets, and green spaces? What's the best _____ for the community?

6. Some people <u>reside</u> in rural areas or suburbs. Other _____ prefer to live in crowded, lively city neighborhoods.

7. It's the <u>connections</u> in computer networks that make cities smart. What technology ___*connects*___ us to the "computing cloud."

8. Various kinds of <u>transportation</u> is used to _____ people in and out of the big city—and from one place to another within it.

9. Community <u>organizers</u> attract, educate, and _____ people; they want to have an impact on powerful people in government and other institutions.

10. How do leaders get grassroots groups to <u>decide</u> which _____ makers to influence?

For more practice, tell or write more nouns from Chapters 1 to 4. Which nouns have related verb forms? What are the related verb forms? Also, you can tell or write some verbs with their related noun forms. (You can check your guesses in a dictionary or online.)

5 Finding Definitions of Vocabulary Items Look at the columns below. In the context of the reading "Communities in Real-Life Locations" on pages 71 to 73, some vocabulary words are between quotation marks because they are being used in possibly new or unusual ways. Match each item with its explanation on the right. The letters in parentheses ( ) are the letters of the paragraphs.

Vocabulary Items

1. __c__ communities (A)
2. _____ organized (A)
3. _____ leader (A)
4. _____ sense of community (A)
5. _____ social housing (B)
6. _____ watching (B)
7. _____ computing cloud (C)
8. _____ smartness (C)
9. _____ regular people (D)

Possible Definitions for the Context

a. person that takes responsibility for others, helping them to participate

b. being there, perhaps observing and sharing information

c. places with no, a few, or a large number of interacting groups

d. a feeling of being part of a group of people that know one another and interact

e. individuals that are not especially powerful or famous

f. designed, arranged, or structured

g. the features of "intelligent cities" that monitor, connect, and organize

h. information and knowledge sent to and from computers and other wireless devices over a network

i. apartments for individuals and families that have low incomes

6 Focusing on High-Frequency Words Read the paragraph below and fill in each blank with a word from the box.

arrangement	effects	tend
century	environments	urban
connections	resources	
economic	spaces	

The Effects of Urban Design on City Residents

Social scientists believe that huge _____ areas have
1

negative _____ on people; for instance, residents of large cities
2

_____ to be more depressed and nervous than people in rural
3

_____4____. City planners in the twentieth _____5_____,
therefore, designed "beautiful cities." _Urban design_ involved the
_____6_____ of attractive structures (mostly tall buildings), public
_____7_____, pleasant parks and other green areas, necessary
_____8_____, and industrial areas outside the city. Its purpose was
to make _____9_____ between people and places, their movements,
and nature. In the twenty-first century, in contrast, community organizers
consider such huge urban and suburban areas wasteful (too expensive) to
keep up in difficult _____10_____ times.

7 **Making Connections** Choose 4 words from Chapters 1–4 in this book. Do
a Google search. What comes up? Do any wikis, like Wikipedia, come up? Click on
some of the items that come up and find words in the same meaning category. Fill in
the chart.

Word	Sites	Meaning Category Words

TOEFL® iBT

FOCUS

Answering Negative Fact Questions On Tests

Similarity of meaning (see Part 3 of this chapter) is tested on many reading tests. Questions may ask you to choose the closest synonym or the most exact paraphrase for some part of the reading passage. Another type of question approaches the same skill in a different way. A negative fact question asks you to judge which of several choices is NOT similar to the rest. The TOEFL® iBT frequently asks negative fact questions. The structure of these questions uses such common expressions as *is not mentioned, except,* and *is not true.* Can you think of other phrases that are common in negative fact questions?

Answering Negative Fact Questions Read the following passage and answer the questions that follow it. Then compare your answers with those of one or two other students.

Creating Communities:
The Immigrant Experience

A   The experience of living in a community, where individuals and families share the common goal of having a normal, everyday life that includes raising children, working, and enjoying social activities with friends and family in the safety and peacefulness of their environment, isn't a unique experience. However, being an immigrant in a new country such as the United States has always been a difficult and complicated experience which native-born citizens take for granted. Why has the integration of the immigrant life into the native culture and community been such a source of hardship for newcomers?

B   The first reason is the language barrier. Many immigrants who arrive in America have little or no knowledge of the English language because as they grew up they never had the chance to learn it. Another major obstacle is the difference in the experience of American life from that normally experienced in the immigrant's home country. For two hundred years, the American way of life has centered on a strong work ethic and a desire to spend money on new products that give us pleasure and improve the quality of our lives. Americans also find enjoyment in a social atmosphere, where individuals who share common interests gather to explore those activities, such as dancing, writing fiction, hiking, and traveling. Another difference that can prevent an immigrant from seamlessly becoming a member of the community is the laws, which can be very different from the laws of a newcomer's own country. American laws promote freedom within a solid but slightly flexible framework that highlights the opportunity for citizens to do as they desire as long as it doesn't cause undue harm to others. American laws ensure freedom to action while maintaining peace and order in society. The final challenge for an immigrant can be the lack of other immigrants of the same or similar ethnicity.

C   Since the early days of immigration, however, this last problem has been dealt with by creating enclaves or ghettos, pockets of land within a city where individuals and families of the same nationality live, work, and socialize. The first immigrants to establish these areas were the Germans and Irish in the 19th century. Eventually, Asians and Eastern Europeans continued this tradition. Well-known areas in New York City where ghettos originated include the Lower East Side, Brighton Beach (home to a large Russian population) as well as Chinatown and Little Italy. The value of culturally-related immigrants living together is in the closeness of the community's shared beliefs, traditions, and language. In these communities the immigrants' native language has little chance of being replaced entirely by English, but this can be problematic when immigrants go out beyond the boundaries created by using only their native language. Another positive side to these enclaves is the shared heritage and traditions that will not be lost under the pressure of the new but often confusing traditions that American life offers. These native traditions keep the culture in all its beauty alive. But a negative effect to staying within the boundaries fostered is that residents fear or shy away from people living on their borders who are culturally different; this prevents the American ideal—of sharing unique identities, beliefs, and traditions—from being fulfilled.

1. Which of the following is NOT mentioned in Paragraph C as an example of a New York City enclave?

   (A) the Lower East Side   (C) Brighton Beach

   (B) Greenwich Village   (D) Chinatown

2. All of the following are positive reasons for living in an enclave EXCEPT:

   (A) having a shared community of beliefs and traditions

   (B) using a common language to communicate and express yourself

   (C) keeping old traditions alive

   (D) engaging only in the culture and heritage of your ethnicity

3. Which of the following is NOT a negative effect of living in an enclave?

   (A) a feeling of closeness in the group's shared ethnic culture

   (B) only using the native tongue of the immigrant community to communicate

   (C) not going beyond its borders to experience the various forms of American culture

   (D) not going outside the community to share the immigrant culture with other American citizens

Self-Assessment Log

Read the lists below. Check (✓) the strategies and vocabulary that you learned in this chapter. Look through the chapter or ask your instructor about the strategies and words that you do not understand.

Reading and Vocabulary-Building Strategies

☐ Identifying paragraph and whole reading topics
☐ Identifying main ideas by asking questions
☐ Using punctuation to recognize supporting details
☐ Skimming for topics and main ideas
☐ Paraphrasing information
☐ Getting meaning from context: finding illustrations of words
☐ Recognizing words with similar meanings and meaning categories
☐ Recognizing nouns and verbs
☐ Finding definitions of vocabulary items

Target Vocabulary

Nouns

- applications*
- arrangement*
- comments*
- content*
- dependence
- design*
- harassment
- infrastructure
- level*
- location*
- motivation
- network*
- observers
- organization*
- reality*
- resources*
- responsibilities*
- retirement
- risk*
- sensors
- sites*
- steps*
- suburbs
- technology*
- transportation

Verbs

- connect*
- contribute*
- exist*
- interact
- monitor
- observe
- organize*
- participate
- recognize*
- tend (to)*

Adjectives

- committed
- compact
- delayed
- geographical
- huge*
- informal
- intentional
- involved
- low-income
- organized
- physical*
- real-life
- rural*
- spiritual
- structured
- suburban
- urban*
- virtual
- wireless

Adverbs

- forever
- however*
- relatively
- therefore*

Phrases

- even so
- general truth
- socially acceptable

* These words are among the 2,000 most frequently used words in English.

Home

> "Home is the place where, when you have to go there, they have to take you in."

Robert Frost , poet

In this
CHAPTER

In Part 1, you will read about similarities and differences among homes throughout history. In the rest of this chapter, you will read about, explore, and discuss ideas about housing, home, and family.

Connecting to the Topic

1. What kind of home is this? Describe what you see.
2. Would you be comfortable in this home? Why or why not?
3. What kind of home do you feel most comfortable in?

At Home in World History

Before You Read

 1 **Previewing the Topic** Which time period does each image represent? Write the number of photo in the timeline. Then answer the questions below with your group.

Stone Age	Middle Ages	Industrial Revolution

Present Time	Future

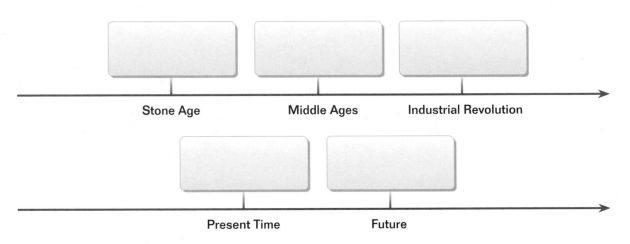

1. Describe each photo. What details helped you decide which time period each photo is from?

2. What similarities do you see in the pictures of home life from different periods of history? What differences do the photos suggest?

3. Describe two other periods in history that you know. What kinds of homes existed then?

2 Predicting Make predictions by discussing possible answers to these questions.

1. Why has shelter been a basic human necessity throughout history?

2. Through the centuries, how have housing design and construction been related to the natural environment? What about history and culture?

3. How do today's attitudes about homes compare with past ideas about human needs? How do you think this will change in the future?

3 Previewing Vocabulary Read the vocabulary items below from the first reading. Then listen to the words and phrases. Put a check mark (✓) next to the words you don't know. Don't use a dictionary.

Nouns		Verbs	Adjectives
architects	manufacturing	construct	ancient
branches	necessity	develop	durable
camp/camper	pipes	discover	flat
centuries	plaster	entertain	fortified
civilizations	property	fill in	hardened
clay	protection	form	homeless
frames/framing	shelter	produce	permanent
generations	tools	range from…to	prehistoric
invention	weapons		temporary
mansions			

Read

4 Reading an Article Read the following article. Then read the explanations and do the activities that follow.

At Home in World History

Prehistoric Times: Shelter as Basic Human Necessity

A   After food and clothing necessary for survival, the most important basic need is *shelter*. Throughout human history, people have needed **protection** from "the elements" (wind, rain, storms, cold, sun). Before they **discovered** how to build structures, human beings found shelter in trees, which provided protection from extreme weather, insects, wild animals, and other dangers. 5 The earliest people began to "feel at home" in caves. In the Stone Age, a **prehistoric** period of about two million years, human builders arranged **branches** on top of one another to make themselves places to live. With stone **tools**, prehistoric builders created tents out of animal skins, or they put big stones together to build shelters. Later **generations** created homes from 10 the earth itself; they **formed** bricks out of **clay** and dried them in the sun. The first roofs (building coverings) were of earth and plants. Everywhere in the world where there were human beings, **necessity** led to **invention**.

The Centuries BCE (B.C.): Housing in Ancient Civilizations

B   As **centuries** passed, housing styles depended on the natural environment: the climate and available resources of various areas of the world. The **architects** of ancient **civilizations**—like those of Egypt around 3000 B.C., Assyria from perhaps 2000 to 600 B.C., Greece in the centuries before and after 500 B.C., and Rome from the 8th century B.C.—designed flat-topped houses; the clay blocks of their structures were baked in ovens and glazed. Then came slanted roof coverings of glazed clay tile for rain and snow to **slide off**, central heating from **pipes** with hot water or air moving through them, and heavy wooden **frames filled in** with **hardened** earth. Later ancient generations **constructed** houses of durable wooden **framing** filled in with **plaster**, brick, or stone.

The Middle Ages CE (A.D.): Houses of the Common People Vs. the Powerful

C   In the European Middle Ages, beginning in the 5th century, most structures were cold, wet, and dark; sometimes it was warmer and lighter *outside* a home than within its walls. The simple, one-room houses of the poor had only small windows without glass (covered with wood at night), hard-earth floors, and plant roofs, which could catch fire when occupants were cooking or heating inside. Common people with greater resources could build more durable homes that included stone or mud-brick walls, hard tiled floors, framed windows, safer fireplaces, and protection against the elements and dangerous outsiders. Some groups of buildings developed into fortified castles. With their thick stone walls, the main purpose of these fortresses for the wealthy and powerful was security—not only of their owners but also of their families, workers, animals, food, weapons, and valued resources.

The 18th to 20th Centuries: Improvements and Choices in Housing

D   The discoveries and inventions of the 18th and 19th century *Industrial Revolution*—a time of worldwide changes in technology, led to great improvements in housing construction. With **manufacturing** and the availability of more kinds of materials, architects designed with three goals in mind: durability, practicality, and beauty. Accommodations **ranged from** the simplest of shelters—such as tents (covered frames) or caves, **to** durable wood, stone, or brick construction for "common people" **to** huge **mansions** with land for the very rich or powerful.

The Modern World: Attitudes Towards "Home"

E   For most people, home has been a place to take care of the young or to feel safe while growing up. In the modern world, this is still true. However, the types of housing people live in varies widely. Housing may be **permanent**: a family house or apartment; or **temporary**: a place to camp for a season, a student dorm room, or a shelter for a **homeless** family. Wherever the place, humans have a strong attachment to "home;" thus the saying, "There's no place like home." People often **develop** feelings of *homesickness* (discomfort, depression, or health problems) when they are away from the familiar things and people of home. Most world travelers feel homesick eventually; only a few individuals say they can "feel at home" anywhere—or call anyplace in the world their home. The question "What makes a house a home?" is likely to **produce** a large variety of answers.

The World Today: Laws and Social Values Related to Housing

F   In some areas of the world, basic government laws and social values have guaranteed and may continue to give people a legal right to some kind of shelter. This guarantee also appears in the 1948 United Nations "Universal Declaration of Human Rights." In some places, there are "fair housing" laws to protect against housing discrimination based on race, nationality, sex, health, family situation, or lifestyle. Even so, most people's housing situations depend on their ability to pay under economic conditions of the time: personal, national, or worldwide. A large number have lost their homes because they cannot pay their mortgages (money owed on their **property**) or the rising costs of renting.

▲ A houseboat

Nature continues to play a role: some people are homeless because of natural disasters like earthquakes or hurricanes; "unsheltered" people need warmer climates or pleasant weather to sleep outside. Others—in the past, mostly young men but now more and more women and children—find shelter in cars or **campers**, in temporary camps, in homeless or warming shelters, or simply "on the street." Throughout world history, a general definition of *homelessness* has been "the condition of people without a regular place of night-time residence." There have been different solutions to the problem in the past; these will continue to vary.

The Future: Housing Design and Purposes

G   Social scientists, researchers, and architects that think about future housing agree: it is likely to look and feel different from today. Modern designers and thinkers have suggested housing under or above the earth, perhaps connected to trees, caves, stone, or other natural features in creative ways. They base their ideas on past, present, and possible future human "necessities," such as physical health, energy efficiency, and use of technology. Another goal may be survival, including protection against natural disasters, extreme weather, and dangers created by other humans. Also, many people

want to decrease the environmental impact of their housing, perhaps with buildings that produce their 95 own energy. Housing plans and construction in the future are likely to involve the latest technological discoveries and inventions. Even so, it may have a lot in common with 100 housing of the past—and there will always be the human need to call someplace, "home."

▲ Architects consider family lifestyles, energy efficiency, and use of technology when designing a modern home.

After You Read

Strategy

Recognizing Topics in a Reading About History
Readings about history usually begin with introductory material. Each paragraph after that may tell about various *periods* of history—probably in chronological (time) order. The last paragraph may add predictions or ideas about the future. Each paragraph, however, will still have its own topic.

5 **Recognizing Topics in a Reading About History** The headings of the six paragraphs A–G in the reading "At Home in World History" all give the name of a period of history followed by a short topic phrase. Fill in the missing words in the blanks. The first blank is filled in as an example.

General Time Frame:	Topic Phrase
A. _Prehistoric Times_	Shelter as Basic Human Necessity
B. _____	Housing in Ancient Civilizations
C. _____	Houses of the Common People vs. the Powerful
D. The 18th to 20th Centuries	_____
E. The Modern World	_____
F. _____	_____
G. _____	_____

6 **Recognizing the Main Ideas** Which title below tells the topic or subject of the whole reading "At Home in World History?" Choose the correct answer. Give reasons for your answer.

    Ⓐ Early vs. Later Centuries: How Ideas about Basic Human Necessity Have Nothing in Common

    Ⓑ From the Beginning to Nowadays: Natural Materials in Beautiful, Useful Fortress Design

    Ⓒ Before the Common Era vs. the Years of Our Lord: Protection from Danger and Disaster with Tools and Weapons

    Ⓓ From Prehistoric Times to the Future: People's Needs, Building Ideas, and Attitudes Toward Their Homes

7 **Recognizing and Asking for Main Ideas** Focus on the most important information and ideas in the reading "At Home in World History," Add words in the blanks of these main-idea questions. (The letters A-G are the letters of the seven paragraphs.) The first item is done as an example. Then answer the main-idea question.

A. Why did _prehistoric humans_ need _shelter_? How did they _get it_?

B. How was housing in the _____ dependent on the

_____? What were some kinds of _____?

C. In the European _____, what was housing

_____ vs. _____ like?

D. In the _____ centuries, what kinds of _____

were there were in housing?

E. What were or are people's _____ about home in

_____? What do they think or _____ about it?

F. Which _____ related to people's shelter

rights and situations in _____?

G. How are living accommodations in _____ likely to

_____?

Main-Idea Question About the Whole Reading: In all of human history, what have been, are, and will be _____?

8 **Changing False Statements to True Statements** Below are incorrect summaries of Paragraphs A-G of "At Home in World History." Change the underlined words to make these false statements true. Then use the statements as correct answers to the seven questions in Activity 7.

A. In prehistoric times, the third most important survival need was for <u>social networking</u>. The earliest humans built <u>fortresses</u> and later created homes out of natural materials like stone and clay.

B. In ancient civilizations, <u>government</u> greatly influenced housing design and construction. Inhabitants built houses with branches, clay, and hardened earth. In later generations, people used <u>the same materials</u>.

C. In the Middle Ages, poorer common people had <u>huge smart houses</u>. The wealthy and powerful lived in <u>huts and tents</u>.

D. The discoveries of the Industrial Revolution led to changes in <u>fair housing laws</u>. Advances in <u>agriculture</u> allowed architects to design for durability, practicality, and beauty.

E. In the modern world, <u>there is no longer a strong attachment</u> to "home." Whether a home is temporary or permanent, people <u>never</u> find a place to call "home" and miss it when they are away.

F. Although some parts of the world have laws to help give people shelter, people's housing situation depends largely on their own <u>governments</u>. Once a person is homeless, <u>there is an easy solution</u> to help them.

G. Housing in the 22nd and following centuries is <u>unlikely to differ</u> from living accommodations in the Middle Ages. It will focus on three key areas: <u>agriculture</u>, <u>wealth</u>, and <u>safety</u>.

Strategy

Graphic Organizer: Using a Timeline to Take Notes on Time and Time Order

In reading about history, you can look for details that tell when things happened. Writers indicate time in (chronological order) these ways:

- naming years such as *1948, or the year 2000*
- naming of long, general time periods like *prehistoric times, the earliest centuries, the Middle Ages, the 19th century, modern times, today, the future.*
- connecting points of time with a dash (–) or *from… to*, as in *1925–1955* or *from ancient times to the future*
- including phrases like *long ago, since the beginning of human history, in the past, for centuries, during the Stone Age, after the Industrial Revolution*, and *at the end of time*
- using time words (usually adjectives, adverbs, and conjunctions) like *early, ancient, before, after, later, then, recently*

9 **Identifying Time and Time Order Details** Read the list of events and developments in the history of human housing. Then write the numbers of the statements, two to each box, in the correct seven places of the timeline that follows.

Events and Developments from the Reading "At Home in World History"

1. In the Middle Ages, both one-room and larger structures tended to be cold, wet, and dark. Houses had features that ranged from cut-out to framed windows, earth to tile floors, open fires to brick fireplaces, and plant to glazed roofs.

2. For survival, prehistoric humans tried to get protection from the elements, wild animals, and other dangers by climbing into trees. Some lived in caves.

3. Protection against danger was the main purpose of the fortified castles of the rich and powerful—security for themselves, their workers and animals, their food, etc.

4. In the 18th and 19th centuries, manufacturing and the availability of new building materials led to improvements of all kinds of housing, from the simplest of shelters to luxurious mansions with private land around them.

5. Later Stone Age generations used tools to build shelters out of branches, animal skins, stones, dried clay bricks, and earth—with plant coverings on top.

6. In human history BCE, the natural environment (the climate and resources in different areas) played a big role in housing development.

7. In ancient civilizations such as in Egypt, Assyria, Greece, and Rome, there were houses with flat and slanted roofs, central heating through pipes, and wood framing filled in with hardened materials. There were also tent-like structures of animal skins on frames and pit houses underground.

8. Beginning with the Industrial Revolution, people have chosen their living accommodations for a variety of reasons: not only protection but also security, privacy, space, comfort, and modern technology.

9. In the world today, there are few guarantees to adequate housing as a human right, but it may be against the law to be homeless. "Fair housing" laws may protect against discrimination based on race, sex, health, or lifestyle.

10. In the modern 20th and 21st centuries, there were and are many different kinds of places to live—or simply to sleep at night. These range from tents in camps, shared rooms in residence halls, and single apartments to huge, luxurious mansions with private land around them.

11. Some important features of future housing may be its relationship to nature, its practical or creative use of technology, its networking connections, its decreasing environmental impact, and its ability to produce its own energy.

12. Modern attitudes toward "home" vary greatly, too. People that feel "there's no place like home" may spend most of their time there; others return to their "home spaces" only when there's nowhere else to go.

13. Recent natural disasters like earthquakes and extreme weather like hurricanes have made many people homeless. Nowadays, economics (the inability to make mortgage or rent payments) have also put individuals and families out "on the street."

14. As in the past, human beings will continue to need homes for survival in the future.

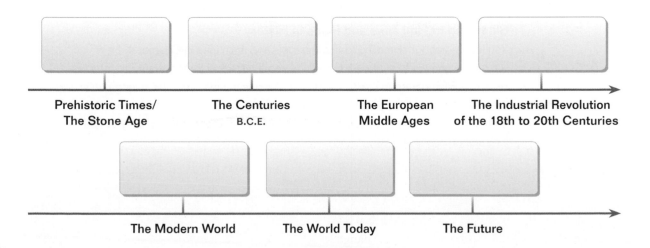

Prehistoric Times/
The Stone Age

The Centuries
B.C.E.

The European
Middle Ages

The Industrial Revolution
of the 18th to 20th Centuries

The Modern World

The World Today

The Future

10 Discussing the Reading Talk about your answers to these questions.

1. In the past, what kinds of homes have you lived in? Where do you live now? What were and are the main reasons for your choices of living situations?

2. Here are some quotations regarding people's attitudes about home and home life. Which of these are similar to your own views? Which are different? Explain.

   a. "I long, as does every human being, to be at home wherever I find myself. (Maya Angelou)

   b. "Home is a place you grow up wanting to leave, and grow old wanting to get back to." (John Ed Pierce)

   c. "When you're safe at home you wish you were having an adventure; when you're having an adventure you wish you were safe at home." (Thorton Wilder)

   d. "Be grateful for the home you have, knowing that at this moment, all you have is all you need." (Sarah Breathnach)

   e. "To be an ideal guest, stay at home." (Edgar Watson Howe)

   f. "The worst feeling in the world is the homesickness that comes over a man when he is at home." (Johann Wolfgang Von Goethe)

PART 2 | Main Ideas and Details

A Short History of...

Before You Read

 ## Strategy

Skimming to Find Time and Place in History
You learned about skimming to find the topic and main idea in Chapter 4. Now you will have a chance to skim short readings about historical topics related to the idea of *home*. Each paragraph tells events and changes in time order, from long ago in the past to future possibilities. You may be able to discover a trend (a direction in developments) through *skimming*—that is, by reading the material quickly to find information.

1 Previewing Vocabulary Read the vocabulary items. Then listen to the words and phrases. Put a check mark (✓) next to the words you don't know. Don't use a dictionary.

Nouns
- descendents
- forefathers
- obligation
- offerings
- offspring
- punishments
- slaves
- society
- trend
- youngsters

Verbs
- beat
- control
- feed
- guide
- obey
- reside
- sacrifice
- spoil

Adjectives
- adequate
- global
- independent
- wealthy

2 Skimming for Topics Read the four topics below. Then skim the four paragraphs in the article "A Short History of…" Match each paragraph from the article to one of the topics below. Write the paragraph letter A, B, C, or D before each phrase.

_____ A Short History of Laws Related to Housing

_____ A Short History of the Changing Family

_____ A Short History of Homelessness

_____ A Short History of Parenting (Raising Children)

Read

3 Skimming for Main Ideas Quickly read Paragraphs A-D again. Answer the question about the main idea that follows each paragraph. Then explain the reasons for each of your choices.

A Short History of…

A   What has the word "family" meant in history? From prehistoric to modern times, the idea has most often had to do with shared living facilities. The first "families" were simply groups of people that shared general survival goals in a common residence; their main purposes were to produce and protect **offspring** (new humans) to continue the race. Then in   5 religious civilizations B.C. (before the birth of Christ), human beings were seen as **descendents** of the various gods—or of the **forefathers** (first heads) of their peoples. In ancient Roman society, men headed family groups that included wives, growing and grown children, and **slaves** with their offspring. Later, in pre-industrial Europe, there were both "nuclear family" structures   10 (parents and their children) and larger "extended families" of more than two generations. A family's size depended on how long its members lived and could care for one another; its social standing or class depended on property ownership and power over other groups of people. Because of new work and living conditions in the Industrial Revolution, however, people began connecting outside their families; government, **society**, and social institutions started to play a role in meeting human needs. In modern times, some family forms have been like those of the past, but there have also been many individuals **residing** alone; unmarried, childless, and same-sex couples sharing homes; single-parent, joined, and communal living groups; and so on. There has never been one "true" family form: the idea of "family" is likely to continue developing in the future, but it will probably stay connected to the idea of "home."

What is the main idea of Paragraph A?

(A) The main difference between Stone Age and ancient families has been the existence of religion, gods, and slaves; these guaranteed the survival of the rich and powerful.

(B) Throughout history, nuclear and expanded family forms have proven much more successful than early unmarried, childless, single-parent, same-sex, and communal living groups without property.

(C) The definition of "family" has changed through the centuries; even so, its main purpose has been the survival and protection of the human race in safe living accommodations.

B   Social scientists have identified several main "methods" of *parenting* ("child rearing") throughout history. Up to about the 4th century A.D., it was acceptable to **sacrifice** (make **offerings** of) the young to the gods for religious purposes. Families without the resources to **feed** or take care of their offspring sometimes threw them into rivers, wild areas, or pits to die; some of those that survived were used as slaves. In following centuries, from around the 5th to the 13th, parents used to send their children away for years—to wet nurses that could give them milk or to religious communities like monasteries. Poorer families used to make their growing youngsters live with and work for the **wealthy**—or they sold their young. Around the 14th century, both poor and rich parents began developing closer ties to their offspring, but their main goal was to *control* them. It was common to bind up babies in clothing so they couldn't move, to tie children to heavy furniture, or to **beat** them so they would **obey** (follow orders). The next **trend** started in the 18th century, when there was less child beating and **punishment** but more parental control in raising children (acceptance or love only in exchange for obedience). By the end of the 19th century, in contrast,

parents were starting to consider their youngsters' needs and personalities 45
by "**guiding**" their development rather than controlling it. They were still
careful not to "**spoil**" their children, however. And in modern times, the
focus has been on relationships, values, and helping—so that the young can
grow into responsible, **independent** adults able to raise their own offspring.
Some even try to "raise **global** children" that feel at home with worldwide 50
technology, culture, and networking.

What is the main idea of Paragraph B?

(A) Because the rich and powerful tend to beat and punish their offspring
or use them as slaves (rather than accept or love them), only poor people
should have and raise children.

(B) Through the centuries, acceptable methods and trends in child rearing
have ranged and changed from killing, giving away, or selling the young
to controlling—and later helping—their development into adults.

(C) The child rearing methods of modern times are much worse than those
of prehistoric and ancient times, when children obeyed, worked hard, and
were never spoiled.

C   In prehistoric times, groups of humans simply built the shelters they
needed for survival--or they competed over land, natural materials, and
resources for secure places to live. But in ancient civilizations, land ownership
became the base of wealth and power; everyone lived on the land but few 55
people owned or controlled it. The idea of land ownership and private
property became even more important in the Middle Ages, when the
common people "paid rent" by working for—or giving things to—wealthy or
powerful landowners. Through the centuries, it was mostly religious leaders
and organizations that recognized an **obligation** to help the very poor, the 60
needy, and the homeless. The 1948 United Nations' "Universal Declaration
of Human Rights" tried to "guarantee" the right to **adequate** housing (more
than four walls and a roof) as part of an economic, social, and cultural right
to a standard of living. But in modern times, there have been few societies
where housing was simply *given* to those that needed it. In some countries, 65
there have been "fair housing" laws to prevent discrimination based on race,
nationality, sex, health, age, family form, or economic situation. Even so, in
today's world economy, there are many individuals and families unable to
find, own, rent, or share the housing necessary for an adequate standard of
living. 70

What is the main idea of Paragraph C?

(A) Since land and property ownership became the base of wealth and power in ancient times, it has been impossible to guarantee everyone housing for an adequate standard of living. Religion, universal declarations, and laws are not enough.

(B) Most individuals and families don't want comfortable housing because private land or home ownership is too much trouble. They prefer to spend their money on more basic human necessities like food, clothing, and the Internet.

(C) To guarantee the survival of the human race, all governments should give people "four walls and a roof" to live in but no more than that. Homelessness should be illegal, like it was in prehistoric times.

D   Since human history began, people have needed shelter for survival and safety. Even so, not everyone has been able to live their lives in four-walled roofed structures. Reasons for homelessness have varied: perhaps poverty (not having or being able to get enough money to pay for basic necessities); physical or mental illness; drug abuse (misuse of harmful substances); 75 natural disasters or fires; war, crime, or abuse by government or people in power; discrimination; relationship problems; the construction of expensive accommodations in place of low-cost ones; or economic conditions. In some places, there have been terrible punishments for "living on the street." In 14th century England, for instance, "unsheltered" people could be put in 80 prison, beaten, made slaves, sent to other countries, or even killed. Hundreds of years later, the government tried to shelter some of the homeless in "workhouses," miserable places to live. In more recent centuries, communities that recognized the problem opened old buildings for the neediest men to sleep in dormitory style; until it became illegal to do so, some people slept 85 in public places such as churches, libraries, and government buildings. These "solutions" were never enough, however; neither are today's homeless or warming (winter) shelters for adults and families. Many thousands of years since the beginning of human society, there are still millions of people without housing for an adequate standard of living. 90

What is the main idea of Paragraph D?

(A) Some of the problems caused by homelessness are poverty, illness, drug abuse, earthquakes, hurricanes, fires, war, crime, discrimination, government power, bad relationships, and a terrible economy.

(B) Shelter has always been a basic human necessity. But because the homeless problem has had so many causes, neither government nor social groups have been able to solve it.

(C) The best places for the wealthy and powerful to live have been—and will continue to be—four-walled roofed structures like prisons, churches, libraries, and government buildings

Summaries: Historical Information and Ideas

You learned how to write a summary in Chapter 3. Here we'll look at how you can summarize readings about history.

- Is there a general point in the history—a trend or clear development? If yes, then begin with that general point.

- Next, *paraphrase* (restate in other words) the important events and developments (the supporting details) in support of that general point.

Here is an example summary of the information in Paragraph A on pages 95-96.

From the beginning of human history, the main purpose of sharing living accommodations has been to survive and to produce and protect offspring; the idea of "family" came from these basic human necessities. Even so, more specific ideas of "family" have had to do with religious beliefs or property ownership and power. Some of the family forms that have existed through the centuries have been the nuclear family; the extended family; unmarried, childless, or same-sex couples; communal living groups, and others.

4 **Writing a Summary** Using your own words, write a summary of the main idea and important details of Paragraph A on pages 95-96. Compare your paragraph with a partner. Does it give you ideas on how to improve your own writing? If so, rewrite your original paragraph.

5 **Paraphrasing** Work in groups of three. Each person chooses one of the other Paragraphs B, C, or D from the reading "A Short History of..." Read it carefully. Reread the main idea. In a few sentences, tell your group the summary of your paragraph.

6 **Discussing the Reading** Discuss these questions about the parts of the reading "A Short History of…" with a partner. Then tell the class some of the most important information.

1. For you, what is the meaning of the word "family?" What kinds of families have you belonged to in the past? What kinds do you hope to have in the future?

2. In your view, what are the best methods of bringing up children? Why do you feel that way?

3. Do you feel that there is—or should be—a universal right to shelter or housing as part of an adequate standard of living? If so, how might government or society provide it?

4. What are your opinions about worldwide homelessness in the past, present, and future? Do you feel it is a natural human condition or a social problem to be solved? Give reasons for your views.

Strategy

Getting Meaning from Context: Punctuation and Phrase Clues
There are many kinds of clues to the meanings of new vocabulary. For example, short definitions of new vocabulary items sometimes appear between or after certain punctuation marks such as parentheses ( ) dashes --, or commas ,.
The definitions might also be in another sentence part after a semicolon ; or a colon :.
The phrases *in other words* and *that is to say* or the abbreviation *i.e. (that is)* can come right before a definition.

1 **Getting Meaning from Context** On the lines, complete or write definitions from the reading selection "At Home in World History" on pages 87–90.
(The letters in parentheses are the letters of the paragraphs.)

1. shelter: (A) structures that provide _____

   _____

2. the elements: (A) kinds of weather like _____

   _____

3. The Stone Age: (A) a prehistoric _____

   _____

4. roofs: (A) earth, plant, or tile _____

5. ancient civilizations: (B) long-past societies in places like _____

   _____

6. castles: (C) _____

   _____

7. The Industrial Revolution: (D) in the 18th and 19th centuries, _____

   _____

8. homesickness: (E) _____

   _____

9. "fair housing" laws: (F) protections against discrimination in housing based on

   _____

10. mortgages: (F) _____

11. homelessness: (F) _____

12. ways of "saving the earth": (G) _____

   _____

Vocabulary Building: Recognizing Similar and Opposite Meanings:

For most vocabulary items, there are words with the same or similar meanings—such as *human beings, humans,* and *people* or *shelters, structures, buildings,* and *houses.*

For some items, there are also words of phrases with *opposite meanings*—that is, completely different, or contrasting, definitions. Examples of opposites are *dangerous* and *safe, increase* and *decrease,* or *up* and *down.*

To explain and learn new vocabulary quickly, you can learn both words with similar meanings and words with opposite meanings.

② **Identifying Words with Similar and Opposite Meanings** In each of the following pairs of words or phrases, do the vocabulary items have the same or similar meanings? If so, write *S* for *Similar* on the line. Or do the vocabulary items have opposite meanings? If so, write *O* for *Opposite* on the line.

1. _____ protection / security
2. _____ huge / small
3. _____ ancient / modern
4. _____ architects / designers
5. _____ formed / constructed
6. _____ prehistoric / modern

7. _____ wealthy / rich
8. _____ clay bricks / mud blocks
9. _____ materials / natural resources
10. _____ cold and wet / warm and dry
11. _____ tiled roofs / building coverings
12. _____ common people / the rich and powerful

Recognizing Nouns and Adjectives

A very useful vocabulary-learning strategy is to recognize parts of speech. Some words can be more than one part of speech. As examples, in the sentences that follow, the words *prehistory, shelter, necessity,* and *survival* are nouns; the words *necessary, prehistoric,* and *sheltered* are adjectives related to three of those nouns. *Survive* is a verb.

Example

Beginning in *prehistory, shelter* was a *necessity* basic to human *survival.* It was *necessary* for *prehistoric* humans to be *sheltered* to *survive.*

3 **Identifying Nouns and Adjectives** Below are some sentences with related words—nouns and adjectives—on the topic of the reading material of this chapter. Within each pair of parentheses ( ), circle the correct word form for the context. Then write the missing words in the chart that follows. Not all words from the sentences are in the chart. Some words are provided as examples.

1. After the food and clothing (necessity / necessary) for basic (survival / survive), the most (importance / important) human need is (protection / protect) from the elements and other (dangers / dangerous).

2. Before they discovered how to build (structures / structural), (prehistory / prehistoric) humans found (shelter / sheltered) in trees.

3. The (architects / architectural) of ancient (civilizations / civilized) used materials from the (nature / natural) (environment / environmental) like earth, plants, and (wood / wooden).

4. (Accommodations / Accommodate) ranged from the simplest of shelters to (durability / durable) stone castles or (fortresses / fortified) for (wealth / wealthy) and (power / powerful) landowners.

5. The (discoveries / discovered) and (inventions / invented) of the (Industry / Industrial) Revolution led to great (improvements / improved) in housing (construction / constructed).

6. Because more kinds of materials were (availability / available), housing was designed with three goals in mind: durability, (practicality / practical), and (beauty / beautiful).

Noun	Related Adjective	Noun	Related Adjective
necessity	_____	_____	wooden
importance	_____	_____	durable
danger	_____	_____	wealthy
structure	_____	_____	powerful
prehistory	_____	_____	improved
architect	_____	_____	invented
nature	_____	_____	available
environment	_____	_____	beautiful

For more practice, tell or write more nouns from Chapters 1 to 5. Which nouns have related adjective forms? What are they? Also, tell or write some adjectives with their related noun forms. (You can check your words in a dictionary.)

4 **Focusing on High-Frequency Words** Read the paragraph on page 103 and fill in each blank with a word from the box.

goals	history	modern	protect	society
groups	living	produce	religious	

What has the word "family" meant in _____? From
1
prehistoric to _____ times, the idea has most often had
2
to do with shared _____ facilities. The first "families"
3
were simply _____ of people that shared general survival
4
_____ in a common residence; their main purposes were to
5
_____ and _____ offspring (new humans) to
6   7
continue the race. Then in _____ civilizations B.C. (before
8
the birth of Christ), human beings were seen as descendents of the various
gods—or of the forefathers (first heads) of their peoples. In ancient Roman
_____, men headed family groups that included wives, growing
9
and grown children, and slaves with their offspring.

Using the Internet

Researching History Online

You can search for specific information about history online. For example, if you want
to find information about housing in the world from prehistoric times to the future, type:

| Housing + Middle Age | | Submit |

Your search results may look like this:

- May 15 Information about types of housing used during the medieval period.
  www.historyonthenet.com/Medieval_Life/houses.htm

- Most medieval homes were cold, damp, and dark. Sometimes it was warmer and
  lighter outside the home than within its walls. For security purposes, windows,...
  www.learner.org/exhibits/middleages/homes.html

- Take a tour of this lost medieval village, read about the homes, and view drawings
  of living quarters. This site includes several articles on...
  www.learner.org/exhibits/middleages/morehome.html

- A Peasant's Hut In The Middle Ages. Peasants homes were simple wooden huts.
  They had wooden frames filled in with wattle and daub (strips of wood woven...
  www.localhistories.org/middle.html

5 **Researching Historical Information** Do an Internet search about housing from TWO different time periods. You can type in *housing + (future, today, 1700s, Roman times, or your idea)*. Take notes on the information. How were or are the architectural styles in the two historical times or places similar? How are they different? Tell a partner or the class what you learned.

PART 4   Focus on Testing

FOCUS

Understanding Definitions and Explanations

The TOEFL® iBT contains a great deal of very difficult vocabulary. Part 3 of this chapter discusses punctuation marks and phrases that signal definitions in a reading. This strategy can be extremely useful on the TOEFL® iBT.

Readings for the TOEFL® iBT are about as difficult as textbooks in a first-year college class. Even university students who are native speakers of English may not understand every word in a reading. Because the vocabulary level is so high, the text often contains definitions or explanations of unusual vocabulary. The hardest "definitions" to find are really explanations or examples, not obvious definitions.

Finding Definitions and Explanations Reread "At Home in World History" on pages 87—91. Try to recognize definitions when you see them. Then answer the questions below.

1. Which of the following is closest in meaning to *shelter*, as it is used in Paragraph A?

   Ⓐ trees for climbing into to stay away from dangerous animals

   Ⓑ caves

   Ⓒ human-built structures to keep people safe from nature's various elements

   Ⓓ roofs made of clay and plants

2. Which of the following is an explanation of the term *Industrial Revolution*, as it is used in Paragraph D?

   Ⓐ changing over from a technological to an agricultural means of working

   Ⓑ working toward building houses that can withstand the elements

   Ⓒ building shelters and homes that are durable, practical, and beautiful

   Ⓓ a time of global technological improvement in the 18th and 19th centuries

3. Which of the following is closest in meaning to *homesickness*, as it is used in Paragraph E?

   Ⓐ enjoying the company of friends and relatives when you are in a new home

   Ⓑ missing home life when you are at work all day in an office

   Ⓒ experiencing sadness and mental health issues when away from home

   Ⓓ moving to a new city or country and not missing your old friends and family

4. Which of the following is closest in meaning to *homelessness*, as it is used in Paragraph F?

  (A) having several places to go "home" to at night after work

  (B) helping those in need of shelter to find homes

  (C) lacking a single permanent residence to live and sleep in at night

  (D) working for charitable causes that try to solve the problems of those who live on the streets all year long

Self-Assessment Log

Read the lists below. Check (✓) the strategies and vocabulary that you learned in this chapter. Look through the chapter or ask your instructor about the strategies and words that you do not understand.

Reading and Vocabulary-Building Strategies

☐ Recognizing topics and main ideas
☐ Recognizing topics in a reading about history
☐ Using a timeline to take notes
☐ Skimming to find time and place in history
☐ Summarizing historical information and ideas

☐ Getting meaning from context: punctuation and phrase clues
☐ Recognizing words with similar and opposite meanings
☐ Recognizing nouns and adjectives
☐ Researching history online

Target Vocabulary

Nouns

- architects
- branches*
- camp/camper
- centuries*
- civilizations
- clay
- descendents
- forefathers
- frames/framing
- generations*
- invention
- mansions
- manufacturing
- necessity
- obligation

- offspring
- property*
- protection*
- punishment
- shelter
- slaves
- society*
- tools*
- trend*
- weapons*
- youngsters

Verbs

- beat
- construct

- control*
- develop*
- discover*
- entertain
- fill in
- form*
- guide
- impress
- obey
- produce
- punish
- range from...to
- reside
- sacrifice
- spoil

Adjectives

- adequate
- ancient*
- attached
- durable
- flat*
- global
- hardened
- homeless
- independent*
- permanent*
- prehistoric
- temporary
- wealthy

* These words are among the 2,000 most frequently used words in English.

Cultures of the World

"No culture can live, if it attempts to be exclusive."

Mohandas K. Gandhi, nonviolent activist and political leader

In this
CHAPTER

In Part 1, you will read about the opinions of a group of students who are discussing culture. In the rest of this chapter, you will read about, explore, and discuss cultural differences and the characteristics of various cultures from around the world.

Connecting to the Topic

1. Look at the two groups of women in the photo. How are they different?

2. What is your definition of *culture*? Think of some examples of your definition.

3. Other than language, why do you think people from different cultures sometimes have misunderstandings?

Cross-Cultural Conversation

Before You Read

 1 **Previewing the Topic** Look at the photos and discuss the questions in a group.

1. What does the scene show? Who is taking part in a group conversation?

2. Describe each of the five photos. How does each photo relate to the theme of "culture?"

3. What do you think the students are saying about culture?

▲ Students in a discussion about culture

 2 **Predicting** Think about and discuss possible answers to these questions. Write down your answers. If you don't know the answers, make predictions. You can look for the answers when you read "Cross-Cultural Conversation."

1. What is a "cultural legacy" from the past? What elements might it include?
2. What are some technical or scientific achievements of ancient cultures?
3. In what ways do you think culture is universal in today's world?
4. In what ways do you think modern cultures vary around the world?

3 Previewing Vocabulary Read the vocabulary items below from the first reading. Then listen to the words and phrases. Put a check mark (✓) next to the words you don't know.

Nouns	Verbs	Adjectives	
architecture	agree	amazing	social
cathedrals	contradict	ancient	soft
civilization	contribute	clear	
contradiction	describe	cultural	**Adverbs**
discoveries	develop	enthusiastic	convincingly
legacy	experience	excellent	politely
literature	grin	knowing	
media	interrupt	opposing	
medicine	invent	pleasant	
societies		proud	
weapons		scientific	

Read

4 Reading an Article Read the following article. Then do the activities that follow.

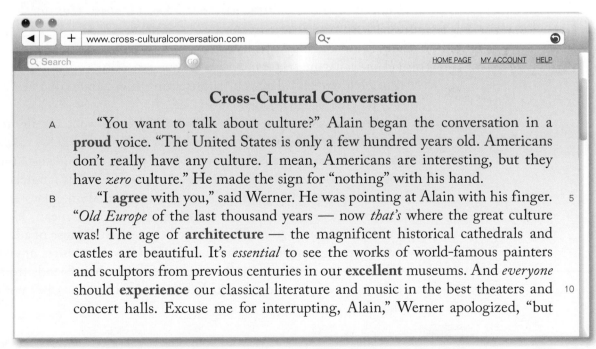

www.cross-culturalconversation.com

Q Search   GO   HOME PAGE   MY ACCOUNT   HELP

Cross-Cultural Conversation

A   "You want to talk about culture?" Alain began the conversation in a **proud** voice. "The United States is only a few hundred years old. Americans don't really have any culture. I mean, Americans are interesting, but they have *zero* culture." He made the sign for "nothing" with his hand.

B   "I **agree** with you," said Werner. He was pointing at Alain with his finger. "*Old Europe* of the last thousand years — now *that's* where the great culture was! The age of **architecture** — the magnificent historical cathedrals and castles are beautiful. It's *essential* to see the works of world-famous painters and sculptors from previous centuries in our **excellent** museums. And *everyone* should **experience** our classical literature and music in the best theaters and concert halls. Excuse me for interrupting, Alain," Werner apologized, "but

5

10

▼ Historical architecture is one example of "culture."

I just gave a perfect example of a long and significant cultural history!"

Kamil spoke up. "You know, we don't call a short millennium a cultural history. The *real* beginning of culture — I mean, *significant civilization* — was in the Middle East and Africa over five thousand years ago." He continued, waving both hands in the air, "Ancient communities not only knew how to create magnificent architecture and art; they also made **amazing scientific** and technological discoveries. They *invented* things. For instance, they figured out how to write and do mathematics; they studied astronomy — the science of the skies, the sun and the planets; they invented the calendar. They even had **medicine**; the ancient religions came from that area, too. *Their* achievements made world civilization possible. *Those* were the civilizations that gave humanity the most meaningful cultural **legacy**!"

D   Mei agreed with Kamil. In a **soft** but **knowing** voice, she added, "But the *really* important science and technology began to **develop** in Asia and the Americas. While the ancient Chinese were building walled cities, they organized the first governments. They invented tools for work and weapons for protection. And the native peoples of the Americas had very, very old civilizations and societies. *That* was ancient traditional culture."

E   "Ancient culture? That's a **contradiction** in definitions." Grinning, Karen objected in an **enthusiastic**, friendly way. She gave a contrasting opinion. "It's *impossible* for culture to be old or traditional," she argued. The *opposite* is true! Culture isn't dead — it's *alive*. Culture is *modern!* Culture is *now!*"

F   Kenji was starting to fall asleep, but suddenly he was fully awake. "I agree!" he said, interrupting Karen enthusiastically.

G   "You tell them!" said Karen, appreciating the support for her point of view. For emphasis, she nodded vigorously.

H   "Culture is worldwide — it's universal!" Kenji went on in his **clear** speaking style. He had a wide smile on his face. "I mean, like — take today's food culture. With our global fast food, I have to say, everyone eats the same. And because of the worldwide **media** — movies, TV, CDs (compact discs), the Internet — everybody knows the same information, plays the same music, enjoys the same stories — even the jokes! And I mean, it's like — people everywhere want to buy the same clothes — all because of advertising. A beautiful young couple in jeans and bright Hawaiian shirts anywhere in the world, eating hamburgers and French fries with their friends from many countries — *finally*, we have a global culture! And *tradition* has nothing to do with it!"

I   Nadia, however, was of another opinion. "You want to call modern movies, music, food, and clothes *culture*?" she said, sweetly but **convincingly**. "Those things don't **describe** culture. Culture isn't about the *sameness* of people in communities around the world; it's about their *differences*. Like — it's important for people to *greet* one another in various ways, and they need to use different titles and follow a variety of **social** rules in their relationships. Some **societies** are formal, while others are informal, or casual. Some groups are friendly, and others aren't. And another example is the diverse use of language — is it direct or indirect? How do communication styles include motions, gestures, facial expressions, and other body language? And *customs* are so interesting! They're what people of different national groups *do* in their everyday lives and on special occasions like holidays or celebrations. Culture means *cultural diversity*. What makes life amusing? It's the *variety* of cultures around the world, its contradictions and opposites!" 60 65

J   "Yeah, maybe so," contributed Alain as **politely** as possible. "On the other hand,…" he started to say. 70

K   "That *does* make some sense," interrupted Werner, beginning to smile, "as long as you don't forget the arts — architecture, painting, literature, music…"

L   "And if you also include ancient civilizations and traditions," added Kamil with a **pleasant** expression on his face. He didn't like to **contradict** Nadia or any of his female friends. 75

M   "Well, we can certainly have **opposing** viewpoints," concluded Karen, "and yet we still enjoy exchanging ideas." Everyone was smiling, and they wanted to talk a lot more.

After You Read

FOCUS

Understanding Reading Structure: Conversation in Paragraph Form
Explanatory material can appear in various forms. For instance, opinions and views on a topic can be in the form of a conversation — with the words of each speaker between quotation marks (" ") in a different paragraph.

5 **Understanding Reading Structure: Conversation in Paragraph Form** In the reading "Cross-Cultural Conversation," the speakers talk about different definitions of the concept (idea) of "culture." For each section of the reading, check (✓) the topic. (The letters in parentheses ( ) refer to the paragraphs.)

1. (A, B)

_____ the long cultural legacy of the arts in European history

_____ the importance of international education through the centuries

2. (C, D)

_____ humanity's scientific and technological discoveries and achievements

_____ the business practices of cultural groups in Africa and the Americas

3. (E, H)

_____ the differences among ancient cultures on various continents

_____ the cultural sameness and similarities among modern peoples

4. (I, J, K, L))

_____ definitions of the word—according to various world cultures

_____ polite, friendly ways of discussing ideas and telling opinions

Which phrase below best tells the topic, or subject, of the whole reading "Cross-Cultural Conversation?" Give reasons for your answer.

(A) relationships among humans in a variety of family structures

(B) college students are interested in education, food, community, and family

(C) opinions about the meaning and importance "culture"

(D) variety in contrast to sameness in the global community of the Internet

6 **Understanding the Point** Following are some false statements about the points of the reading selection "Cross-Cultural Conversation." To make them into true statements, change the underlined words. Number 5 is about the whole reading. The first item is done as an example.

1. Some people believe that countries with s~~hort~~ _long_ histories have more cultural legacy than ~~old~~ _young_ countries — especially in their ~~communication styles and body language~~. _technology and religion_

2. For other thinkers, civilization didn't include only old architecture and art; it also meant opinions and statements in mathematics, astronomy, medicine, weapons, city building, and the like.

3. Young people around the world don't want to think about food, media, music, or clothes as culture because those things are ancient, and nobody seems to like the same kinds.

4. According to others, diversity is less significant than sameness in discussions about culture; such speakers say that people should decrease and forget about their differences.

5. People from various cathedrals and castles around the world have exactly the same views on the meaning and importance of the concept "culture." In fact, it's common for them to express their ideas in similar ways.

FOCUS

Recognizing Important Details: Opinions

Clearly, the speakers in "Cross-Cultural Conversation" have diverse opinions and views about the value and importance of their various concepts of culture.

• Some words in their speeches are in italics: speakers use italics to show that the words are important to the point.

• An **exclamation point**, a punctuation mark that looks like this (!), also shows strong emphasis.

7 **Recognizing Important Details: Opinions** What did the speakers in "Cross-Cultural Conversation" value within their concepts of culture? Circle the letters of *all* the correct answers to each question.

1. Alain and Werner felt that the age of a culture added to the value of its fine arts. Which parts of culture were essential to them?

   a. fast food and junk food

   b. old paintings and sculpture

   c. literature and classical music

   d. human feelings and emotions

   e. the architecture of buildings and structures

   f. things in museums, theater plays, and concerts

2. Kamil and Mei most valued the ancient civilizations of the Middle East, Africa, Asia, and the Americas. What things did they include in "a cultural legacy?"

   a. international business

   b. magnificent architecture and art

   c. scientific discoveries and invention

   d. writing and mathematics

   e. the study of astronomy

   f. protected cities and government structure

3. Kenji was happy that modern culture is worldwide and similar all over the planet. Which features did he find most important?

   a. ancient religions

   b. the historical structure of the family

   c. food from global chains

   d. Indian rock tools and weapons

   e. the media of movies, TV, and the Internet

   f. advertising for clothes and other things

4. Nadia preferred cultural diversity to sameness. What things did she include in her concept of culture?

   a. greetings, including titles and names

   b. relationships and other social rules

   c. formality in contrast to informality

   d. directness and indirectness in language

   e. body language and movements

   f. everyday and special occasion customs

5. In what ways did the group members discuss their ideas and opinions with one another?

   a. proudly and enthusiastically

   b. with various hand and arm gestures

   c. in a moderate or a soft voice

   d. grinning or smiling

   e. with a clear speaking style

   f. agreeing or disagreeing

8 **Discussing the Reading** Discuss these questions in small groups.

1. In your view of the concept of culture, which parts or qualities are essential — or very important? Why?

2. According to your experience, in what ways are world cultures similar or alike? Which features are different? Explain your views.

3. Which is better for humanity and the future of the world — one global culture or cultural diversity all over the planet? Explain your reasoning or logic.

PART **2** Main Ideas and Details

Clues to World Cultures

Before You Read

1 **Previewing Vocabulary** Read the vocabulary items below from the next reading. Then listen to the words and phrases. Put a check mark (✓) next to the words you don't know. Don't use a dictionary.

Nouns	Verbs	Adjectives	Adverbs
attention	beg	afraid	backwards
bite	clean (his) plate	annoyed	loudly
customer	greet	insulted	patiently
guest	hitchhike	mean	rudely
host	ignore	rude	
pain	serve	successful	
pharmacist	shout	terrible	
pharmacy	wait on (someone)	tourist (places)	
service	whisper	unwelcome	

Understanding Anecdotes

An *anecdote* is a very short story with a humorous or interesting point. Reading material on the topic of world cultures often includes anecdotes. These descriptions of cultural situations tell what happened to create cross-cultural misunderstanding or learning. Most reading of this kind is about topics such as the following:

_____ • greetings and introductions; meeting new people

_____ • visiting a family at home; eating and drinking with people from other cultures

_____ • body language — gestures, hand movements, and facial expressions

_____ • concepts of time and timing — doing things in a certain order or at the same time

_____ • formality and informality, directness and indirectness in communication

_____ • ideas about individual and group responsibility and rights

2 **Reading Stories with Anecdotes** Following are three short stories with the general title "Clues to World Cultures." Read the stories through once, and then, on the lines before *three* of the topics listed in the box above, write the story letters A, B, and C. (There are no stories about the other three topics in this part of the chapter.)

On your second reading of each story, look for "culture clues"—pieces of information that suggest differences between members of cultural groups. These possible differences in customs, attitudes, and beliefs are the *point* of the material.

Following each paragraph are some questions about the "cross-cultural meaning" of the experience. Fill in the best answer—A, B, or C. Then give your answers and the reasons for them.

Clues to World Cultures

A　　An Irish woman was visiting **tourist** places in a Latin American city when she got a **terrible** headache. She knew what medicine she needed, so she went to a local pharmacy. The pharmacist was waiting on another **customer** when she came in. The Irish woman **patiently** waited her turn.

While she was standing there, two other customers came in, then another, and then three more. Each time, the pharmacist turned his **attention** to the new people. He did not **greet** the Irish woman; he never said, "I'll be with you in a minute."

After about 20 minutes, the woman couldn't stand the **pain** in her head any longer. "Hey, I've been here a long time," she said **loudly**, very **annoyed** and insulted. "Why is everyone ignoring me? I need service, too!" she shouted **rudely** (impolitely).

1. Why didn't the pharmacist pay attention to the Irish woman when she came into his store?

   (A) He didn't know her, and he didn't like her looks.

   (B) She didn't greet him or ask for attention; she just stood there quietly.

   (C) He was probably not waiting on a customer at all — just talking to a friend.

2. Why was the Irish customer insulted, angry, or hurt?

   (A) She had a terrible headache; her pain reduced her patience.

   (B) She expected the pharmacist to greet her and wait on her in turn (in order).

   (C) She didn't want to buy medicine; it was too expensive at the pharmacy.

3. What is the cultural point of the story?

   (A) In some cultures, people wait their turn for greetings and attention, but in others, they ask for these things in some clear way.

   (B) In stores in all countries, people need to be patient: they have to stand quietly in line and wait for service — often for a long time.

   (C) Pain is different in various parts of the world; some people can stand it better than others.

B   A Middle-Eastern businessman and his brother invited an American guest to their family home for dinner. The American got there on time and enjoyed the interesting conversation, the tea, and the attention. But as time passed, he got very, very hungry. Finally he politely whispered to his host, "Excuse me, but are we going to eat dinner?"

"Of course!" answered his host. "We usually serve the evening meal around 9:00, and when we have guests, we enjoy the long conversation before dinner."

At the dinner table everything was delicious, and the hungry American guest ate quickly. He emptied his plate, and his host put more food on it. As soon as he cleaned his plate a second time, the host gave him more. After several plates of food, he could eat no more. He was going to burst! "Please, please, please — don't give me any more food," he begged them. "I finished the food on this plate, but I can't eat another bite!"

Even then, his host insisted. The guest accepted a little more and ate it with difficulty. Finally, the supper dishes were removed. There was more conversation — with more tea and coffee. At about midnight, the server brought a pitcher of ice water. The tired American knew it was OK to thank his hosts and leave.

1. Why did the host family serve the evening meal so late?

   (A) They were waiting for the guest to say he was hungry.

   (B) After an hour or two of conversation with guests, supper is usually served around 9:00.

   (C) The hosts were busy talking to the guest, so dinner wasn't ready yet.

2. Why did the American guest eat more food than he wanted?

   (A) He was very, very hungry because there was no food in his house and he never went to restaurants.

   (B) In the dinner conversation, his hosts talked and talked; he didn't get a chance to answer, so he paid attention only to the food.

   (C) His host kept putting food on his plate; he didn't want to leave food or seem impolite, so he ate it all.

3. What is the cultural point of the story?

   (A) In some cultures, there is a lot of social conversation before and after the evening meal with guests; also, servers put food on guests' plates every time they are empty.

   (B) All over the world, dinner guests should eat a lot; if they leave anything on their plates, their hosts will think they don't like the food.

   (C) In some cultures, guests eat more than their hosts; in others, it is impolite to eat a lot at other people's houses.

C

▲ A student hitch-hiking to Italy

A group of international students was attending college in Europe. They had a long time between semesters for travel, so they decided to hitchhike as far as they could in other countries. In many places, they were **successful**. They put their thumbs out or pointed them backwards and smiled; friendly drivers stopped. As soon as the first traveler got a "yes" answer from a driver, he motioned with his hand or fingers for his friends to come — or he held both thumbs up in an "OK" sign or made a circle with the thumb and the next finger of one hand. The young tourists saved money, saw a lot of the countryside, and had interesting conversations and experiences.

On the other hand, in Greece and Turkey, the visitors were not so lucky. Few drivers stopped to give them rides; instead, most people ignored them. Others gave them mean looks from their cars; they seemed almost insulted that the visitors were begging for rides. A few drivers shouted terrible words at the travelers; two even got out of their truck and started a fight. The students thought the drivers were very **rude**. They felt confused, afraid, and unwelcome. After a few days the students took the bus back to the countries where they were studying.

50

1. Why did the young travelers get rides successfully in many places in Europe?

   (A) Drivers knew they were trying to "thumb rides" because they recognized the meanings of their hand gestures.

   (B) All the travelers were good-looking young men, and the drivers that stopped were single women.

   (C) Most people knew the students had money; they expected payment for the rides in their cars and trucks.

2. Why weren't the student tourists so lucky in Greece and Turkey?

   (A) In those countries, there are laws against hitchhiking, so drivers aren't allowed to give rides to travelers.

   (B) In certain places, the custom is to ask for rides with printed signs: the signs should tell the place the travelers want to go.

   (C) The "hitchhiking" thumb gesture has an insulting meaning in those cultures: drivers thought the young people were being rude and disrespectful.

3. What is the cultural point of the story?

   (A) Hand gestures are rude because they are kinds of body language: visitors to other cultures should always ask for things with words.

   (B) Travelers should hitchhike only in their home cultures: drivers are afraid to give rides to foreigners.

   (C) The same gestures (hand positions and movements) can have very different meanings in various cultures — even opposite meanings.

After You Read

Strategy

Summarizing an Anecdote

When you summarize an anecdote to make a point:

- Retell the story in your own words.
- Include the "message" (or point) of the story.

3 **Summarizing an Anecdote** Work in groups of three. Choose an anecdote from the reading selection "Clues to World Cultures." Summarize the anecdote. Remember to focus on the point, or message.

4 **Discussing the Reading** In small groups, talk about your answers to these questions. Be prepared to tell the class some of the highlights from your discussion.

1. In your community, city, or country, do people pay attention to others one at a time or all at the same time? Who gets attention first — the people already in conversation or the new people?

2. At dinner parties in your culture, what are some of the "rules" or customs? How do hosts offer or serve food? How do guests ask for food — or ask for more?

3. What are some hand, finger, or thumb positions or movements in your culture? What do they mean — and do they have the same meanings in all situations? Do people from other communities or countries use the same gestures in the same ways? Explain.

4. What is a "cross-cultural situation?" What kinds of things might cause misunderstandings between members of two different cultures?

5 **Talking It Over** Below are some statements about cultural attitudes and customs. In your opinion or experience, which sentences are true for typical situations in your social group, your community, your country, or your culture? Check (✓) those items and explain your choices. Where do you think the other statements might be true? Why do you think so?

1. _____ To greet each other, people bow the head or bend the body forward. This body movement shows respect. Shaking hands or kissing and hugging are not common forms of greeting.

2. _____ Young people usually dress informally. Even for business or special occasions, they can wear comfortable clothes, like jeans and bright Hawaiian shirts.

3. _____ Families invite guests to their homes for dinner parties; they prepare special meals. They rarely meet guests in restaurants.

4. _____ Guests come on time for dinner parties, but hosts don't usually serve food right away. Instead, people enjoy drinks and conversation for a long time before the meal.

5. _____ People give gifts of money for special occasions, like birthdays, weddings, and holidays. They bring food or wine gifts to dinner parties.

6. _____ On social occasions, people smile a lot. They give compliments; that is, they say nice things to others about their clothes, their appearance, their houses, and so on.

7. _____ On the street and in public places like stores, people are not usually very polite; they try to be first and to get what they want. They may shout or use rude gestures.

8. _____ In classes at schools and colleges, students try to be first to answer questions. They tell their ideas and say their opinions on many topics. They may contradict the teacher.

9. _____ The individual is more important than the group or the community. Each person is responsible for his or her own needs, achievements, and successes.

10. _____ Time is very important in society because time means money; most people are in a hurry all the time.

Add a statement about another cultural custom, habit, attitude, or action. Share your statement with the class. When other students share their ideas, give your opinion.

PART 3

Vocabulary and Language-Learning Skills

Strategy

Understanding New Vocabulary in Context

In the reading "Cross-Cultural Conversation" on pages 109 – 111, the speakers talk about two kinds of culture. One meaning of *culture* is "a society's achievements in the arts, science, or government." Werner has that meaning in mind when he talks about the cathedrals, castles, and museums of Europe. Another meaning of *culture* is "the values, beliefs, and customs of a society." Nadia has that meaning in mind when she talks about greetings, titles, and social rules. Look back at the reading and determine what meaning of *culture* the speaker has in mind based on the context.

1 **Understanding New Vocabulary in Context** Below are some sentences with important vocabulary from the reading selection on pages 109 – 111. From the context, answer the questions about the underlined items. Then choose the meaning that seems the most logical in the context. To practice what you've learned about getting meaning from context, figure out the meanings of words from the clues in the paragraph.

1. Some examples of the architecture of old Europe are the magnificent cathedrals and castles. The design and building styles of modern architecture are excellent too.

What are some examples of old *architecture*?

_____

What are some examples of modern *architecture*?

_____

What does the noun *architecture* mean in these sentences?

   Ⓐ the form and plan of buildings and other structures

   Ⓑ the art and science of designing the study of classical literature

   Ⓒ people that study the culture of old Europe and other societies

2. Perhaps the real beginning of civilization — with its scientific and technological discoveries and inventions — was in the Middle East and Africa. Over five thousand years ago, those ancient civilizations had astronomy, mathematics, medicine, government, and so on.

Where and when did *civilization* begin?

_____

_____

What kinds of things did ancient *civilizations* have?

_____

Which word is a synonym of the word *civilization*?

   Ⓐ astronomy   Ⓑ technology   Ⓒ culture

3. The cultural legacy of ancient Chinese and Indian peoples included walled cities, the first governments, tools for work, and weapons for protection. Modern peoples built on this legacy.

Does a *legacy* come from the past, the present, or the future?

_____

What kinds of things might a *legacy* include?

_____

_____

What is a possible explanation of the word *legacy*?

   Ⓐ a gift of money that somebody gives to another person

   Ⓑ ideas and achievements passed from earlier generations to modern society

   Ⓒ the state or condition of being legal; not against the law

4. "For me, the idea of ancient culture creates a contradiction in definitions," said Karen, going against Mei's views. "Only modern things can be part of culture. Of course, people that like classical art and music will contradict me."

According to Karen, what kinds of things are part of culture?

_____

Does Karen think that people who like classical art and music agree with her?

_____

Do Karen and Mei have the same or different opinions?

_____

What might the noun *contradiction* and the verb *contradict* mean?

   Ⓐ (noun) the opposition of two opinions; (verb) to say that someone's ideas are wrong or not true

   Ⓑ (noun) the short forms of two words together; (verb) to put words together

   Ⓒ (noun) wearing a Hawaiian shirt in an ancient culture; (verb) to eat hamburgers with French fries

5. Because of the worldwide <u>media</u>—movies, TV, and the Internet — everybody knows the same information, plays the same music, and enjoys the same jokes.

What are some examples of "the worldwide media?"

_____

What are some things that _the media_ give to people around the world?

_____

How might you define the phrase _the media_?

   Ⓐ events that appear in the daily news and that everyone knows about

   Ⓑ the tradition of being in the middle — not on the extremes of possible views

   Ⓒ the combination of visual, sound, and printed ways to send ideas around the world

Strategy

Recognizing Nouns, Verbs, and Adjectives

If you don't know the meaning of a new vocabulary item, it helps to figure out its part of speech.

- Is the word a **noun** (a person, place, thing, or concept)?
- Is it a **verb** — a word for an action or a condition?
- Maybe the word is an **adjective**; in other words, its function might be to describe a noun or pronoun.

One way to tell the part of speech of an item is to recognize its function or purpose in the sentence — what does the word _do_ or _serve as_? Another is to figure out what question the item answers. Below is a summary of these clues to parts of speech.

Part of Speech	Function or Purpose	Question the Word Answers	Examples
A noun	serves as the subject of the sentence is the object or complement of a verb or is the object of a preposition	Who? (What person?) What? (What thing, place, or concept?)	<u>Karen</u> writes long <u>letters</u> to a good <u>friend</u> in <u>France</u>.
A verb	names an action, an activity, or a condition (a state of being)	What does the subject of the sentence do?	Karen <u>writes</u> long letters to a good friend in France.
An adjective	describes a noun or pronoun	How is it?	Karen writes <u>long</u> letters to a <u>good</u> friend in France.

2 **Recognizing Nouns, Verbs, and Adjectives** In the blanks of the sentences on the left, write the missing noun, verb, and adjective from the parts of speech chart. Then give the parts of speech of the words. The first item is done as an example.

1. Our class discussed the definition of modern culture, but there were a lot of ___opposing___ (adjective) views. The main ___opposition___ (noun) came from Carmel. She _____d (verb) everything we said.

Noun	Verb	Adjective
opposition	oppose	opposing

2. Can you _____ a typical cross-cultural situation? In your _____ , use as many _____ words as you can.

Noun	Verb	Adjective
description	describe	descriptive

3. To attract tourists, cities advertise the _____ of their architecture. They say that the buildings _____ in their beauty. They talk about the _____ artwork, too.

Noun	Verb	Adjective
excellence	excel	excellent

4. Are you an _____ traveler? Do you like to _____ the customs and habits of people in other cultures? Do you enjoy new _____ ?

Noun	Verb	Adjective
experiences	experience	experienced

5. One definition of the word _____ is "a high level of culture." Does a good education _____ people? Does it make them more _____?

Noun	Verb	Adjective
civilization	civilize	civilized

6. When did ancient civilizations _____ the calendar? Which _____ people figured it out? What were some of their other _____ ?

Noun	Verb	Adjective
inventions	invent	inventive

7. People of the same cultural background don't always _____ on the values of society. Even _____ people aren't in _____ all the time.

Noun	Verb	Adjective
agreement	agree	agreeable

8. Every _____ (group of people of the same culture) has _____ problems to solve. It also has to _____ its young people.

Noun	Verb	Adjective
society	socialize	social

9. Sometimes two cultural values seem to _____ each other. For instance, individual achievement may be _____ to the interests of families. It may create _____ .

Noun	Verb	Adjective
contradictions	contradict	contradictory

10. When did global advertising begin to _____ through the Internet? The _____ of the Internet is a significant achievement all over the globe, including in _____ nations.

Noun	Verb	Adjective
development	develop	developing

Understanding Adverbs of Manner

Adverbs are parts of speech that answer the question "how?" or "when?" or "where?" "Adverbs of manner" tell *how* or in *what way* something happens:

- Most often, adverbs of manner are closely related to adjectives. Some examples of adjectives are *easy* and *loud*.
- Adverbs of manner usually end in the letters –*ly*. For example, the adverb *easily* means "in an easy way." *Loudly* is an adverb of manner with the meaning "in a loud way."
- Adverbs for adjectives with the –*ly* ending, like *friendly*, can be difficult to pronounce. More often, such adjectives appear in noun phrases, such as *in a friendly tone*.

3 **Using Adverbs of Manner and Adjectives** Below are some sentences with pairs of related words — one adjective and one adverb of manner in each pair. In each blank, write the missing word — the adjective related to the underlined adverb or the adverb related to the underlined adjective. The first item is done as an example.

1. A <u>proud</u> Frenchman began the conversation about culture _____*proudly*_____. His friend was very _____*patient*_____, so he responded <u>patiently</u>.

2. A German student answered him in a _____ and _____ voice. She spoke <u>clearly</u> and <u>pleasantly</u>.

3. An American member of the group had a _____ way about her. She answered questions <u>knowingly</u>. She didn't find the questions <u>rude</u> so she didn't respond _____ .

4. A Middle Eastern woman with an _____ voice said she found ancient civilizations <u>amazing</u>. "_____, the ancients studied astronomy thousands of years ago," she explained <u>enthusiastically</u>.

5. An angry man stated his opinions _____. He was so <u>loud</u> that students in the next room heard him!

6. "The _____ mind looks at problems and situations <u>scientifically</u>," said someone from a well-developed Asian culture.

7. "But _____ scientists don't always know how to communicate <u>successfully</u>."

8. "I'm afraid I have to disagree with you," a nice African man answered _____. "According to the rules of their culture, most people try to be <u>polite</u>."

9. In a _____ voice, a young Chinese student stated his opinion; but he said it too <u>softly</u> for the others to hear.

10. Finally, the most _____ and <u>convincing</u> member of the group ended the discussion <u>enthusiastically</u> and _____.

4 **Focusing on High-Frequency Words** Read the paragraph below and fill in each blank with a word from the box.

another	ignoring	pain
attention	local	patiently
customer	minute	terrible

An Irish woman was visiting tourist places in a Latin American city when she got a _____ headache. She knew what medicine she
        1
needed, so she went to a _____ pharmacy. The pharmacist was
        2
waiting on another _____ when she came in. The Irish woman
        3
_____ waited her turn.
    4

While she was standing there, two other customers came in, then _____, and then three more. Each time, the pharmacist
    5
turned his _____ to the new people. He did not greet the Irish
      6
woman; he never said, "I'll be with you in a _____."
        7

After about 20 minutes, the woman couldn't stand the _____
        8
in her head any longer. "Hey, I've been here a long time," she said loudly, very annoyed and insulted. "Why is everyone _____ me? I need
        9
service, too!" she shouted rudely (impolitely).

5 Making Connections Do an Internet search about a culture that you don't know well. You can use a search engine and type in the country's name and the word *culture*, for example, *Mexican culture*.

Identify at least five things that you learn about that culture. It can be anything like food, language, sports, music, types of greetings, gestures, money, architecture, etc.

Tell your classmates what you learned about that culture. What do these things indicate about cultural norms or customs in that country? Are these things similar to or different from things in your culture?

Culture: _____

Website(s): _____

Five things I learned about this culture: _____

_____

_____

_____

_____

_____

Similarities to my culture: _____

_____

Differences from my culture: _____

_____

PART 4 | **Focus on Testing**

FOCUS

Practicing Vocabulary Questions

A well-developed English vocabulary is one of your best tools for doing well on the TOEFL® iBT. For each passage in the reading section, there will be two or three direct vocabulary questions.

Each direct vocabulary question on the TOEFL® iBT is asked in the following way: "Which of the following is closest in meaning to _____ (vocabulary item) used in Paragraph X?" Part 3 of this chapter discusses getting meaning from context.

Notice that the question emphasizes a context (". . . in Paragraph X"). In some cases, the word you are considering has several meanings. You must choose the meaning that fits the context specified in the question.

Practicing Vocabulary Questions Below is a new reading, "Cultural Anthropology." Using the skills you practiced in Part 3 of this chapter, try to answer the TOEFL® iBT–like questions that follow. The target vocabulary words — those asked about in the questions–are highlighted in the reading and the question.

Cultural Anthropology

A   The science of anthropology is divided into several branches, one of which is cultural anthropology. This branch looks at the basic beliefs, possessions, and behavior common within a society. For example, the crops a group plants or the ways in which a society catches and cooks fish are concerns of the cultural anthropologist.

B   One of the main goals of cultural anthropology is to discover relationships among groups that presently seem very distant from each other. Such discoveries, along with other evidence, may show that such disparate cultures come from the same origins. A cultural anthropologist may see, for example, that owning cattle has a huge significance in two African societies that are now separated by thousands of miles. This fact, together with other evidence, could indicate that both cultures came from the same Bantu ancestor in the past.

C   Cultural anthropologists and linguists each contributed evidence in determining the origin of a large group of cultures — the Malayo-Polynesian. Since the late 18th century, scholars knew of similarities among peoples from Madagascar (off the east coast of Africa), through Southeast Asia and New Zealand, to Easter Island just west of South America. There were some similarities in appearance but, more importantly, also similarities in beliefs and practices. Still, it seemed hard to believe that one culture was the ancestor to so many people in different parts of the world. And even if they were all related, where did they come from?

D   Linguists (who study language patterns and structure) used research and reasoning to pinpoint the island of Formosa (present-day Taiwan) as the origin of Malayo-Polynesian languages. It is there that such languages exist in the greatest number in relatively small areas. This means that the peoples of Formosa have had the longest time of all the Malayo-Polynesians to develop distinct local languages.

E   Cultural anthropologists were interested, but they needed more evidence. They found it in two items of food—millet and pork. Millet, a kind of cereal grain, is part of an agricultural tradition carried from Formosa to vastly different climates, where it remains a cultural staple of traditional Malayo-

Polynesian societies. The same goes for domesticated pigs. Malayo-Polynesians continue to raise and eat pigs even in areas that probably had no native pig species until the arrival of humans came from the Formosans.

F   Current customs might seem to cast doubt on this theory. Modern Malays, for example, usually avoid any contact with pigs or their meat. The Malayo-Polynesians, however, arrived in Malay lands thousands of years ago, before Muslim missionaries brought their religion's rules. The strongest evidence comes from small, traditional cultures in these regions, not from the Islamized or Westernized larger societies.

1. Which of the following is closest in meaning to concerns as it is used in Paragraph A?

   A worries

   B goals

   C interests

   D branches

2. Why does the author twice use the phrase with other evidence (Paragraph B)?

   A to show that other evidence tells cultural anthropologists what to study

   B to show the relationship between two widely separate cultures

   C to show an important tradition among anthropologists

   D to show that cultural anthropologists do not draw conclusions from one fact alone

3. Which of the following is closest in meaning to disparate as it is used in Paragraph B?

   A different

   B similar

   C distant

   D nearby

4. Which of the following is closest in meaning to practices as it is used in Paragraph C?

   A exercises

   B workplaces

   C activities

   D ideas

5. Which of the following is closest in meaning to cast doubt on as it is used in Paragraph F?

   A make clear

   B cause some questioning of

   C say terrible things about

   D make unclear

Self-Assessment Log

Read the lists below. Check (✓) the strategies and vocabulary that you learned in this chapter. Look through the chapter or ask your instructor about the strategies and words that you do not understand.

Reading and Vocabulary-Building Strategies

☐ Understanding reading structure: conversation in paragraph form
☐ Recognizing supporting detail: opinions
☐ Understanding anecdotes
☐ Summarizing an anecdote
☐ Understanding new vocabulary in context
☐ Recognizing nouns, verbs, and adjectives
☐ Understanding adverbs of manner

Target Vocabulary

Nouns	Verbs	Adjectives	Adverbs
architecture	agree*	amazing	convincingly
attention*	contradict	annoyed	loudly
civilization	describe*	clear*	patiently*
contradiction	develop*	enthusiastic	politely
customer*	experience*	excellent*	rudely
legacy	greet	knowing	
media*	ignoring*	local*	
medicine	invent	opposing	
pain*		pleasant	
societies*		proud	
		rude	
		scientific*	
		social*	
		soft*	
		successful*	
		terrible*	
		tourist	

* These words are among the 2,000 most frequently used words in English.

7 Health

"He who has health has hope, and he who has hope has everything."

Arabian proverb

In this CHAPTER

In Part 1, you will read about people who live long lives, and the secrets to their longevity. In the rest of this chapter, you will read about, explore, and discuss health issues such as diet, activity, and avoiding disease.

Connecting to the Topic

1. Look at the photo. What is this grandmother doing with her grandsons? What do you think her secret is to a long and healthy life?

2. Would you want to live to be 100 years old or older? Why? Why not?

3. Eating nutritiously is important for good health. What are five other things people can do to stay healthy?

The Secrets of a Very Long Life

Before You Read

1 **Previewing the Topic** Look at the photos and discuss the questions in your groups.

1. What is the relationship of the two people? What are they doing?

2. Describe the lifestyle of the couple. What do they probably do all day? Do you think they are healthy? Why or why not?

3. Do you know any very old people? Do they have any "secrets" of a long life?

▲ An elderly couple kayaking

2 **Predicting** Talk about these questions with a partner. When you read "The Secrets of a Very Long Life," look for the answers.

1. What places in the world are famous for people who live a very long time?

2. What is the environment like in places where people live a long time?

3. What kind of diet do you think people in these places have?

3 Previewing Vocabulary Read the vocabulary items below from the first reading. Then listen to the words and phrases. Put a check mark (✓) next to the words you don't know. Don't use a dictionary.

Nouns
- altitude
- average
- benefits
- claims
- disease
- environment
- inhabitants
- length
- longevity
- population
- preservatives
- streams
- stress
- theories

Verbs
- consume
- cure
- prevent
- solve
- theorize

Adjectives
- active
- available
- different
- famous
- long-lived
- moderate
- unpolluted
- valid

Connectors
- as a result
- furthermore
- however
- in addition
- moreover
- nevertheless
- therefore
- thus

Read

4 Reading an Article Read the following article. Then do the activities that follow.

The Secrets of a Very Long Life

Introduction

A   There are several places in the world that are **famous** for people who live a very long time. These places are usually in mountainous areas, far away from modern cities. Even so, doctors, scientists, and public health experts often travel to these regions to **solve** the mystery of a long, healthy life. In this way, the experts hope to bring to the modern world the secrets of **longevity**.   5

Hunza in the Himalayan Mountains

B   Hunza is at a very high altitude in the Himalayan Mountains of Asia. There, many people over 100 years of age are still in good physical health. Additionally, men of 90 are new fathers, and women of 50 still have babies. What are the reasons for this good health? Scientists believe that the people   10 of Hunza have these three main advantages or benefits: (1) a healthful, **unpolluted environment** with clean air and water; (2) a simple diet high in vitamins, fiber, and nutrition but low in fat, cholesterol, sugar, and unnatural chemicals; and (3) physical work and other activities, usually in the fields or with animals.   15

The Russian Caucasians and Vilcabamba

C   People in the Caucasus Mountains in Russia are also famous for their longevity. Official birth records were not available, but the community says a woman called Tsurba lived until age 160. Similarly, a man called Shirali

▲ An inhabitant of the Caucasus mountains

probably lived until 168; moreover, his widow was 120 years old. In general, the people not only live a long time, but they also live well. In other words, they are almost never sick. Furthermore, when they die, they not only have their own teeth but also a full head of hair, and good eyesight too. Vilcabamba, Ecuador, is another area famous for the longevity of its **inhabitants**. This mountain region — like Hunza and the Caucasus — is also at a very high altitude, far away from cities. In Vilcabamba, too, there is very little serious **disease**. One reason for the good health of the people might be the clean, beautiful environment; another advantage is the **moderate** climate. The temperature is about 70° Fahrenheit all year long; furthermore, the wind always comes from the same direction. In addition, the water comes from mountain **streams** and is high in minerals: perhaps as a result of this valuable resource, the region is rich in flowers, fruits, vegetables, and wildlife.

Differences in the Diets of People with Unusual Longevity

D   In some ways, the diets of the inhabitants in the three regions are quite different. Hunzukuts eat mainly raw vegetables, fruit (especially apricots), and chapatis — a kind of pancake; they eat meat only a few times a year. In contrast, the Caucasian diet consists mainly of milk, cheese, vegetables, fruit, and meat; also, most people there drink the local red wine daily. In Vilcabamba, people eat only a small amount of meat each week; their diet consists mostly of grain, corn, beans, potatoes, and fruit. Even so, experts found one surprising fact in the mountains of Ecuador: most people there, even the very old, consume a lot of coffee, drink large amounts of alcohol, and smoke 40 to 60 cigarettes daily!

Similarities in Diet

E   However, the typical diets of the three areas are similar in three general ways: (1) The fruits and vegetables are all natural; that is, they contain no preservatives or other chemicals. (2) Furthermore, the **population** uses traditional herbs and medicines to **prevent** and cure disease. (3) The inhabitants consume fewer calories than people do in other parts of the world. A typical North American eats and drinks an average of 3,300 calories every day, while a typical inhabitant of these mountainous areas takes in between 1,700 and 2,000 calories.

Other Possible Reasons for Healthy Longevity

F   Inhabitants in the three regions have more in common than their mountain environment, their distance from modern cities, and their low-calorie natural diets. Because they live in the countryside and are mostly farmers, their lives are physically hard and extremely active. Therefore, they do not 60 need to try to exercise. In addition, the population does not seem to have the stress of fast city work and recreation. As a result, people's lives are relatively free from worry — and therefore, illness or other health problems. Thus, some experts believe that physical movement and a stress-free environment might be the two most important secrets of longevity. An 65 additional health advantage of life in these **long-lived** communities may be the extended family structure: the group takes care of its members from birth to death.

The Validity of Longevity Claims

G   Nevertheless, some doctors theorize that members of especially long-lived populations have only one thing in common: they don't have **valid** official 70 government birth records. These health scientists think there is a natural limit to the **length** of human life; in their theories, it is impossible to reach an age of more than 110 years or so. Therefore, they say, **claims** of unusual longevity in certain groups are probably false.

After You Read

Strategy

Recognizing Reading Structure Using a Mind Map
You can organize the topics and main ideas of a reading by using a mind map.
It can be used to review and recall material.

- A mind map shows the relationship of the topics, main ideas, and supporting details.
- The main topic is placed in the center of the map.
- The most general parts of the reading can appear in big circles connected to the central topics.
- The main idea for each paragraph can appear in smaller circles connected to these general parts.
- Supporting details are connected to the main ideas.
- You can use color to help organize the material.

5 **Recognizing Reading Structure Using a Mind Map** Look at the example of a mind map for the material in Paragraph B of the reading "The Secrets of a Very Long Life." Then answer the questions that follow the mind map below.

A Mind Map of Paragraph B

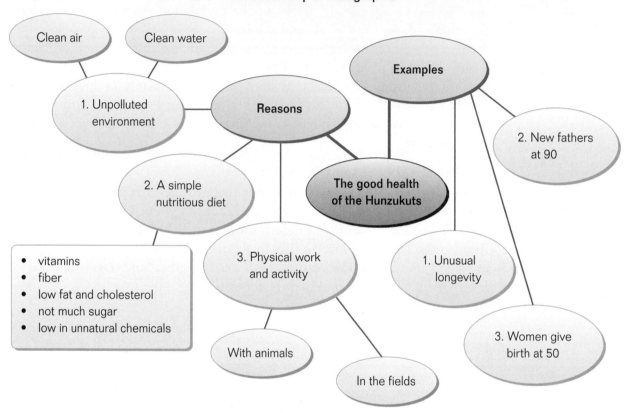

1. What is the main topic of the diagram? (the title).

   _____

2. What are the two general divisions? _____ *1. Examples*

   _____ *2. Reasons*

3. What are the three examples given?

   _____

   _____

   _____

4. How many main reasons are there for the good health of the people of Hunza?

   _____

   What are these reasons? _____

   _____

   _____

5. What are two characteristics or elements of an unpolluted environment?

_____

_____

6. How many characteristics of a simple nutritious diet are there in the diagram?

_____

List three of them:

_____

7. "In the fields" and "with animals" are two details of what reason for good health?

_____

6 **Completing a Mind Map** Read and complete the mind map below about "The Secrets of a Very Long Life." Choose your answers from the phrases in the box on page 138. Then answer the question about the main idea.

A Mind Map of "The Secrets of a Very Long Life"

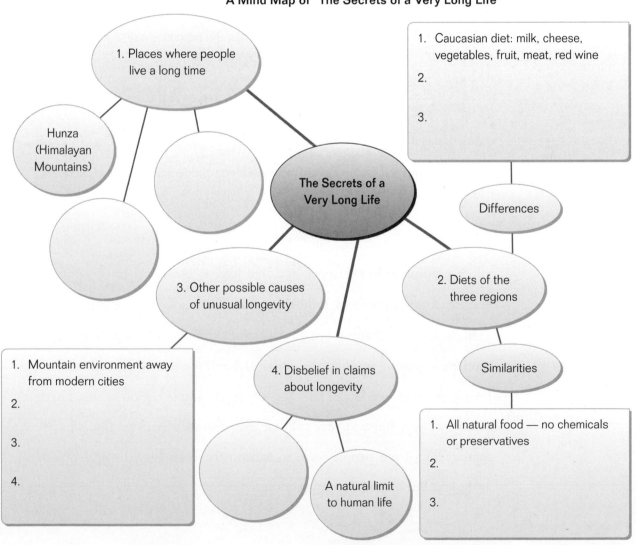

1. Places where people live a long time

Hunza (Himalayan Mountains)

The Secrets of a Very Long Life

3. Other possible causes of unusual longevity

4. Disbelief in claims about longevity

A natural limit to human life

1. Mountain environment away from modern cities

2.

3.

4.

1. Caucasian diet: milk, cheese, vegetables, fruit, meat, red wine

2.

3.

Differences

2. Diets of the three regions

Similarities

1. All natural food — no chemicals or preservatives

2.

3.

- Hunzukut diet: raw vegetables, fruit, *chapatis*
- The Caucasus Mountains in Russia
- fewer calories
- stress-free lives
- Vilcabamba, Ecuador

- Ecuadorian diet: grain, vegetables, fruit, coffee, alcohol, cigarettes
- no valid birth certificates
- hard physical activity
- extended family structure
- traditional herbs as medicine

Answer the question.

What is the main (the most general) topic of the reading?

- (A) places in the world where people live a long time
- (B) some possible secrets of the mystery of longevity
- (C) a comparison of the health of people in the Caucasus Mountains and Ecuador
- (D) the typical diet of the inhabitants of mountain regions

7 Understanding the Main Idea Finish the main-idea question about the reading selection "The Secrets of a Very Long Life."

Main-idea question:

Why do people in some areas of the world _____

_____ ?

In the paragraph below, change the underlined words so that the paragraph answers your main-idea question.

According to health specialists that <u>have</u> longevity, there are <u>no</u> possible reasons for a <u>short</u> and <u>unhealthy</u> life. The first requirement might be a high level of hard <u>mental</u> work and activity <u>without</u> freedom from modern worries. Second, the physical environment makes <u>no</u> difference: people seem to live longer in a <u>low desert or jungle</u> region with <u>a changing</u> climate of <u>very hot and very cold</u> air temperatures. And finally, diet <u>doesn't matter</u>: long-lived people seem to eat mostly foods high in <u>fat, cholesterol, and sugar</u> but low in <u>vitamins and nutrition</u>.

Strategy

Recognizing Supporting Details After Punctuation, Numbers, and Connecting Words

Punctuation, numbers, and connecting words can show the relationship of main ideas to supporting details. They also show the relationship of general points to more specific ones.

- A colon (:) before a list often indicates the relationship of the following material to the previous point.

- Numbers in parentheses within a paragraph, like (1), (2), and so on, come before separate items that all relate to the same main point.

- Connecting words and phrases also give clues to the relationships among points. The phrase *for instance* means that the following sentence part will give instances, or examples, of a previous statement.

- There are connecting words such as *and* or *furthermore* that show addition. They introduce similar facts or concepts or give additional evidence or arguments.

- Some connecting words, such as *but* or *however*, mean that differences, opposites, or contradictions will follow. Still other vocabulary of this kind indicates causes, reasons, or results. Examples include *thus* and *therefore*.

Read the commonly used connecting adverbs and phrases below.

Addition or Similarity	Contrast or Contradiction	Causes, Reasons, or Result
and	but	thus
also	while	therefore
too	instead	for this reason
in addition	even so	as a result
additionally	however	because of this
furthermore	nevertheless	
moreover	in contrast	
in the same way	on the other hand	
similarly		

8 **Recognizing Supporting Details After Punctuation, Numbers, and Connecting Words** Use punctuation clues, numbers in parentheses, and connecting words to help you find the answers to these questions. You will find the answers in the reading selection "The Secrets of a Very Long Life." On the lines, write the answers in your own words.

1. High mountain regions where people live to a very old age are far away from modern cities. For what two reasons might medical scientists and health specialists travel there?

_____

_____

_____

2. According to scientists, what are three reasons for the good physical health of the people of Hunza?

_____

_____

_____

3. Who were two people similar in their longevity to the Caucasian woman Tsurba?

_____

_____

_____

4. In what ways do the people of the Caucasian region live well even in old age?

_____

_____

_____

5. What are four or five healthful elements or features of the environment in Vilcabamba, Ecuador?

_____

_____

_____

6. In what three general ways are the diets of inhabitants of the Hunza, the Caucasus, and Vilcabamba similar?

_____

_____

_____

7. In addition to diet, what are three other possible reasons for the healthy longevity of the populations discussed in the reading?

_____

_____

_____

8. Why don't all doctors believe the longevity claims of these groups of people?

_____

_____

_____

9 Discussing the Reading In small groups, talk about your answers to the following questions.

1. Do you believe that the people discussed in the reading selection really lived to over 150 years of age? Why or why not?
2. Do you hope or plan to live to a very old age? Why or why not?
3. Can you suggest any other things that might lead to a long, healthy old age?

PART 2 | Main Ideas and Details

Claims to Amazing Health

Before You Read

1 Previewing Vocabulary Read the vocabulary items below from the next reading. Then listen to the words and phrases. Put a check mark (✓) next to the words you don't know. Don't use a dictionary.

Nouns		Verbs	Adjectives
▨ advice	▨ folk medicine	▨ color	▨ accurate
▨ bacteria	▨ genes	▨ correct	▨ dishonest
▨ birth defects	▨ geneticists	▨ determine	▨ elderly
▨ characteristics	▨ joints	▨ oppose	▨ fraudulent
▨ cherry juice	▨ length	▨ recommend	▨ genetic
▨ combination	▨ parasites	▨ take	▨ proven
▨ cure	▨ patients	advantage of	▨ sour
▨ damage	▨ physiologist		
▨ decisions	▨ senior citizens		
▨ engineering	▨ specialists		
	▨ viruses		

Read

2 Understanding Facts and Opinions With a topic like health care or medicine, personal beliefs may contradict proven scientific fact. A definition of the word *fact* might be "reality as opposed to opinion."

Following are four readings on the general topic of "Claims to Amazing Health." They tell the views of some healthcare and medical experts; all of these opinions come from a combination of proven fact and personal belief.

Skim each paragraph. Then answer the question above each paragraph about the topic. Choose A, B, or C. Then read each paragraph a second time. Read the question below the paragraph and fill in the letter of the statement that best tells the point.

Claims to Amazing Health

Which title best expresses the topic of Paragraph A?

(A) The Value of a Variety of Valid Views

(B) Long on Longevity: Free but False

(C) Internet Help and Hope: Health Benefits vs. Costs

A   On the subject of physical health and medical research, there are thousands of amazing websites where people can get information. However, when does the amount of available information affect its validity and health benefits? The Internet is greatly influencing people's attitudes about their own health care: probably, this worldwide cultural trend improves global health. Because computer users can look up almost any topic of interest to them, they become their own researchers. In the busy modern world, doctors don't always take the time to explain illnesses and possible remedies to their **patients**; they may not give scientific details in words that are easy to understand, either. For this reason, many hopeful people take advantage of Internet resources to find the facts they need for good medical **decisions**. But are the beliefs of "experts" always completely **accurate** or real? Are they helpful to everyone that needs advice on a specific medical condition? The health products or books that seem the most wonderful are often the most fraudulent — that is, **dishonest** or false. Do sick or worried people expect too much when they look for clear, easy answers to difficult health questions or problems on the computer?

▲ Using the Internet to research a health problem

Which sentence best states the point of the facts and beliefs in Paragraph A?

(A) The great amount of medical information (facts and opinions) available on the Internet may improve people's attitudes about health; on the other hand, some claims might be inaccurate or dishonest— and therefore dangerous.

(B) To find out the easiest and best ways to solve difficult health problems and cure diseases, everyone should go online — that is, people ought to look up the topics that interest them on the Internet.

(C) Doctors are too busy to help their patients, especially the people that are the oldest or the sickest; therefore, these people have to take advantage of the Internet to find help.

Which title best tells the topic of Paragraph B?

   (A) The Cure for All Cancers: Causes and Cases

   (B) Theories and Advice from Medical Specialists

   (C) The Personal Problem of Parasites in Patients

B   Many specialists have their own theories about illness and health. As an example, a California physiologist (someone who studies biology) has written books with the titles *The Cure for All Diseases* and *The Cure for* 25 *All Cancers.* She says there are only two causes of disease: (1) pollution of the environment and (2) parasites (harmful plants and animals that feed on living things) inside the human body. To prevent or cure the illnesses that these parasitic bacteria and viruses cause, she offers (tries to sell) two kinds of health products on the Internet and in other places: electronic 30 machines and herbal medicines. The two beneficial effects of these items in humans and animals, this scientist claims, are (1) to clean out the body, freeing it of parasites and (2) to rebuild new healthy living cells. According to her theories, people will feel better and live longer as a result. In addition, other medical experts recommend kinds of natural, nontraditional, or 35 non-Western remedies for modern health disorders such as heart disease, cancer, asthma, nervousness, depression, and so on. Their advice might include (1) special diet plans with added vitamins and minerals, (2) folk medicine, (3) environmental changes, or (4) unusual therapies that patients don't get from traditional doctors. 40

Which sentence best states the point of the facts and beliefs in Paragraph B?

   (A) In the human body, parasites are dangerous viruses and bacteria; for this reason, everyone must use electronic machines and herbal medicines to fight against them.

   (B) Nontraditional and non-Western remedies are more effective cures and remedies for health problems than the methods of doctors that offer information over the Internet.

   (C) Many medical specialists have their own theories about illness and health, including the causes of disease and the beneficial effects of certain products and therapies.

Which title best tells the topic of Paragraph C?

   (A) Colorful Cures for Continuing Care: Natural Food Remedies

   (B) A Variety of Theories vs. Advice from Medical Experts

   (C) Family and Folk Falsehoods — Physical Facts and Figures.

C   In a small-town farm market, hundreds of **elderly** people drink a glass of **sour** dark cherry juice every day. These happy senior citizens, some of them over the age of 90, claim that the natural fruit juice cures — or at least decreases — the pain of their arthritis, a disease of the joints of the aging body. It's a folk remedy, not a **proven** medical therapy. Nevertheless, science is beginning to figure out why sour cherry juice might work to improve the health of patients with arthritis. The secret is in the substance that gives the cherries their dark red color. It belongs to a classification of natural nutrients that color blueberries, strawberries, plums, and other fruits — and vegetables too. Moreover, these coloring substances may help to prevent serious health disorders like heart disease and cancer. In other words, vitamins and fiber are not the only reasons to eat fruits and vegetables. "To take advantage of natural whole foods," advise nutritionists and health researchers, "think variety and color."

Which sentence best states the point of the facts and beliefs in Paragraph C?

(A) Color makes people happy, so it improves their health and state of mind; therefore, families should wear colorful clothes at meals.

(B) Like vitamins and fiber, the substances in foods that give them color may offer an important health advantage.

(C) Dark red foods are the best for nutrition, but bright yellow and green vegetables are more effective for elderly people that have arthritis pain.

Which title best tells the topic of Paragraph D?

(A) Claims of the Advantages of Genetic Research and Engineering

(B) Defects in Gene Structure and Insect Damage to Foods

(C) Characteristics of Folk Remedies vs. Beliefs of Geneticists

D   What are **genes** and why are medical researchers always trying to find out more about them? Genes are part of the center (that is, the nucleus) of every living cell; in the form of DNA (deoxyribonucleic acid), this biological **genetic** material determines the characteristics (features) of every living thing—every plant, animal, and human being—on Earth. Medical geneticists are scientists that study DNA and genes for many purposes: (1) to learn how living things such as parasites, viruses, and bacteria cause illness; (2) to find the gene or **combination** of genes that cause certain diseases to pass from parents to their children; (3) to prevent or **correct** (repair) birth defects; (4) to change gene structure to improve health and increase the length of human life (longevity); and (5) to change the biological characteristics of animals and humans in ways that are beneficial to society. Another use of genetic technology that some

▲ model of a DNA strand

scientists support is changing the genes of the food farmers grow. Genetic engineers claim that these differences in DNA structure will increase food production, prevent **damage** from insects, and improve world health; in contrast, others **oppose** the use of genetic **engineering** not only in plants but also in animals and humans.

Which sentence best states the point of the facts and beliefs in Paragraph D?

(A) Deoxyribonucleic acid is not as beneficial as DNA—the biological material related to genetics—in research on the causes of birth defects.

(B) Genetic engineers and other specialists claim that research into the gene structure of living things can improve human health in many ways.

(C) Because there is a natural limit to the length of human life, only changes in gene structure can increase longevity in senior citizens that drink cherry juice.

After You Read

Strategy

Summarizing Using a Mind Map

You learned how to summarize in previous chapters. Another way to summarize is to use a mind map.

- First, figure out the topic, the main ideas, and the supporting details. You can make a mind map showing the relationship of the points to one another.
- Then create a short summary from the items on the map.

Below is an example of a mind map of Paragraph A from the reading "Claims to Amazing Health." A summary based on the mind map follows.

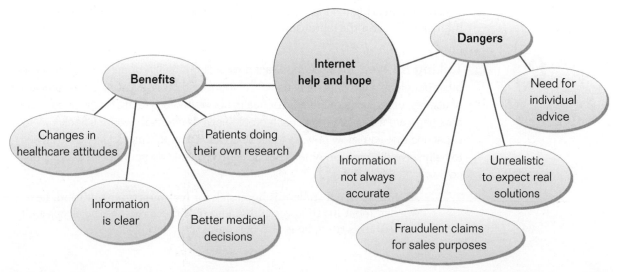

FOCUS

Summary: Benefits vs. Limits of Internet Health Information

On the Internet, people can find many medical facts and beliefs. Their availability can improve world health: people may change their attitudes about health care when they get information in clear language through their own research. Then they can make better medical decisions. However, the information on the Internet may not always be accurate or helpful to all individuals. There may even be fraudulent (false or deceptive) claims about products to increase sales. Is it realistic to expect real solutions to difficult health problems from the Internet?

3 Summarizing Using a Mind Map Work in groups of three. Each person chooses a different paragraph (B, C, or D) from the reading "Claims to Amazing Health." Read your paragraph carefully. Make a mind map about your paragraph. Place the topic in the middle of the mind map. Then complete the map.

Next, from your mind map, summarize the information in as few sentences as possible, paraphrasing the important points in your own words.

Then tell or read your summary to your group.

4 Discussing the Reading In small groups, talk about your answers to these questions. Then tell the class the most interesting information or ideas.

1. Do you go to the Internet for information about health and medicine? Why or why not? In your view, what are the benefits and limits of this kind of research?

2. What natural, nontraditional, or non-Western remedies for modern health disorders have you heard about? What do the experts that offer these cures claim? Do you believe their claims? Why or why not?

3. Do you believe that natural chemicals in food, including substances that give color, can decrease pain or help prevent serious disease? Why or why not? If so, which foods do you recommend for these reasons?

4. In your opinion, is genetic research beneficial for global health? How about genetic engineering (changing the gene structure of plants, animals, and humans)? Explain the reasons for your views.

5 Talking It Over Many people want advice about health or medicine. Experts or other people might recommend beneficial foods and other substances, helpful kinds of activity, other kinds of therapy, or health books and products. Below and on the next page are some common health problems in the modern world. Check (✓) the situations that you know or want to know about. Then, talk as a class. Give advice to help solve the problem or tell your opinion. (You can do your own research, of course.)

1. _____ An international student is homesick for his country; in addition, he worries about his finances and grades. For these reasons, he sleeps a lot but still feels tired; he is also nervous.

2. _____ A young man in a cold northern climate gets depressed during the long, dark winter months. He is irritable and moody. He thinks he has SAD (Seasonal Affective Disorder).

3. _____ During times of forceful winds from the mountains, a Japanese woman seems to have more asthma attacks. She can't breathe very well, and she feels afraid.

4. _____ The members of a family often get colds or the flu (influenza)— not only during the winter but also during changes in the seasons. Occasionally, someone gets pneumonia.

5. _____ A professor is having memory problems. From the Internet, she learned that foods with the substance lecithin and B-vitamins can help, so she eats a lot of broccoli, soybeans, and nuts. Even so, she often forgets what she is doing.

6. _____ A brother and sister disagree on the best kinds of foods to eat for good health. He follows a famous high-protein diet plan that allows only certain foods at certain times. She wants to eat what tastes good.

7. _____ A Czech woman serves nutritious salads and other vegetables to her family, but her husband won't eat them. He prefers high-calorie meat and dairy dishes with rich desserts, and he is getting very fat. She is afraid he will die of a heart attack.

8. _____ A young male athlete feels strong and healthy, but he is worried about his longevity because of his relatives' diseases. For this reason, he welcomes research into genetic engineering.

9. _____ A 70-year-old man drinks a lot of coffee and smokes cigarettes; he also enjoys alcoholic drinks. He likes to go walking in his mountain community; however, he is often in pain from his arthritis.

10. _____ A couple is going to have a baby. Because there is a history of genetic defects in several generations of their extended families, they are worried about the child's chances for good health and long life.

PART 3 Vocabulary and Language-Learning Skills

Strategy

Getting Meaning from Context

As you learned in Chapter 6, even without definitions or explanations in the same sentence or paragraph, you can figure out new vocabulary. There may not be definitions, words with similar or opposite meanings, illustrations, or punctuation clues to help. Even so, the message or meaning of the reading may lead to useful guesses about the meaning of unfamiliar or difficult vocabulary.

1 Figuring Out New or Difficult Vocabulary Read the following sentences with vocabulary from the reading selection. From the context, answer the questions that follow. Then use logic to figure out a definition of each word. Fill in the letter of the explanation closest to yours.

1. To discover the secrets of <u>longevity</u>, health specialists are studying people that reach ages well over 100. These <u>long-lived</u> individuals enjoy good health all their lives, too.

   Who is trying to find out about *longevity*? _____

   _____

   Why might these scientists want to know such "secrets"? _____

   _____

   Whom are these researchers studying? _____

   _____

   What does the noun *longevity* mean?

   (A) health researchers

   (B) a hundred different ages

   (C) many years between birth and death

   (D) old people in the mountains

   What is the meaning of the adjective *long-lived*?

   (A) living a long time

   (B) dying at an early age

   (C) the altitude of the Himalayan Mountains

   (D) having a full head of hair and healthy teeth

2. Scientists believe the people of certain high mountain regions have the benefit of a healthful <u>environment</u> with clean air and water and <u>moderate</u> temperatures — not very hot or very cold.

   What is an *environment* in this sentence?

   (A) clean air and water

   (B) a healthful place in the desert

   (C) unnatural or extreme atmospheric conditions

   (D) the conditions of a place that influence people

   What two things can an *environment* have? _____

   Where might an *environment* be? _____

   What kinds of temperatures are not *moderate*? _____

   What is the meaning of the adjective *moderate*?

   (A) very hot and very cold

   (B) not extreme; in the middle

   (C) related to the air and water of a region

   (D) of the modern world

3. A woman named Tsurba and a man named Shirali were among the long-lived inhabitants of the Caucasus Mountain region of Russia. Other people that inhabit the area don't seem to get sick often either.

Were Tsurba and Shirali *inhabitants* of or visitors to the mountains?

_____

Are *inhabitants* people, places, things, or actions? _____

_____

Who are the *inhabitants* of a place?

Ⓐ people that live there

Ⓑ people that live there in summer

Ⓒ people that study the environment in that region

Ⓓ hardworking, physically active farmers

What is the meaning of the verb *inhabit*?

Ⓐ to make an action difficult

Ⓑ to work during the day in a place

Ⓒ tto have scientific interests in common

Ⓓ to live in (a region or area)

4. A healthful environment includes unpolluted clean water; the water might come from high mountain streams and contain a lot of minerals.

If an environment has clean water, is the water *polluted*? _____

_____

What do high mountain *streams* bring to a healthful environment? _____

_____

What is high in minerals? _____

_____

What does the adjective *unpolluted* mean?

Ⓐ dirtying of the earth and air

Ⓑ high in preservatives and chemicals

Ⓒ having a lot of vitamins and minerals

Ⓓ not containing unhealthful substances

What are high mountain *streams*?

Ⓐ small rivers of moving water

Ⓑ regions with little serious disease

Ⓒ widows that keep birth records for communities

Ⓓ to move a lot from one place to another

5. According to some doctors, long-lived populations have only one thing in common: their members don't have valid birth records. Because the government didn't write down when these people were born, their claims of unusual longevity are false.

What do *populations* contain? _____

What are *populations*?

(A) members of government

(B) ideas that are widespread

(B) all of the people living in specific areas

(C) kinds of freedom from worry

Do *all* health experts believe that certain populations have unusual longevity?

_____

What don't these long-lived people have? _____

What does the adjective *valid* mean?

(A) officially legal or accepted

(B) of high value in the community

(B) to prove something is correct

(C) of the region of Vilcabamba

Do certain populations make *claims* about unusual longevity? _____

Do people in these communities believe the *claims*? _____

What is the meaning of the noun *claims* in this context?

(A) to state something is right and real

(B) attempts to get money that is legally yours

(B) something important about a person

(C) statements of the truth of information

For more practice, you can look for and figure out the general meanings of other vocabulary items, such as *benefits, preservatives, an average,* and *stress.* For each item, explain the logical reasoning for your guesses at the definition.

2 Identifying Synonyms Read the vocabulary words in Column A. Select the word in Column B that has the same or a similar meaning as the vocabulary word.

Column A	Column B
1. _d_ cure	a. measured distance
2. _____ length	b. verified
3. _____ patients	c. disagree with
4. _____ solve	d. remedy
5. _____ oppose	e. not allow
6. _____ accurate	f. not truthful
7. _____ dishonest	g. find an answer
8. _____ elderly	h. not sweet, tart
9. _____ proven	i. sick people
10. _____ sour	j. correct
11. _____ prevent	k. old

Recognizing Parts of Speech From Word Endings: Suffixes

One way to tell the part of speech of a vocabulary item is to recognize its function or purpose. (Remember: nouns serve as sentence subjects or objects; verbs name actions; adjectives modify nouns; adverbs modify verbs.)

Another useful clue to the part of speech of a word is its ending, or *suffix*. Below are a few of the common word endings that may indicate if a word is a noun, an adjective, or an adverb.

Nouns		Adjectives		Adverbs	
Suffixes	*Examples*	*Suffixes*	*Examples*	*Suffixes*	*Examples*
-ance	ignorance	-ant	ignorant	-ly	slowly
-ence	differences	-ent	different	-ward	backward
-ity	availability	-able	available		
-ment	amusement	-ible	responsible		
-ness	happiness	-ive	active		
-sion	decision	-ic(al)	economical		
-tion	vacation	-ous	famous		

3 **Identifying Parts of Speech from Suffixes** Read some important nouns, adjectives, and adverbs (or related words) below from the reading selections in Chapters 1 to 7. On the line before each item, indicate the part of speech: Write *n* for noun, *adj* for adjective, or *adv* for adverb. You might want to underline the ending (suffix) that indicates the part of speech. A few words are done as examples.

1. _*n*_ ability
2. _*adj*_ active
3. _*adv*_ actively
4. _____ activity
5. _____ agreement
6. _____ agreeable
7. _____ agreeably
8. _____ biological
9. _____ beneficial
10. _____ civilization

11. _____ contradiction
12. _____ convenient
13. _____ discussion
14. _____ element
15. _____ influence
16. _____ longevity
17. _____ nutritious
18. _____ pleasant
19. _____ politely
20. _____ preference

21. _____ probably
22. _____ religious
23. _____ requirements
24. _____ residence
25. _____ similarly
26. _____ slowly
27. _____ supportive
28. _____ theoretical
29. _____ typical
30. _____ visual

4 Choosing Word Forms with Suffixes Read the sentences below from the readings in Chapter 7. Circle the correct word form in parentheses ( ). Then write the missing words in the *Parts of Speech Chart* that follows — except for the boxes with Xs. Some of the items are done as examples. Not all of the words from this activity appear in the chart.

1. Three (mountains /(mountainous))regions of the globe are (fame /(famous)) for the (longevity / long) of their inhabitants. There may be (variety / various) reasons for their long lives.

2. According to (science / scientific) research, many elderly inhabitants of the Himalayan Mountains are still in good (physics / physical) health. One (reason / reasonable) for their amazing condition might be the low level of (pollution / polluted) in their (environment / environmental).

3. Is a simple, (nature / naturally) (nutrition / nutritious) diet (benefits / beneficial) to human health? Is physical work also (advantages / advantageous)?

4. Farmers in the countryside (usual / usually) lead (action / active) lives — that is to say, they fill their days with (activity / actively) and physical (move / movement).

5. Official birth records of (special / especially) long-lived people are seldom (availability / available). Nevertheless, health specialists are in (agreement / agreeable): These amazing people are (general / generally) in good health in their old age.

6. In some regions, the (types / typical) diet of the inhabitants consists of (most / mostly) meat and dairy products; in contrast, other groups consume (main / mainly) fruits and vegetables and use (tradition / traditional) herbs as medicine.

7. How (importance / important) is the (environment / environmentally) to human health? There is some (confusion / confused) about the (validity / valid) of the research into the matter.

8. The amount of (availability / available) medical (information / informative) on the Internet is amazing. This (combination / combined) of proven fact and opinion is changing (culture / cultural) attitudes of people about their own health care.

9. Some patients are (ignorance / ignorant) of the facts they need to make the best (medicine / medical) (decisions / decisive). These people may benefit from the (recommendations / recommend) of a number of health experts.

10. Many scientists believe in the (value / valuable) of (genes / genetic) research and engineering. They hope they can make (defects / defective) genes healthy and prevent (biology / biological) diseases.

Parts of Speech		
Noun	Adjective	Adverb
advantages	advantageous	
availability	*available*	
activity	active	
biology		biologically
	confused	
culture		culturally
defects		
decisions	decisive	
fame		famously
genes		genetically
generalities		
humanity		
		ignorantly
importance		importantly
	natural	
mountains		
	typical	*typically*
		traditionally

5 **Focusing on High-Frequency Words** Read the paragraph below and fill in each blank with a word from the box. One of the words is used twice.

characteristics	damage	increase	purposes
combination	engineering	prevent	structure

What are *genes* and why are medical researchers always trying to find out more about them? Genes are part of the center (that is, the *nucleus*) of every living cell; in the form of DNA (deoxyribonucleic acid), this biological genetic material determines the _____ (features) of every living thing—every plant, animal, and human being—on Earth. Medical geneticists are scientists that study DNA and genes for many _____ : (1) to learn how living things such as parasites, viruses, and bacteria cause illness; (2) to find the gene or _____ of genes that cause certain diseases to pass from parents to their children; (3) to _____ or correct (repair) birth defects; (4) to change gene _____ to improve health and increase the length of human life (longevity); and (5) to change the biological characteristics of animals and humans in ways that are beneficial to society. Another use of genetic technology that some scientists support is changing the genes of the food farmers grow. Genetic engineers claim that these differences in DNA structure will _____ food production, prevent _____ from insects, and improve world health; in contrast, others oppose the use of genetic _____ not only in plants but also in animals and humans.

6 **Making Connections** Find advice about health on the Internet. Look for tips on one aspect of health. You can look for tips on healthy eating, running, walking, dieting, doing yoga, living a long life, quitting smoking, or anything else that interests you.

Type in *tips* on _____ . Look at a couple of websites. Write down at least three tips that you agree with. Write down at least three that you disagree with or question. Tell the class what you have learned.

Topic : _____

Tips I agree with	Tips I disagree with

FOCUS

Focusing on Timed Readings and Note-Taking

In the reading section of the TOEFL® iBT, you have 20 minutes to read and answer the questions for each reading. During that time, you can reread parts of the passage if you need to. You can check your answers by looking back at the text. You can skip difficult questions and come back to them later. All this is possible only in the reading section.

The best note-taking strategy is to concentrate on main ideas. Also, if you have time, list supporting details under them. Use lots of abbreviations and don't worry about spelling in your notes.

Taking Notes on a Timed Reading Read the following passage and answer the questions. Before you begin, set a timer for 20 minutes. You have that much time to read the essay, take notes, and respond to all the questions. If you have time at the end, go back and check answers to any questions you were unsure about.

Calorie Counting

A   In discussions about healthy eating, there are not many points of agreement. Almost everyone, however, recognizes that people should take in about as many calories as they use up. A calorie is not a substance but a measure of heat. In the context of eating, calories tell how much energy the body can get by burning up a certain food item. Balancing the calories in food with the body's energy needs is the central goal of any long-term diet program.

B   It should be clear that calories in food are not a bad thing. In fact, we would die without them. Archaeologists suspect that many healthy civilizations either died or relocated because they could no longer get enough calories from their food. The Anasazi of the American Southwest, for example, probably suffered a huge loss in their calorie intake, and their health, when deforestation slowly removed deer and pine nuts from their diet. Our appetite for food, a problem for many modern humans, is a natural drive for survival. In fact, some of the most irresistible foods — those high in fat or sugar — have a special hold on humans because ancient impulses tell us to consume them. Our bodies see them as a calorie bonus, as a survival resource.

C   Modern humans have trouble with weight mostly because the body has not adapted to the constant food supply much of the world enjoys. In humans, physical evolution takes a lot more time than social evolution. Prehistoric Europeans or North Americans had to worry about hunting down enough deer, or catching enough fish, or raising enough beans. Modern humans in prosperous nations have a ready supply of affordable calories at the nearest grocery store. Nevertheless, our bodies tell us to store up extra calories, just in case.

D   Responding to that urge causes no problems if a person uses those extra calories. Our ancient ancestors probably did. The walking, hunting, tree-felling, clothes-washing, and other physical activities of a low-tech civilization used up a lot of calories. Modern life is far less active. Even a moderately active person in a wealthy society today has to deliberately exercise to even come close to such a level of activity.

E   So how many calories does an average person need? That question cannot be answered. There is no average person. Calorie needs vary because each person processes food in a slightly different way, depending on body chemistry. And calorie needs are greatly influenced by height, weight, age, and other factors. Still some estimates can be made if we put certain numbers into a long formula from the U.S. Department of Agriculture (USDA). Let's assume two healthy, moderately active young people, each 20 years old. The man is 6 feet tall and weighs 160 pounds. The woman is 5 feet, 6 inches tall and weighs 120 pounds. According to the USDA formula, the man would need to take in about 2,750 calories each day. The woman should take in about 2,002 calories each day.

F   These target levels include the energy it takes simply to operate the body — breathing, pumping blood, raising one's arms, etc. They also include the energy needed for moderate activity (such as walking one or two miles each day, cutting the grass, or walking up and down stairs). Each of these activities uses few calories. Walking for about 30 minutes, for example, burns up only about 140 calories. Running for 30 minutes burns up twice as many calories, but that's still under 300. Compare that to the energy in a good-sized turkey sandwich with mayonnaise — about 450 calories. And that's just lunch.

1. Which of the following best expresses the main idea of the reading as a whole?
   - (A) A healthy diet should balance the number of calories the body takes in with the number it uses.
   - (B) Early humans had a healthier way of living than modern people do.
   - (C) Modern humans are healthier than their ancient ancestors.
   - (D) People do not agree about which foods should be part of healthy eating.

2. Which of the following best expresses the main idea of Paragraph B?
   - (A) The Anasazi civilization lost two important sources of calories.
   - (B) Humans cannot survive unless they take in enough calories.
   - (C) Civilizations have died because they depended on fats and sugars.
   - (D) Humans naturally seek high-calorie foods.

3. Which of the following best expresses the main idea of Paragraph C?
   - (A) Some of the body's survival techniques do not fit in with modern society.
   - (B) The human body cannot evolve in ways that keep it healthy.
   - (C) The human body has stopped evolving, but societies continue to evolve.
   - (D) The food-supply system in modern societies is better than that in earlier societies.

4. Why does the author mention walking in Paragraph D?

    (A) It is the most important activity of humans in low-tech societies.

    (B) It is the most important source of exercise for modern humans.

    (C) As an example of the activities common in low-tech societies.

    (D) As an example of the activities that are not part of life in modern societies.

5. Which of the following best expresses the main idea of Paragraph E?

    (A) There is no way to estimate how many calories a person should take in.

    (B) Personal traits like weight, height, and age have to be considered in any calculation of calorie needs.

    (C) Men need to take in more calories each day than women need to take in.

    (B) The USDA has a formula for figuring out how many calories a person should take in every day.

6. Which of the following best expresses the main idea of Paragraph F?

    (A) Most people get all of their calories by eating lunch.

    (B) Moderate activity burns up most of the calories a person takes in.

    (C) The energy needed for breathing and other basic body functions is greater than the energy needed for moderate exercise.

    (D) Food contains so many calories that it is hard to burn them all up.

Self-Assessment Log

Read the lists below. Check (✓) the strategies and vocabulary that you learned in this chapter. Look through the chapter or ask your instructor about the strategies and words that you do not understand.

Reading and Vocabulary-Building Strategies

- ☐ Recognizing reading structure using a mind map
- ☐ Understanding the main idea
- ☐ Recognizing supporting details after punctuation, numbers, and connecting words
- ☐ Understanding facts and opinions
- ☐ Summarizing using a mind map
- ☐ Figuring out new or difficult vocabulary
- ☐ Identifying synonyms
- ☐ Identifying parts of speech from suffixes
- ☐ Choosing word forms with suffixes

Target Vocabulary

Nouns
- ■ characteristics*
- ■ claims*
- ■ combination*
- ■ cure
- ■ damage*
- ■ decisions*
- ■ disease*
- ■ engineering*
- ■ environment*
- ■ genes
- ■ inhabitants
- ■ length*
- ■ longevity
- ■ patients*
- ■ population*
- ■ purpose*
- ■ streams
- ■ structure*

Verbs
- ■ correct
- ■ improve*
- ■ increase*
- ■ oppose
- ■ prevent*
- ■ solve

Adjectives
- ■ accurate

- ■ dishonest
- ■ elderly*
- ■ famous*
- ■ genetic
- ■ long-lived
- ■ moderate
- ■ proven
- ■ sour
- ■ unpolluted
- ■ valid

* These words are among the 2,000 most frequently used words in English.

8

Entertainment and the Media

"Whoever controls the media controls the mind."

Jim Morrison
musician

In this CHAPTER

In Part 1, you will read about the effects of visual media (television, movies, and the Internet) on people and society. In the rest of this chapter, you will read about, explore, and discuss typical story plots and your opinion of the visual media.

Connecting to the Topic

1 Look at the photo. Describe what you see. What kind of video or film do you think they are making?

2 Do you think movies, video games, and TV can influence the way people act and feel? If so, how?

3 What are some popular movies, TV shows, and video games? Why do you think they are popular?

How the Visual Media Affect People

Before You Read

1 **Previewing the Topic** Look at the photos and read the questions below. Discuss them in small groups.

1. What are the people doing?

2. How are the photos similar? How are they different?

3. Are either of the scenes similar to a scene that you know? Why or why not?

▼ A family relaxing with media

▼ Reading in the park

2 **Predicting** Discuss possible answers to these questions. If you don't know the answers, make predictions. You can look for the answers when you read "How the Visual Media Affect People."

1. What are some examples of visual media?

2. How might the amount of time spent in front of a TV or computer have a negative effect on family life? In what ways can watching television be helpful in people's lives?

3. What might low-quality programming do to the human brain? What might it do to people's lives?

4. What are some possible effects of violent movies or TV programs on people's personalities and behavior?

5. What are some signs of possible addiction to visual media like TV and computers?

3 Previewing Vocabulary Read the vocabulary items below from the first reading. Then listen to the words and phrases. Put a check mark (✓) next to the words you don't know. Don't use a dictionary.

Nouns
- ▨ addiction
- ▨ adults
- ▨ behavior
- ▨ disadvantages
- ▨ hospitals
- ▨ images
- ▨ personalities
- ▨ practice
- ▨ programming
- ▨ reality
- ▨ stars
- ▨ tension
- ▨ viewers
- ▨ violence
- ▨ visual media

Verbs
- ▨ concentrate
- ▨ envy
- ▨ focus
- ▨ improve
- ▨ reduce
- ▨ replace
- ▨ scare
- ▨ shout

Adjectives
- ▨ addicted
- ▨ aural
- ▨ average
- ▨ boring
- ▨ dissatisfied
- ▨ elderly
- ▨ emotional
- ▨ envious
- ▨ exciting
- ▨ immoral
- ▨ nursing
- ▨ reality
- ▨ unlimited

Read

4 Reading an Article Read the following article. Then do the activities that follow.

How the Visual Media Affect People

Introduction: Benefits of the Visual Media

A   How do television and the other **visual media** affect the lives of individuals and families around the globe? Media can be very helpful to people (and their children) who carefully choose what they watch. With high-quality **programming** in various fields of study—science, medicine, nature, history, the arts, and so on—the Internet, TV, and DVDs increase   5
the knowledge of the average *and* the well-educated person; they can also **improve** thinking ability. Moreover, television and other visual media benefit **elderly** people who can't go out often, as well as patients in **hospitals** and residents of **nursing** facilities. Additionally, it offers language learners the advantage of "real-life" audiovisual instruction and **aural** comprehension   10
practice at any time of day or night. And of course, visual media can provide almost everyone with good entertainment—a pleasant way to relax and spend free time at home.

Media Replaces Other Activities

B   Nevertheless, there are several serious disadvantages to the visual media. First of all, some people watch the "tube" or are online for more hours in a day than they do anything else. In a large number of homes, TV sets and computers—as many as five or more in a single household—are always on. Many people watch TV for many hours a day or spend hours playing games or surfing on their computers; they download music, movies, and other forms of entertainment. Instead of spending time taking care of their kids, parents often use a video screen as an "electronic babysitter." As a result, television and video can easily **replace** family communication as well as physical activity and other interests.

The Effects of TV on the Mind

C   Second, too much TV—especially programming of low educational value—can reduce people's ability to **concentrate** or reason. In fact, studies show that after only a minute or two of visual media, a person's mind "relaxes" as it does during light sleep. Another possible effect of television and videotapes on the human brain is poor communication. Children who watch a lot of TV may lose their ability to focus on a subject or an educational activity for more than 10 to 15 minutes. Maybe it is because of the visual media that some kids—and **adults** too—develop attention deficit disorder (ADD), a modern condition in which people are unable to pay attention, listen well, follow instructions, or remember everyday things.

The Effects of Violence in the Media

D   A third negative feature of the media is the amount of **violence** on the screen—both in real events in the news, and in movies, TV programs, and video games. It **scares** people and gives them terrible nightmares; the fear created by media images and language can last for a long time. On the other hand, frequent **viewers** of "action programming" get used to its messages: they might begin to believe there is nothing strange or unusual about violent crime, fights, killing, and other terrible events and **behavior**. Studies show that certain personality types are likely to have strong **emotional** reactions or dangerous thoughts after some kinds of "entertainment." They may even copy the acts that they see on violent shows—start fires, carry and use weapons, attack people in angry or dangerous ways, or worse.

Dissatisfaction with Normal Living

E   Because of the visual media, some people may become **dissatisfied** with the reality of their own lives. To these viewers, everyday life does not seem as exciting as the roles actors play in movies or TV dramas. They believe they aren't having as much fun as the **stars** of comedy shows. Furthermore, average people with normal lives may **envy** famous media personalities, who seem to get **unlimited** amounts of money and attention. Also, media watchers might get depressed when they can't take care of situations in real life as well as TV stars seem to. On the screen, they notice actors solve serious problems in hour or half-hour programs—or in twenty-second commercials.

Boredom with Real Life

F   Yet another negative feature of modern television is called "trash TV." These daily talk shows bring real people with strange or **immoral** 55 lives, **personalities**, or behavior to the screen. Millions of viewers— including children—watch as these "instant stars" tell their most personal secrets, shout out their 60 angry feelings and opinions, and attack one another. TV watchers seem to like the emotional atmosphere and excitement of this kind of programming—as well as 65 the tension of the real but terrible stories on TV "news magazine" shows. A newer version of this kind of entertainment is called "**reality** TV." In shows like *Survivor, The* 70 *Amazing Race, American Idol,* and *The Apprentice,* "real people" compete for attention, fame, and other rewards. What effect does frequent viewing of such programs 75

▲ Watching certain types of programs can make normal living seem boring.

have on people's lives? It makes television seem more real than **reality**, and normal living begins to seem **boring**.

Disadvantage of the Media: Addiction

G   Finally, the most negative effect of all of these kinds of visual media might be **addiction**. People often feel a strange and powerful need to watch TV or go online to watch videos or a movie even when they don't enjoy it or 80 have the free time for entertainment. Addiction to a TV or computer screen is similar to drug or alcohol dependence: addicts almost never believe they are **addicted**. Even so, truthful media addicts have to answer *yes* to many of these questions:
- Do you immediately turn on the TV set or computer when you arrive 85 home from school or work?
- Do you watch a lot of programming that requires little focus or thinking ability?
- Can you concentrate on another topic or activity for only 10 to 15 minutes at a time? 90
- Do you enjoy the action and violence of the media more than activity in your own life?

- Do you feel **envious** of the lives of well-known TV or screen personalities or the participants in "reality TV" shows?
- Do you feel closer to the people on TV than to your own family members and friends? 95
- For you, is TV or video the easiest—and, therefore, the best—form of relaxation or fun?
- Would you refuse to give up your TV viewing and Internet connection for a million dollars? 100
- Would you like to compete on a reality TV show more than do anything else?

After You Read

Strategy

Recognizing Reading Structure: Using an Outline
We learned in Chapter 7 how to use a mind map to help review and organize information in a reading. Here we're going to learn how to use an outline.

- An outline shows the relationship of the topics, main ideas, and supporting details or examples.
- The topic is usually the title of the outline.
- The main ideas and subtopics of the reading can appear after numbers like this: I, II, III, IV.
- The supporting details or examples are written under the main ideas after capital letters like this: A, B, C.
- Sometimes the supporting details have more details. Those can be written after numbers like this: 1, 2, 3.

5 Completing an Outline On the next page is an incomplete outline for the reading "How the Visual Media Affect People." The reading gives two opinions about the visual media. Look at the outline and first answer these questions:

What is the topic? _____

What are the two main subtopics about the topic? _____

_____

Now read the phrases below that will complete the outline. They are the positive and negative effects of the visual media. Read each phrase and scan the article to find the one or two paragraphs where the information appears. Write the letter(s) of the paragraph in the parentheses ( ). Then write the phrases in the outline below.

- Increase people's knowledge and thinking ability   (A)
- Benefit the elderly and the sick   (   )
- Take too much time from family life and other activities (B)
- Reduce people's ability to concentrate, focus, or reason (   )
- Scare people or get them used to violence   (   )
- Provide language learners instruction and practice   (A)
- Offer good entertainment during free time   (   )
- Cause dissatisfaction in normal people's lives   (   ) and (   )
- Addict people to TV and video   (   )

Effects of the Visual Media

I. _____Advantages_____

   A. _____

   B. _____

   C. _____

   D. _____

II. _____Disadvantages_____

   A. _____

   B. _____

   C. _____

   D. _____

   E. _____

6 **Understanding the Point and Recognizing Supporting Details**
Finish the main-idea question about the material of the reading selection "How the Visual Media Affect People." In the paragraphs that follow, change the underlined words so that the paragraphs accurately answer the question.

A   Television and other visual media probably influence people's lives in positive but ~~not~~ *and* negative ways. Here are examples of their possible benefits: (1) <u>Low-quality</u> programming in various fields provides education value to <u>only scientists, doctors, naturalists, historians, and artists</u>. It can <u>damage</u> thinking ability. (2) Also, elderly and sick people who rarely go out <u>can't ever</u> enjoy the Internet, TV, and DVDs. (3) <u>In contrast</u>, students get <u>no</u> educational benefit from shows in the languages they are trying to learn. (4) Another advantage is that TV can help people to <u>get nervous and tense</u> in their free time at home. 5

B   <u>In exactly the same way</u>, there are serious disadvantages to the visual media: (1) An "electronic babysitter" is likely to <u>bring children and their parents closer together</u> and <u>increase</u> the amount of time they spend on other activities. (2) Second, too much television or work on a computer may make it <u>easier</u> for the overly relaxed brain to pay attention, concentrate, or reason. (3) Third, violent or horrible TV images and language can give frequent viewers <u>beautiful dreams</u>, making them fearful of <u>technology, medicine, or the arts</u>; or people may begin to think of terrible events or acts as <u>very strange or unusual</u>. (4) A fourth possible disadvantage of too much television, video, and other kinds of visual media is that people may become <u>too satisfied</u> with the reality of their <u>exciting and fun</u> lives. (5) And finally, the most negative effect of the visual media is probably viewer <u>independence</u>. TV and video watchers <u>will</u> be able to get away from the media easily; they <u>can never</u> become addicted. 10 15 20

7 Discussing the Reading In small groups, talk about your answers to the questions. Then tell the class the most interesting information and ideas.

1. In your opinion, is it a good use of time to watch TV, download music and other entertainment, and/or make use of videos and DVDs? Why or why not?

2. In general, do you believe that television and other visual media improve or damage the brain? How? Give reasons for your opinions.

3. In your view, how does violence on TV affect people? Explain.

4. Have you ever watched "trash TV"? Do you enjoy reality TV? If not, why not? If so, what do you think of the people on those shows? Why?

5. Look back at the list of questions about TV addiction on pages 163–164 of the reading. For how many of the questions did you answer *yes*? Do you believe you are addicted to TV? Give reasons for your answers.

Stories from the Screen

1 **Previewing Vocabulary** Read the vocabulary items below from the next reading. Then listen to the words and phrases. Put a check mark (✓) next to the words you don't know. Don't use a dictionary.

Nouns	Verbs	Adjectives	
▪ adulthood	▪ capture	▪ bloody	▪ scary
▪ adventure	▪ inherit	▪ computerized	▪ shadowy
▪ bankruptcy	▪ investigate	▪ decent	▪ suspenseful
▪ drama	▪ recover	▪ desperate	▪ wealthy
▪ investigator	▪ sink	▪ natural	
▪ murderer	▪ stabs	▪ powerful	
▪ passion	▪ transport	▪ pregnant	
▪ relationship		▪ run-down	

2 **Classifying Stories and Putting Events in Order** Most programs in the visual media include stories that tell what happened, most often in time order. Below are the kinds of stories that most often appear in movies and TV series.

Vocabulary Tip

Story **plot summaries** are short descriptions of the actions or events of a movie, TV show, or story.

1. _____ adventure or action
2. _____ crime or mystery
3. _____ authentic history
4. _____ serious drama
5. _____ suspense or horror

6. _____ science fiction or fantasy
7. _____ comedy
8. _____ animated cartoon
9. _____ musical
10. _____ biography or people's personal experiences

Skim the four story plots of well-known movies and TV shows. On the lines before some of the listed story types above, write the letters of the story plots A, B, C, and D. You can write the same letter more than once, but you will not find stories for all 10 types.

3 **Finding the Main Idea** After you read each plot description, answer the question that follows.

Stories from the Screen

Story Plot A

Marion, who works in a real estate office, is depressed about her life—especially her unhappy love **relationship**. Because she is feeling ill,

her supervisor lets her leave early; he gives her $40,000 in cash from a house sale to put in the bank on her way home. However, temptation gets the best of the moody young woman. With the cash in an envelope, she packs her bags and drives out of town. On a dark, lonely road, a severe thunderstorm forces her to stop at the run-down Bates Motel. There is a **scary** old house high on a hill behind the motel, with the form of an old woman in a rocking chair at the window. Norman Bates, the motel owner, is happy to sign in a guest, but his mother shouts at him angrily. After a conversation with Norman, Marion goes to her room. When she is in the shower, the bathroom door opens. In a very famous, very **bloody** murder scene, the **shadowy** figure of an old woman pulls aside the shower curtain and stabs the motel guest to death. Horrified, Norman cleans up the room, puts Marion's body in her car, and pushes the car into the swamp.

Worried about her and the stolen money, Marion's sister, lover, and boss send out an investigator, who finally arrives at the Bates Motel. Suspicious of Norman's strange behavior, the investigator goes into the scary house, where the dark shape of an "old woman" at the top of the stairs kills him too—with a long knife. Others come to **investigate**. After many **suspenseful** scenes, they discover that Norman's "mother" is a skeleton. The murderer in the old woman's clothes was Norman Bates himself, who has turned more and more into his mother.

In what movie does the sequence of events in Story Plot A above occur? Choose the title that best fits the plot summary.

(A) *The Public Enemy* (a drama about the social forces that cause violent crime)

(B) *Psycho* (a psychological suspense film directed by Alfred Hitchcock in 1960)

(C) *Gone with the Wind* (a world-famous 1939 American Civil War drama)

Story Plot B

After a hurricane sinks their ship off the coast of Africa, a British couple finds their way to land with their baby son. However, the parents are killed by a wild animal. A gorilla (the largest of the humanlike primates) finds the baby, brings him home to her mate, and raises the helpless human in the jungle. As a result, he grows to **adulthood** in the **natural** ape community.

Nevertheless, the young man's peaceful life in the jungle soon changes. To study African wildlife in its natural environment, Professor Porter arrives with his daughter, Jane, and a hunter named Clayton. When the explorers meet the jungle man, at first they think he is "the missing link" (a being halfway between an animal and a human being). Therefore, they are surprised to discover that he is as human as they are. When he begins to feel strange, unfamiliar emotions towards Jane, the man that grew up in the jungle becomes very confused. He wants to be with his own kind but doesn't want to leave the gorilla family that raised him—especially since Clayton sees the apes not as friends but as animals to hunt and kill. When Jane has to leave with her father, the ape man is very sad and upset. Even so, he saves the humans when they are captured, and Jane stays with him in the jungle.

In what movie (produced in many versions) do the events in Story Plot B happen?

- (A) *Tarzan, the Ape Man* (the first of a series based on the "Lord of the Jungle" characters)
- (B) *A Night to Remember* (the film about the sinking of the ship *Titanic*)
- (C) *Robinson Crusoe* (an adventure story about a man who lives alone on an island)

Story Plot C

The starship *Enterprise* (a flying vehicle that travels to other galaxies at amazing speeds) stops at a space station for repairs. The four Bynars (beings with **computerized** brains) that are doing maintenance seem worried. Suddenly, they realize the ship is about to explode and order evacuation. Everyone leaves except Picard, the captain, and Riker, the second man in command, who don't hear the alert. After everyone else reaches the starbase (the space station), the problem mysteriously corrects itself, and the ship disappears. As the crew on the starbase try to figure out a way to recover the *Enterprise*, the captain and his helper discover what has happened. They instantly transport themselves to the bridge, where they find the Bynars unconscious, dying, and asking for help.

The ship reaches Bynarus, the Bynars' planet. Because of an exploded star that destroyed the planet's center computer, Bynarus is dead too. The Bynars needed the *Enterprise* to store the data from the planet during the shutdown time. Picard and Riker manage to get into the Bynarus file and restart the computer. The Bynars come back to life. Undamaged, the ship returns to the starbase. 70 75

What popular American TV series are the events in Story Plot C from?

A. *The Twilight Zone* (amazing stories about the effects of the human imagination)

B. *Superman* (the adventures of a being from another planet with superhuman powers)

C. *Star Trek: The Next Generation* (futuristic adventures of travelers in space)

Story Plot D

It is the middle of the 19th century, a very romantic time of honor and passion. Matilde Peñalver y Beristan is an aristocrat, a member of the nobility (the most wealthy, powerful class in society). She falls in love with Adolfo Solis, an army soldier with no fortune. Matilde trusts that her fair, kind father will let her marry her true love. However, Augusta (Matilde's mother) objects; with her powerful connections, she sends Adolfo to prison. Lying, she tells her daughter that Adolfo is married with children. 80 85

Because their family is facing bankruptcy, Augusta wants Manuel Fuentes Guerra, an honorable and handsome young man who has just inherited a vast fortune, to be her son-in-law. Confused and desperate, Matilde marries Manuel. Soon, Adolfo escapes from jail. After a frantic, intense search, he finds Matilde. Posing as the new ranch administrator, he recognizes her husband as an honest, fair, and decent man. At that point, Manuel and Matilde discover Augusta's deceit in their marriage. But in the meantime, Matilde's feelings for Adolfo are beginning to disappear. She is starting to fall in love with Manuel. Heartbroken, Adolfo accepts reality and leaves the ranch. Matilde announces she is pregnant. However,... 90 95 100
To be continued...

Which popular Mexican soap opera is the plot in Story Plot D from?

(A) *Rubí* (a modern melodrama about a beautiful, manipulative woman and her effects on the people around her. Rubí lies, cheats, and steals to get what she wants—especially from rich, attractive men.)

(B) *Amor Real* ("True Love," a historical drama about a young woman who breaks the social code when she falls in love with a poor commoner.)

(C) *Like Water for Chocolate* (a sad and funny love story set in Mexico with cooking as the central theme of passion. Many recipes are included.)

After You Read

Strategy

Summarizing a Story

A reading selection or paragraph that describes a plot (a sequence of events in a story) is most often organized in time order—that is, one event follows another.

- To prepare to summarize a plot, you might number the main events in the reading material.
- Then after an introduction to set the scene, you tell the most important things that happened.

Here is an example of possible event numbering from part of the first story in "Stories from the Screen."

Marion, an employee in a real estate office, is depressed about her life—especially her unhappy love relationship. (1) Because she is feeling ill, her supervisor lets her leave work early; he gives her $40,000 in cash from a house sale to put in the bank on her way home. (2) However, temptation gets the best of the moody young woman. With the cash in an envelope, she packs her bags and drives out of town. (3) On a dark, lonely road, a severe thunderstorm forces her to stop at the run-down Bates Motel. There is a scary old house high on a hill behind the motel, with the form of an old woman in a rocking chair at the window. (4) Norman Bates, the motel owner, is happy to sign in a guest, but his mother shouts at him angrily. (5) After a conversation with Norman, Marion goes to her room.

4 **Summarizing a Story** Work in groups of three. Choose a plot description (Story B, C, or D) from the selection "Stories from the Screen" on pages 169–170. Read it carefully. Number the events like the example in the Strategy Box shows. Then write a summary of the story. After a short introduction, list the main events needed to understand the story in as few words as possible. Then tell or read your plot summary to your group.

5 Discussing the Reading In small groups, talk about your answers to these questions. Then tell the class the most interesting information or ideas.

1. Of the ten media story types in Activity 2 on page 167, which is your favorite, your second favorite, and so on? Give reasons for your preferences.

2. For several of the kinds of stories, tell the titles of some well-known movies or television series. How many of each media type can your group name in three minutes?

6 Talking It Over What are your preferences in media entertainment? Read the choices for each category below. Number your preferences from favorite (1) through least favorite (6). Then explain the reasons for the order you chose. Compare your choices with your partner's preferences. Then share with the class.

Media

_____ television (network, cable)

_____ DVDs at home

_____ feature films in theaters

_____ videos on the Internet

_____ radio programs

_____ other kinds of media

Movies

_____ comedies or animated features

_____ romance

_____ action or thrillers

_____ horror or suspense

_____ serious drama

_____ other kinds of movies

TV Series

_____ situation comedies

_____ science fiction

_____ crime or detective shows; law or hospital dramas

_____ soap operas (highly emotional dramas with continuing story lines)

_____ reality shows

_____ other kinds of series

Other Programming

_____ news or current events

_____ talk shows

_____ game shows

_____ educational programs

_____ travel shows

_____ other kinds of programs

Music

_____ classical music

_____ jazz or blues

_____ popular singers and groups

_____ country music or dancing

_____ international folk music

_____ other kinds of music

Other Entertainment

_____ live theater (plays)

_____ cabarets or dinner theater

_____ stand-up comedy clubs

_____ dance clubs or discos

_____ casino gambling

_____ other _____

PART 3 Vocabulary and Language-Learning Skills

Strategy

Getting Meaning from Context

Getting the general meaning of new or difficult words or phrases can help you understand the meanings of the sentences. You may then be able to understand the details and their relationship to the main ideas of the material.

1 **Understanding New Vocabulary from Context** Read the outline from the reading selection "How the Visual Media Affect People" on pages 161–164. Then read the details that follow. In the questions below, choose the answer that is closest in meaning to the underlined word or phrase. Identify where each detail belongs in the outline and write the number and letter from the outline (for example, I.A.) in the parentheses after the sentence. The first answer is provided.

How the Visual Media Affect People

I. Advantages:
   A. Provide learning in many subjects
   B. Benefit the old and the sick
   C. Help with language instruction
   D. Offer ways to relax

II. Disadvantages:
   A. Take time from family and other activities
   B. Can decrease people's concentration and reasoning abilities
   C. Produce strong or dangerous emotional reactions in people
   D. May create dissatisfaction or boredom in everyday life
   E. Can be addictive

1. At all hours, the media offer language learners "real-life" audiovisual instruction and practice in <u>aural comprehension</u>. [I. C]

   A the answers to test questions

   B understanding spoken language

   C hospital and health information

   D real-life experience

2. Moreover, television helps <u>elderly</u> people who can't go out often, as well as patients in hospitals and residents of <u>nursing facilities</u>. [ ]

   elderly

   A sick people

   B old people

   C people who need help

   D busy people

   nursing facilities

   A homes for doctors and nurses

   B centers for public entertainment

   C normal housing for average people

   D places for older and very sick people

3. High-quality TV <u>programming</u>—a good plan of shows about various fields of study—can increase people's knowledge and improve their thinking abilities. [ ]

   A scientific and medical shows

   B academic lecture courses

   C choice and organization of shows

   D movies with good music

4. Television and video provide almost everyone with good entertainment—a pleasant way to relax and spend free time at home.
   - (A) relaxation through exercise
   - (B) amusement or pleasure
   - (C) fun through serious study
   - (D) freedom from worry and tension

5. Children who watch a lot of TV may lose their ability to concentrate or focus on a subject for very long; sometimes they develop "attention deficit disorder."

   concentrate
   - (A) direct their attention
   - (B) reduce or decrease
   - (C) communicate
   - (D) improve

6. Because of the time it consumes, television and video can easily replace family communication as well as physical activity and other interests.
   - (A) take the place of
   - (B) go back to
   - (C) find the location of
   - (D) contribute to family time

7. Images of violence on the screen scare people, giving them terrible nightmares when they sleep.

   violence
   - (A) bad conditions
   - (B) behavior that hurts people
   - (C) dark, stormy weather
   - (D) physical disabilities

   nightmares
   - (A) frightening dreams
   - (B) the emotion of depression
   - (C) traditional visual images
   - (D) personality types

8. The talk shows of "trash TV" make instant "stars" of real people with strange or immoral ideas, who tell their most personal secrets, shout angrily, and attack one another.

   "trash TV"
   - (A) valuable programs
   - (B) shows without quality
   - (C) negative effects
   - (D) normal life stories

   "stars"
   - (A) movie roles
   - (B) news magazines
   - (C) media addicts
   - (D) famous personalities

   immoral
   - (A) not having values
   - (B) refusing help
   - (C) excited
   - (D) unusual or common

For more practice, you can look for and figure out the general meanings of other vocabulary items in the reading, such as *visual, action programming, likely, normal, boring, truthful,* and so on.

For each item, explain the logical reasoning for your guesses at definitions. Then use each word or phrase in a sentence that tells an advantage or disadvantage of TV watching.

Understanding Suffixes

A useful clue to the part of speech of a word is its ending, or suffix.

- The noun suffixes presented in Chapter 7 were -ance or -ence, -ity, -ment, -ness, and -sion or -tion.
- The adjective endings were -ant or -ent, -able or -ible, -ive, -ous, -ic, and -al.
- The adverbs ended in -ly or -ward(s).

Below are a few additional word endings that may indicate if a word is a noun, a verb, or an adjective. In parentheses are the general meanings of the suffixes. Examples are included.

Noun Suffixes	Examples
-er, -or, -ist (a person or thing that does something)	daughter, calculator, actor, scientist
-ship (having a position or skill)	citizenship, friendship
-hood (a state or time of something)	childhood, widowhood
-ism (a belief or way of doing something)	liberalism, Buddhism

Verb Suffixes	Examples
-ate, -ify, -ize, -en (to make something be a certain way or change it to that quality)	create, decorate, beautify, clarify, realize, energize, strengthen, widen

Adjective Suffixes	Examples
-al, -ar (relating to something)	dental, financial, muscular
-y (full of or covered with something)	rainy, angry, moody
-ful (full of)	careful, beautiful
-less (without something)	careless, endless
-ing (causing a feeling)	interesting, exhausting
-ed (having a feeling)	interested, exhausted

② **Practicing More Word Endings** Here are some of the important nouns, verbs, and adjectives (or related words) from the reading selections before or in Chapter 8. In these words, the suffix (ending) clearly indicates the part of speech. On the line before each item, write *n* for "noun," *v* for "verb," or *adj* for "adjective." Underline the suffix. A few words are done as examples.

1. __n__ chapter
2. _____ behavior
3. _____ classify
4. _____ addicted

5. _____ psychologist
6. _____ concentrate
7. _____ computerized
8. _____ unlimited

9. __v__ visualize
10. _____ universal
11. _____ boring
12. _____ forceful

13. _adj_ truthful	19. _____ researcher	25. _____ specialist
14. _____ childhood	20. _____ dissatisfied	26. _____ shadowy
15. _____ bloody	21. _____ personalize	27. _____ investigate
16. _____ simplify	22. _____ relationship	28. _____ sadden
17. _____ organize	23. _____ emotional	29. _____ natural
18. _____ viewer	24. _____ exciting	30. _____ adulthood

Strategy

Understanding Word Families

Word families are groups of related words of various parts of speech. Read below about word families.

- Within a word family of related forms, some words can be used as more than one part of speech. For example, *increase* can be used both as a noun and a verb.
- There may be two or more nouns with different suffixes: often, one noun names an idea, while a related noun with a different ending is a word for a person—like *psychology* (a field of study) and *psychologist* (a specialist in psychology).
- There may be related words of the same part of speech with meanings that are a little different from each other. Some examples are *vision* (*noun*: a mental picture) and *visionary* (*noun*: a person with clear ideas of the future), *criticize* (*verb*: to judge negatively) and *critique* (*verb*: to evaluate the quality of), *classic* (*adjective*: historically important and popular) and *classical* (*adjective*: based on traditional ideas).

3 Choosing from Word Families Read the sentences below about the topics in Chapter 8. Circle the correct word form in parentheses. Then write the missing words in the charts on page 178—except for the boxes with Xs. There may be more than one possible word for some of the boxes—maybe one noun for a person and another for an idea.

1. Which kinds of shows do you (preference /(prefer)/ preferable)? Do they decrease your ability to (concentration /(concentrate)/ concentrated)?

2. Are you (addiction / addict / addicted) to television or other (visions / visualize / visual) media?

3. Many TV critics and viewers (criticism / criticize / critical) the amount of (violence / violate / violent) in the media.

4. Psychologists worry about the (behavior / behave / well-behaved) of young people who watch a lot of TV during their (children / childhood / childless).

5. (Frequency / Frequent / Frequently) TV watchers may become (dissatisfaction / dissatisfy / dissatisfied) with their normal or average lives.

6. They might (envy / enviable / envious / enviously) the lives of TV or film actors because their lives seem (excitement / excite / excitable / exciting).

7. "Trash TV" brings (reality / realism / realize / real) people to talk shows—people with behavior that may be (immorality / immoral / immorally).

8. Are the guests on these shows telling the (truism / truth / true / truthful) about their lives? Are the people on reality TV showing their real (person / personalities / personalize / personal)?

9. Many of the films of the director Alfred Hitchcock are (psychology / psychologists / psycho / psychological) thrillers. They are very (suspense / suspend / suspenseful / suspensively).

10. Hitchcock usually (strength / strengthens / strong) the (scare / scary / scared) mood of his movies with frightening details.

Noun	Verb	Adjective
preference(s)	prefer	preferred preferable
	concentrate	concentrated
addiction(s) addict	addict	
vision(s)		
		critical
		violent
behavior		(well-) behaved
		childish childless
	frequent	
		dissatisfied

Noun	Verb	Adjective
envy		
	excite	
		real
		immoral
truth		
personality personalities		
		psychological
	suspend	
		strong
scare		

For more vocabulary practice with word endings that indicate parts of speech, try to think of more words (nouns, verbs, and adjectives) with the suffixes listed on page 176. You can check your guesses in a dictionary. Can you use your words in sentences that show their meanings?

4 Focusing on High-Frequency Words Read the paragraph below and fill in each blank with a word from the box.

advantage	elderly	media	programming
average	improve	practice	provide

Introduction: Benefits of the Visual Media

How do television and the other visual _____ affect
the lives of individuals and families around the globe? Media can be very
helpful to people (and their children) who carefully choose what they
watch. With high-quality _____ in various fields of study—
science, medicine, nature, history, the arts, and so on—the Internet, TV,
and DVDs increase the knowledge of the _____ and the
well-educated person; they can also _____ thinking ability.
Moreover, television and other visual media benefit _____
people who can't go out often, as well as patients in hospitals and
residents of nursing facilities. Additionally, it offers language learners
the _____ of "real-life" audiovisual instruction and aural
comprehension _____ at any time of day or night. And of
course, visual media can _____ almost everyone with good
entertainment—a pleasant way to relax and spend free time at home.

5 Making Connections Do an Internet search on a TV show or movie that you
enjoy or would like to see. It can be a comedy, a soap opera, a drama, a mystery, a
talk show, or any other kind of popular entertainment.

You can use a search engine such as Google and type in the name of the show. Take
notes on the plot or topic(s) of the show, the actors, or celebrities in it, and other
interesting aspects of the show. You can use the model on the next page.

Describe what you learned to a partner, a group of classmates, and/or the whole class.
Try to persuade them to watch the show. Did you persuade them? Why or why not?

Website: _____

Name of show/movie: _____

Type of show/movie: _____

Interesting information: _____

_____

_____

_____

_____

What is good about the show/movie? _____

_____

_____

_____

_____

PART 4 Focus on Testing

FOCUS

Focus on Comparison and Contrast in Readings

Part 1 of this chapter focuses on comparison and contrast. The first reading focuses on the positive and negative effects of television. Standardized tests, including the TOEFL® iBT, expect readers to recognize similarities and differences in meaning between ideas, opinions, points of view, and pairs of sentences.

Practicing with Comparison and Contrast Read the following short personal stories about the topic of this chapter's first reading, "How the Visual Media Affect People." Try to recognize the similarities (points in common) and the differences between the two stories. Then answer the questions that follow.

Story 1

My television set is an important piece of equipment for me. I can't get out of the house very often, but my TV brings the whole world to me. From the evening news and the all-news channels, I learn about events in the outside world: politics, the environment, recent changes in technology and medicine, and so on. I like game shows and travel programs, too. Even the talk shows are exciting—all of these strange people telling their life stories and secrets to the whole world! And I love comedies; I think it's important to be able to laugh. I can even watch shows in other languages and "go shopping" by TV. With the major national networks, the educational and cable channels—and the extra sports, movie, science fiction, history, music, and other specialty channels, I have a choice of 50 different programs at the same time! The only programs I don't watch regularly by myself are the children's shows, but when my niece visits, those are fun, too! Maybe I'll get a satellite dish. Then I'll have even more TV choices; and if those aren't enough, I can watch movies or listen to the radio online. How can I ever feel lonely or bored with so much media?

Story 2

We used to have a television set in every room of our house. Our eight-year-old son used to spend *hours* each day in front of the "tube." He was beginning to get strange ideas about reality from the violence and sex on many programs. He was having nightmares; he was losing interest in school, in creative play, in other children, and in his family! We (his parents) were watching too much TV, too. We stopped inviting our friends and relatives to our home and we stopped visiting them. We preferred to watch TV. We didn't even talk to each other that much. Because we weren't communicating enough, our marriage was suffering. Our health was suffering, too. We were getting lazy and becoming old and tired very quickly. So one day we decided to "pull the plug" on our dangerous family addiction. We quit TV "cold turkey"—from that time on, there was no television in our lives! It was a *very* difficult time for all of us. Like most recovering addicts, we had all the signs of withdrawal—feelings of boredom, of loneliness, of emptiness. Our son was always running to the refrigerator to satisfy his need for pleasure. My wife and I went back to smoking, to drinking alcohol, and to some other bad habits. But we finally recovered—and found the perfect solution to our discomfort and emptiness. Now we each have our own computer at home, and we spend all our free time in front of another screen. We are now addicted to the Internet.

1. Which of the previous stories is about the topic "views of the visual media, especially TV"?

   (A) Story number 1

   (B) Story number 2

   (C) both of the stories

   (D) neither of the stories

2. Which of the following might be a good title for Story 1?

   (A) How TV Changes Politics

   (B) Why I Need TV

   (C) How to Get on a TV Talk Show

   (D) Why Shopping on TV Is Convenient

3. Which of the following statements describes the main idea of Story 2?

   (A) There are many kinds of television programs—political, educational, commercial, and musical.

   (B) Television is an important element of a healthy and communicative family life.

   (C) Cold turkey is an excellent cure to feelings of boredom, loneliness, and emptiness in people's lives.

   (D) Addiction to television is difficult to overcome without a replacement or substitute.

4. According to both Stories 1 and 2, TV and visual media _____.

   (A) have very little influence on most of their viewers

   (B) are not a good distraction from real life

   (C) can greatly affect viewers' lives

   (D) are becoming less popular

5. What is the main difference between the points of view of the writers of the first and second stories?

   (A) The first story views television and video as beneficial, but the second focuses on their harmful effects on people.

   (B) In contrast to the first story, the second values the Internet over TV programming.

   (C) The first story's view is overwhelmingly negative; the second's feelings are exactly the opposite.

   (D) There is little difference between the two opinions; both stories explain the visual media in similar ways.

Self-Assessment Log

Read the lists below. Check (✓) the strategies and vocabulary that you learned in this chapter. Look through the chapter or ask your instructor about the strategies and words that you do not understand.

Reading and Vocabulary-Building Strategies

☐ Recognizing reading structure: using an outline
☐ Understanding the point and recognizing supporting details
☐ Classifying stories and putting events in order
☐ Summarizing a story
☐ Understanding new vocabulary from context
☐ Understanding suffixes
☐ Understanding word families

Target Vocabulary

Nouns
- addiction
- adulthood
- adults*
- advantage*
- behavior*
- hospitals*
- media*
- personalities
- practice*
- programming*
- reality*
- relationship*
- stars*
- viewers
- violence*
- visual media

Verbs
- concentrate*
- envy
- improve*
- investigate*
- provide*
- replace*
- scares

Adjectives
- addicted
- aural
- bloody*
- boring
- computerized
- dissatisfied
- elderly*
- emotional
- envious
- exciting
- immoral
- natural*
- nursing
- reality*
- scary
- shadowy
- suspenseful
- unlimited

* These words are among the 2,000 most frequently used words in English.

9 Social Life

The only way to have a friend
is to be one.

Ralph Waldo Emerson,
American author, poet, and philosopher

In Part 1, you will read about how people connect with and meet others in real-life and online. In the rest of the chapter, you will read about, discuss, and explore the different ways people explore friendship and dating both online and offline.

Connecting to the Topic

1. Look at the people in the photo. Where are they? What are they doing?

2. How do young people meet new people and make new friends in your country?

3. What do you think are the three best ways for people to meet a potential boyfriend or girlfriend?

Meeting the Perfect Mate

1 **Previewing the Topic** Discuss the pictures and questions that follow in small groups.

> I joined a computer dating service last week. It's going to be great! Soon dozens of men will be asking me for dates!

> A computer dating service? YECH! That's not very romantic. I prefer to go to clubs or do speed dating. I meet lots of men that way.

> Clubs? Speed dating? How awful! How unnatural! I think it's terrible to plan a romance. Romance should come naturally.

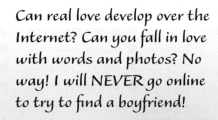

A computer program can't lead to true love. Did Romeo and Juliet have a computer? Did they go to a dance club? Of course not !

These things happen naturally.

Can real love develop over the Internet? Can you fall in love with words and photos? No way! I will NEVER go online to try to find a boyfriend!

So when was your last date?

Three years ago.

1. Who are the people and what are they talking about? How are the three people different from one another?

2. Do you agree with any of them? Why or why not?

3. How do young people you know usually meet their boyfriends/girlfriends or their future mates?

2 Predicting Think and talk with a partner about possible answers to these questions. What will the reading say? Make predictions. When you read "Meeting the Perfect Mate," look for the answers.

1. What was a common kind of marriage in India in the past that still exists today?

2. How do some young people around the world meet the people who become their boyfriends or girlfriends, or fiancés (future spouses)?

3. What is an advantage to each method (way) of meeting people? What is a disadvantage?

"Yeah, there are plenty of people to communicate with in cyberspace," Freddy began, **enthusiastically**. "With the most up-to-date technology—iPads, smart phones, and video, you can do it anywhere—at home, at work and school, at cafés, in the library . . . I text with people a lot, too."

Slowing down, Freddy paused to think. "On the other hand,... I'm not such a good writer. It's hard, you know,... to use those little computer devices. Anyway, well, um... who knows what is real there and what isn't? Who knows... like, who might be dangerous?" he continued, starting to sound a little **discouraged**. It seemed he was talking more to himself than to me. I thanked him, and we said good-bye so I could continue my search for the **perfect** way to find the perfect mate.

"The Internet? Never!" said Julie, a student who works part-time in the campus bookstore. "I prefer to make new friends at places where people have the same interests. I met my boyfriend at the health club, for example, and it seems that the healthy atmosphere of the gym is continuing into the relationship that I have with him." We work out together, hang out at the pool, go to the health-food juice bar, and so on. There are so many active, attractive people there. Hmm... maybe you should try it."

"That sounds interesting," I said.

"Yes," Julie said, "I guess so. But to be honest, there's one problem with meeting someone at the gym."

"What?" I asked.

"The truth is that I really hate to exercise, so I don't want to go to the gym anymore. What's my boyfriend going to think when he finds this out?"

To be continued...

After You Read

FOCUS

Recognizing the Structure of Written Conversations

Even readings that are in conversational form—with the words of each speaker between quotation marks (" ")–should be well organized. There should be a main topic and smaller topics, or subtopics. Each main topic should include details and ideas about the topic.

5 **Recognizing the Structure of Written Conversations** The chart below will help you organize the main topics and supporting ideas of the reading selection "Meeting the Perfect Mate." First, in the column after the speakers' names, write what the person talked about. Choose from the phrases below. (Note: One person talks about two topics.)

- Meeting people in dance clubs
- Arranged marriages
- Going to "speed dating" sessions
- Finding friends in cyberspace
- Meeting in health clubs or the gym

Interviewer's Question *What's the best way to meet a perfect mate?*

Interviewee	His or her method (= main idea)	Speaker's Pros	Speaker's Cons	Your Opinion
Usha	*Arranged marriages*			
Bill				
Freddy			*You don't know what is not real or dangerous about people you meet online.*	
Julie		*You can meet people with common interests.*		

Next, write the pros (advantages) and cons (disadvantages) each person talks about in the chart. Choose from the list below. You can look back at the reading for help. Some answers are in the chart as examples.

- The club atmosphere is exciting, especially on weekends.
- You can dance, talk to people, or just listen to music.
- Husbands and wives may learn to love each other.
- You meet a different potential date every six minutes.
- You list the names of the people you met that you want to see again.
- Spouses may meet for the first time on their wedding day.

- You can go online at home, at work or school, in cafés, and in other places.
- If you're not a fast thinker or talker, there's not enough time to get to know people.
- You can use your smart phone or iPad.
- You can meet people with common interests.
- You don't know what is not real or dangerous about people you meet online.
- People may drink, and shout instead of talk, and become aggressive.
- There are many attractive, active people there to meet.
- If you're not really interested in exercise, there might be a problem.

To tell the main (the most general) idea of the reading, finish this sentence:

There are _____ and disadvantages to the various ways

_____.

6 **Understanding the Main Idea** The main idea of the reading selection "Meeting the Perfect Mate" is in the first sentence of the following paragraph, but it is not quite true. Change the underlined words so that the paragraph correctly tells the point of the reading. A few items are done as examples.

> *advantages and disadvantages*
>
> There are (1) ~~only disadvantages~~ to the various possible ways of meeting
>
> *mates*
> potential (2) ~~classmates or roommates~~. (3) <u>An advantage of</u> arranged
>
> marriages is that mates may not meet until their wedding day; even so,
>
> through the years they may learn to (4) <u>take graduate courses</u> anyway.
>
> (5) At <u>stand-up comedy</u> clubs, you can talk or just listen to (6) <u>soft, relaxing</u>
>
> music; on the other hand, the people in such places tend to (7) <u>listen too</u>
>
> <u>much</u>, so they often act (8) <u>passive</u>. "Speed dating" is an organized way to
>
> meet potential friends, but it's probably most effective for (9) <u>slow-talking,</u>
>
> <u>thoughtful</u> people. Getting to know people in cyberspace is (10) <u>inconvenient</u>
>
> because computers and other electronic devices are (11) <u>nowhere</u>; however,
>
> (12) it is <u>easy</u> to know what is not real or unsafe about the people online. If
>
> you meet potential dates at a place where you have (13) <u>nothing</u> in common,
>
> like the gym, you can share your interest, but what happens if one person
>
> (14) <u>gets interested</u> in the activity?

Strategy

Understanding Left-Out Words and References

1. Left-Out Words

Often, a writer leaves out words because information in other sentences or sentence parts makes them unnecessary. The reader figures out the missing information from the context.

Example

"What's one way to meet a possible husband or wife?" I asked.

"Well," she said, "one method in my country is to have an arranged marriage."

Full meaning:
"One method _____*to meet a possible husband or wife*_____ in my country is to have an arranged marriage."

2. References

Some words refer to ideas that came before them in the reading.

Example

"My parents have had ⌒a good marriage⌒ for the past 30 years. This happens in a lot of arranged marriages."

Note: The word *this* refers to having a good marriage.

---

7 Providing Left-Out Words In the following quotes there are missing words that readers can figure out from the context. Which words are missing? Write them in the blanks. See the Strategy Box above for more help.

1. "I know you can match a tie to a shirt—or _____*match*_____

   two socks, too, after you do the laundry. But _____

   people?"

2. "Sure," she replied. "There are still arranged marriages these days, and there

   were a lot more _____ not too long ago."

3. "Do you mean that the bride and groom weren't in love? That sounds awful!

   Weren't they worried?"

   "They _____ a little bit," Usha said. "But it

   turned out well. They've had a successful marriage for 30 years."

4. "I meet a lot of women in dance clubs," Bill said. "At least I used

   to. The environment was exciting. I used to go _____

   every weekend."

8 **Identifying References** In each of the following sentences, circle the words that the underlined word refers to. The first one is done as an example. See the Strategy Box on page 193 for more help.

1. I've been taking a graduate (seminar) in social structure for the past month. It's a very popular course.

2. "One method is to have an arranged marriage," Usha said. "A what?" I asked.

3. "My grandparents chose their children's mates and arranged their weddings," she explained. "Do you mean they weren't in love?"

4. "Dance clubs seem great," I said. "I thought so too at first," he said a little sadly.

5. "Yeah, there are plenty of people to communicate with in cyberspace, . . . but who knows what is real there and what isn't?"

6. "It seems that the healthy atmosphere in the gym is continuing into our relationship," Julie said. "That sounds wonderful," I said. "Yes," she said. "I guess so."

7. "But the truth is that I hate to exercise. What's he going to do when he finds this out?"

9 **Discussing the Reading** In small groups, talk about your answers to the following questions. Then tell the class the most interesting information or ideas.

1. Do you know anyone who had or has an arranged marriage? Are there arranged marriages in your country or culture? What is your opinion of them?

2. Do you like to communicate with potential friends or dates in cyberspace? Why or why not?

3. Where might people with common interests meet in your community?

PART 2 Main Ideas and Details

Meeting the Perfect Mate (continued)

Before You Read

1 **Previewing Vocabulary** Read the vocabulary items below from the next reading. Then listen to the words and phrases. Put a check mark (✓) next to the words you don't know. Don't use a dictionary.

Nouns		Verbs	Adjective
background	inches (")	fill	optimistic
beach	motorcycling	film	
characteristics	statistics	make a mistake	
computer dating services	supermarkets	miss	
feet (')		tell the truth	
height			

Strategy

Understanding Literal Meaning and Inferences
The first time readers skim a piece of information, they usually read for *literal* (exact) meaning—that is to say, they find out quickly what the material says. Beyond the basic meaning of the words, however, they may be able to *infer* (figure out) other ideas or opinions. On a second, more careful, reading they can recognize and understand thoughts that the writer did not state directly.

2 Reading for Literal Meaning and Inferences Read "Meeting the Perfect Mate, Part 2" for literal (basic) meaning. Then to better understand the writer's meaning, read the material a second time.

Meeting the Perfect Mate, Part 2

"What is the best way to meet the perfect husband or wife? Computer dating services are the answer!" said my friend Sara, who lives down the hall from me in the dormitory. "They provide a great way to meet people! The biggest advantage is that you can have a lot in common with the people you meet through a computer. The computer can match you up with someone   5 of your same intelligence, cultural background or religion, age, personality, values, and so on. If you want, you can meet someone who is famous, exciting, **optimistic**, healthy, polite—any characteristics that are important to you. You can match your

◂ Is online dating a good way to meet people?

preferences in lifestyle, food, nature, sports, movies, and everything else.
And you can ask for a professor, a scientist, a computer specialist, an artist, or…"

"Have you had many successful dates so far?" I asked.

"To tell the truth," she said, "not really. I think I made a big mistake when I filled out the application form. I didn't want to miss a wonderful guy because of an answer that was too specific, so I was careful to write very general answers."

"What do you mean?"

"Well, there was a question about height. I said, 'anyone between 3'5" [3 **feet, 5 inches**] and 7'5".' Then there was a question about recreation. I answered 'yes' to 147 interests, from classic historical architecture to motorcycling. I wrote that I liked tennis, swimming, the beach, the mountains, the desert, health food, junk food, ethnic foods, eating out, cooking, staying home, traveling, the arts, TV comedies, quiz shows, crime dramas, family life, single life, and on and on and on… you know, I think that the computer got confused. It hasn't found a date for me since I sent in the application."

"And what about online video-dating?" asked Sara's roommate, Sandra.

"Online video-dating?" I asked. "How is that possible?"

"Well, I hear that you film yourself and talk about yourself… you know, your background and your interests and things like that. Then you post your video online and people can view it and you can view other people's videos and email the people you want to meet."

"Hmm…," I answered. "More videos in my life."

"Well, you could use Facebook," Sandra continued.

"Facebook?"

"Sure. A friend of mine did that. He wanted to get married, so he figured it out by statistics. He decided that out of every ten women, he liked one. And out of every ten women he liked, he might fall in love with one. Therefore, to get married, he just needed to meet one hundred women. He told his Facebook friends to each introduce him to two single women. Then, he sent those women a friend request."

"Did it work?" I asked.

"He's now married—to one of his Facebook friends!"

Last, I interviewed a guy in the cafeteria. His name was Felix.

"Supermarkets," he told me.

"You're kidding," I said.

"No, I'm serious. I meet a lot of potential dates over the frozen pizzas in the convenience-food section. Also, it's easy to make small talk over the cabbage and broccoli in the produce section. We discuss chemicals and nutrition and food prices. Sometimes this leads to a very romantic date."

I slowly shook my head: it is strange… very strange.

That evening, I talked with my roommate, Usha.

"You know," I said, "I think maybe your parents and grandparents had a pretty good idea. An arranged marriage is beginning to seem more and more attractive to me."

3 **Identifying Literal Meaning and Inferences** As you read in the Strategy Box on page 195, information in a reading can be literal (the author states it clearly) or inferred (the author implies or suggests it). The reader can read for the literal meaning and infer (figure out) the implied meaning.

Read the sentences below. Put a check mark (✓) on the line in front of the ideas that the author stated (clearly said) or implied (suggested) in the reading. Put an (✗) before the ideas that the writer did not state or imply. Look back at the reading selection if necessary.

1. ___✓___ The writer's friend Sara is a student.

2. ___✗___ There is a computer dating service in the dormitory.

3. _____ Sara thinks that computer dating has many advantages.

4. _____ A computer application asks questions about height, interests, and other things, and the computer uses the information to match people for dates.

5. _____ Sara wants to have a date with a doctor who doesn't eat meat.

6. _____ Sara had a lot of success with computer dating so far.

7. _____ If you join an online video-dating club, you meet people on network TV or online.

8. _____ In online video dating, two people can arrange to get together if they like each other's videos.

9. _____ Facebook could be a way to meet people you have something in common with.

10. _____ Dating may be a matter of statistics.

11. _____ The student that the writer interviewed in the cafeteria likes computer dating services and online video-dating clubs too.

12. _____ Felix makes small talk with potential dates in stores.

13. _____ On dates, Felix likes to eat pizza with broccoli and cabbage salad.

14. _____ The writer doesn't think that it is a good idea to date people you meet in the supermarket.

15. _____ The writer agreed with the guy in the cafeteria.

16. _____ She thinks that arranged marriages may have some advantages after all.

Strategy

Summarizing Stories by Identifying Pros and Cons
You learned to summarize stories in Chapter 8 by numbering the main events of a story. Another way to summarize a story is to tell the advantages (pros) and disadvantages (cons) of each side of the story. The story in Parts 1 and 2, "Meeting the Perfect Mate," is fiction, but it contains real information about possible ways to meet potential husbands and wives in many societies in today's world. For Part 2 of this story about ways to meet people, it's a good idea to write the pros and cons in your summary.

4 **Summarizing Stories by Identifying Pros and Cons** Work in groups. Each student should complete two or more of the following items taken from the readings on pages 188–190 and 195–196. Then read your sentences to your group. As a group, put your sentences together in a summary about the pros and cons of different ways to meet a mate.

1. The writer has been interviewing people about relationships. She found out that the mates in arranged marriages _____ _____.

2. The advantages of meeting people at dance clubs are that _____ _____.

   The disadvantages are that _____ _____.

3. Speed dating is _____.

   It may be effective if _____,

   but it probably won't work if _____.

4. It's easy to meet people online because _____.

   On the other hand, it can be a problem if _____ _____.

5. Some people make new friends at places where _____ _____,

   such as a gym. But there might be a problem if _____ _____.

6. An advantage of computer dating is that _____ _____.

   But if you _____,

   the computer might not _____ _____.

7. For online video-dating, _____.

   If you reach out to your Facebook friends, you can meet _____ _____.

8. Some people think the supermarket is a good place to meet potential dates because _____.

9. After interviewing many people about a possible way to meet potential mates, the writer decided _____ _____.

5 **Discussing the Reading** In small groups, talk about your answers to these questions. Then tell the class the most interesting information or ideas.

1. Do you sometimes make conversation with people in places where you have similar interests? Do these people ever become your friends?

2. Do you have online video and/or computer dating services in your country? What do you think of this way of finding dates?

3. Where do you usually meet the people who become your friends? Where or how did or do you meet potential boyfriends or girlfriends?

6 **Talking It Over** Proverbs are old, short, well-known sayings about human nature and life. Here are some well-known English-language proverbs about social life, friendships, and love relationships. First, match the proverbs on the left with their meanings (the paraphrases) on the right. Write the letters on the lines. Then for each proverb, discuss your answers to the questions below with a partner.

Proverbs

1. _____ Love makes the world go 'round.

2. _____ Absence makes the heart grow fonder.

3. _____ All's fair in love and war.

4. _____ Better to love and lose than never to love at all.

5. _____ Love is blind.

6. _____ Any friend of yours is a friend of mine.

7. _____ A friend in need is a friend indeed.

8. _____ The best of friends must part.

9. _____ The course of true love never did run smooth.

Meanings

a. If you don't see someone for a while, you will miss that person.

b. In love relationships, anything is possible.

c. Love motivates people all over the globe.

d. Even after it ends, a failed relationship is better than no relationship at all.

e. When you are in love, you don't see the faults of the other person.

f. In times of need, you find out who your real friends are.

g. Even the closest friends cannot always be together.

h. If you like someone, I will like that person too.

i. There will always be hard times in a real love relationship.

1. Do you agree with the "wisdom" of each proverb? Why or why not? Give some examples from your own experience.

2. Is there a proverb with a similar meaning in your native language? If so, translate it into English for the class and explain it.

3. Do you know any proverbs with an approximately opposite meaning (in English or in any language)? If so, translate one into English for the class and explain it.

Strategy

Identifying Negative Prefixes

A *prefix* (a part added to the beginning of a word) does not show the part of speech; however, a prefix usually changes the *meaning* of the word it is attached to. (In contrast, as you learned in Chapter 8, a *suffix*, an ending added to a word, often indicates its *part of speech*—that is, if it is a noun, a verb, an adjective, or an adverb.)

These are some common prefixes that add negative meanings to words; that is to say, these word beginnings change a word to its opposite.

dis-   *il-*   *im-*   *in-*   *non-*   *un-*

Example

    During our trip, we discussed our <u>dis</u>satisfaction with our relationship. He was <u>im</u>polite, and I was <u>in</u>direct. Even so, the talk was so important and interesting that the miles seemed to <u>dis</u>appear.

In the words *dissatisfaction*, *impolite*, and *indirect*, the prefixes *dis-*, *im-*, and *-in* add a negative meaning. However, the same letters are not negative prefixes in the words *discussed*, *important*, and *interesting*.

The prefix *im-* appears most often before the letters *b*, *m*, or *p*. Words beginning with the letter *l* may take the prefix *il-*. The most common negative prefix is *un-*.

---

1 **Identifying Negative Prefixes** Which of these words below from Chapters 1 to 9 contain a prefix with a negative meaning? Underline those prefixes and write *Neg* on the line before the word. Write *X* on the lines before the words without negative meanings. Use a dictionary if you need help.

1. _____ discover
2. __X__ discussion
3. _Neg_ <u>dis</u>ease
4. _____ dishonesty
5. _____ disorder
6. _____ distance
7. _____ illogical
8. _____ illustration
9. _____ images
10. _____ immediately

11. _____ immoral
12. _____ immortality
13. _____ impatience
14. _____ impolite
15. _____ inability
16. _____ increase
17. _____ indirect
18. _____ ingredients
19. _____ industrialization
20. _____ informal

21. _____ interrupt	26. _____ universal
22. _____ nonsense	27. _____ unlimited
23. _____ nontraditional	28. _____ unpolluted
24. _____ non-Western	29. _____ unusually
25. _____ understanding	30. _____ unwelcome

2 **Filling in the Negative Prefix** From your own knowledge of the vocabulary in this book, write the missing negative prefix (*dis-*, *il-*, im-, *in-*, *non-*, *un-*) in each blank, as in the example. Then you can check your answers in the dictionary.

1. _____ advantage	6. _____ effective	11. _____ natural
2. _dis_ appearance	7. _____ fortunately	12. _____ perfect
3. _____ certain	8. _____ healthy	13. _____ politeness
4. _____ common	9. _____ legality	14. _____ sense
5. _____ consistent	10. _____ mortality	15. _____ specific

3 **Writing Opposites** To make the following paragraph accurate, write the contrasting word (a word with the opposite meaning) over all the underlined items. Be careful: not all words with opposite meanings include negative prefixes—or any prefixes at all.

possible   *new*

Some people looking for impossible husbands and wives try old methods. For instance, they might find it difficult to make small talk with people that look unfriendly or depressed in the produce section of the supermarket, where they are choosing rotten fruits and vegetables. Or they might have a conversation at a slow-food restaurant, where they dislike eating hamburgers, French fries, or other items with high nutritional value. In a similar way, a computer service is incapable of matching singles with married people that are very much unlike them; men and women that get together in this inconvenient way often share many interests. A video-dating center may be unhelpful as well; meeting people on the Internet has benefits, but it can have advantages too. In any case, many ways of meeting people can be unsuccessful all the time.

For more vocabulary practice with the words that begin with prefixes, identify the parts of speech of the items in Activities 1–3 of Part 3. Can you use these words in sentences that show their meanings?

4 Figuring Out Vocabulary from Prefixes and Suffixes: Reading Online Profiles As you've read and discussed in this chapter, some people go online to meet potential mates. Below are four examples of online profiles.

Read the four profiles and circle or highlight the words and phrases that are new or difficult for you. Work with a partner to figure out their general meanings from the word parts— their prefixes and suffixes. Can you think of words with opposite meanings for some of the items? Which people would be a good match? Why or why not?

▼ Photo 1

I run my own photography business, specializing in analog black and white images. I'm looking for a travel partner, collaborator, and friend.

Enthusiastic and energetic teacher looking for a quiet professional guy with creative and athletic interests. I love to travel with my guitar!

▲ Photo 2

Graphic designer and tennis player in search of a funny, creative woman for travel partner. You take pictures, I write the blog!

Student of graphic design and photography seeks friend and partner for conversation and collaboration.

▲ Photo 3

Photo 4 ▶

5 Recognizing Words with Similar Meanings Read the words in each row below. Three of the words have the same or similar meanings. One of the words has a different meaning. Circle the word with a different meaning.

1. aggressive   calm   assertive   strong
2. fast   quick   slow   speedy
3. guy   gal   male   man
4. joyfully   enthusiastically   quickly   happily
5. husband   daughter   spouse   wife
6. inches   pounds   feet   arms
7. question   reply   say   respond
8. arrange   organize   plan   disrespect
9. pessimistic   positive   optimistic   hopeful
10. well-liked   popular   pleasing   unpopular

6 Focusing on High-Frequency Words Read the paragraphs below and fill in each blank with a word from the box.

accepted	generations	interviewing	match (noun)	university
discussing	international	match (verb)	replied	worried

For the past month, I've been taking a _____ graduate
                                              1
course called "Social Structure." It's a very popular class. We've been
_____ friendship, social life, dating, marriage, and other
            2
relationships—through the _____ and throughout the world.
                                      3
One of our assignments is to examine the ways that people meet potential
spouses (husbands and wives). I've been _____ students on
                                                      4
campus all week as part of my study. I'm amazed at what I've been hearing.

First, I talked with my roommate in the dormitory, Usha, an
_____ student from India.
            5
"What's one way to meet a possible mate?" I asked her.

"Well," she said, "one method in my country is to have an
arranged marriage."

"A what?" I asked. "I know you can _____ a tie to a shirt—
                                                  6

or two socks after you do the laundry. Then they're a _____.
7
But people?"

"Sure," she _____. "There are still arranged marriages
8
these days, and there were a lot more not too long ago. My parents, for
example, met each other for the first time on their wedding day. My
grandparents chose their children's spouses and arranged the weddings."

"Do you mean that the bride and groom weren't in love? That sounds
awful! Weren't they _____?"
9

"Maybe a little bit," Usha said, "but they _____ each other.
10
Then, fortunately, they learned to love each other."

7 Making Connections Do an Internet search to find love poems, quotes,
or proverbs about love. You can type "love poems" or "love quotes" in a search
engine. Find a few that you like. What do they mean? Is there a similar poem or
proverb in your language? Choose a favorite one, write it down and explain it to
your classmates.

Website: _____

Poem, Quote, or Proverb: _____

_____

_____

_____

_____

_____

_____

_____

_____

_____

_____

FOCUS

Understanding Inferences and Points of View in Readings

Parts 1 and 2 of this chapter are a fiction story with a point of view. Standardized tests, including the TOEFL® iBT expect readers to understand sentences, paragraphs, and passages beyond their literal meaning. Test-takers should be able to make inferences by figuring out answers from the events and ideas in a story. They also need to recognize the writer's point of view.

Practicing Inferences and Points of View Read this passage about the topic of Chapter 9, Social Life. Try to recognize the real meaning of the story. Then answer the questions that follow.

The Beginning of a Friendship

A   Lucy was a shy and frightened little girl when she first stood in front of Mrs. Campbell's third-grade class. It was Monday. "Now, children, we are very lucky today. I would like you to meet Lucy. She and her family just moved here from Guam. She will be in our class for the rest of the year." Pointing to a two-student desk that was empty, the teacher addressed the new student. "You can have that desk over there."

B   Looking only at the floor and holding her books close to her, Lucy walked over to her desk. However, she stumbled slightly and her books fell on the floor. Some of the kids in the class laughed—because that's the way some kids were. Lucy picked up her books and sat down, alone. The class had an odd number of students, so she was the only one without a desk partner.

C   When it was time for the first recess, all the kids hurried out of the classroom—all the kids but Lucy, that is. She waited until they were gone, got the snack out of her lunchbox, and walked slowly out to the playground. All the children were laughing, running, and playing. Unnoticed, Lucy made her way to a big tree, where she sat down on a bench and ate, alone. She watched the others play, but nobody came over to ask her if she wanted to join them.

D   When lunchtime came, the situation was the same. The girls played hopscotch and the boys played ball, and Lucy sat alone on the bench under the big tree. The only thing any of the kids said to her all day was, "Guam? I've never heard of Guam. I'm from America." Lucy was too shy to say anything. The little boy ran off to tell his friends that people from Guam didn't talk. That's the way some kids were.

E   The next day Lucy told her mom she didn't want to go to school anymore because she didn't have anybody to play with. She wanted to go back to Guam, to her friends. Her mother told her she would make new friends—and to hurry up and get ready. She shoved her lunchbox into her hands and led her out the door. Lucy's second day went just like her first. During recess, she went out to the bench under the big tree to eat her snack. She didn't look up much, but she could hear the sounds of laughter coming from the playground. She was lonely and very homesick. Then, halfway through her apple, she started to cry. Some of the other kids saw her crying, but they didn't ask her what was wrong. They just whispered to one another and pointed at her. Some laughed, because that's the way some kids were.

F   The third day of the week went pretty much the same—and the fourth day too. Lucy talked to nobody. Nobody talked to her. She sat alone during all the recesses and lunch periods. Then she went home and cried.

G   Then on Friday something different happened. In the middle of math class, the teacher was called out of the room. When she returned, she had a little boy with her. She said, "Class, this week we are very, very lucky. We have another new student. His name is Henry. Henry, you can take the other seat at that desk, next to Lucy." The little boy came over and put his book bag on Lucy's desk. He looked at her before he sat down, and he smiled. He smiled at her. It was a shy kind of smile, but it was a nice smile. She smiled back.

H   When lunchtime came, Lucy sat on the bench under the big tree eating her peanut butter sandwich. She didn't feel like crying. She was looking for Henry. There he was—playing ball with some boys. Henry made friends quickly, it seemed. Then he looked over at Lucy and saw her looking at him. Shyly, she looked down, but when she looked up again, there was Henry— standing right in front of her, his lunch bag in his hand. "Can I sit on this bench with you?" he asked. She nodded. For a few minutes they didn't talk at all. But right away Lucy knew she had a friend. Henry was nice. Some kids were just that way...

By Andrew Kirn, 1995

1. What kind of reading passage is this?

    Ⓐ a science fiction or fantasy story

    Ⓑ a personal story—either fiction or a narrative based on a real situation

    Ⓒ a factual history of elementary school education in the United States

    Ⓓ an opinion essay about conditions in our public schools today

2. According to the passage, what is most important about Lucy, the main character of the story?

    Ⓐ She couldn't relate to the other children because of her poor English skills.

    Ⓑ She missed her family and friends and home, so she paid no attention to the kids on the playground.

    Ⓒ She needed time—and a friend—to get over her shyness and discomfort in a new situation.

    Ⓓ She didn't like the lunches and snacks at her new elementary school.

3. According to the passage, what is most important about the other characters in the story?

- (A) They were all mean, vicious children that needed discipline and punishment from school officials and their parents.
- (B) They treated Lucy as she deserved to be treated—like an outsider that didn't belong to their group.
- (C) They were as nice and kind to Lucy as possible, but she didn't respond to their efforts.
- (D) They acted like typical kids their age when they meet someone new or different—except for a friendly boy that understood Lucy's feelings.

4. A good title for this story might be _____.

- (A) Changing Children's Attitudes Toward Newcomers
- (B) The Mistakes of Teachers and Parents of Third-Graders
- (C) The Differences Between Girls and Boys in a Typical School
- (D) How Friendship Can Make a Difference

5. Who might most appreciate and learn from the point of this story?

- (A) shy people at any age that feel uncomfortable in a new environment
- (B) students that don't know how to relate to people from other cultures
- (C) both A and B
- (D) neither A nor B

Self-Assessment Log

Read the lists below. Check (✓) the strategies and vocabulary that you learned in this chapter. Look through the chapter or ask your instructor about the strategies and words that you do not understand.

Reading and Vocabulary-Building Strategies

- ☐ Recognizing the structure of written conversations
- ☐ Understanding left-out words and references
- ☐ Understanding literal meaning and inferences
- ☐ Summarizing stories by identifying pros and cons
- ☐ Identifying negative prefixes
- ☐ Figuring out vocabulary from prefixes and suffixes
- ☐ Recognizing words with similar meanings

Target Vocabulary

Nouns
- ☐ feet
- ☐ generations*
- ☐ guy
- ☐ inches
- ☐ match*
- ☐ mates
- ☐ socks
- ☐ spouses

Verbs
- ☐ arrange*
- ☐ interview
- ☐ match*
- ☐ reply*

Adjectives
- ☐ aggressive
- ☐ arranged
- ☐ discouraged
- ☐ discuss*
- ☐ optimistic
- ☐ perfect*
- ☐ popular*
- ☐ speedy*
- ☐ worried*

Adverbs
- ☐ enthusiastically
- ☐ fortunately

* These words are among the 2,000 most frequently used words in English.

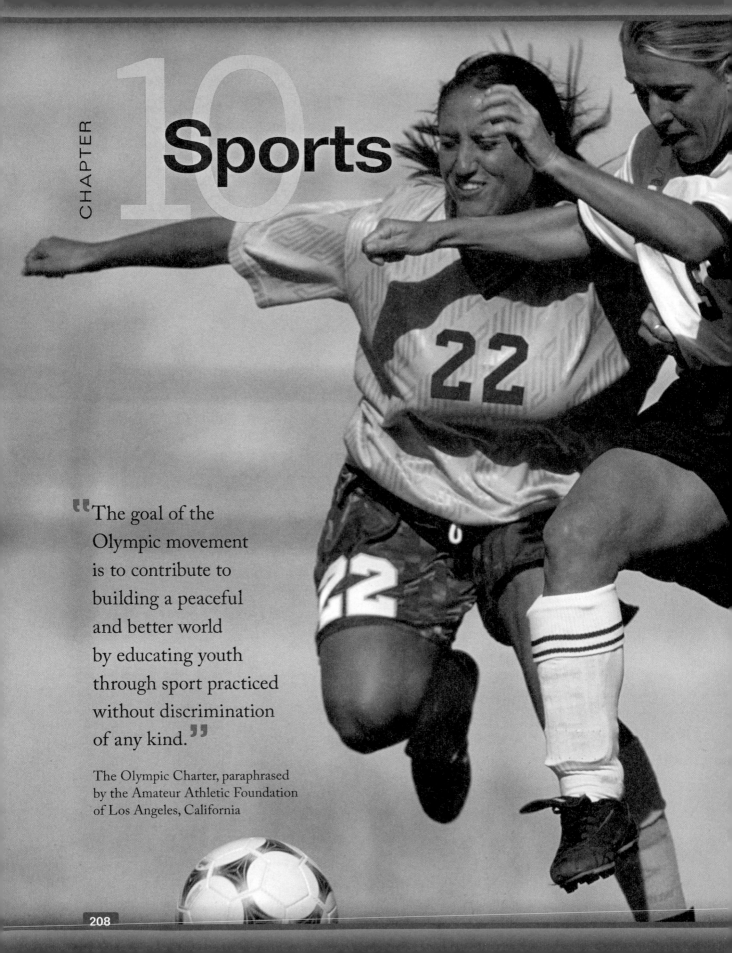

10 Sports

"The goal of the Olympic movement is to contribute to building a peaceful and better world by educating youth through sport practiced without discrimination of any kind."

The Olympic Charter, paraphrased by the Amateur Athletic Foundation of Los Angeles, California

In this **CHAPTER**

In Part 1, you will read about the ancient vs. the modern Olympics. In the rest of this chapter, you will read about, explore, and discuss issues related to sports competitions.

 Connecting to the Topic

1 Look at the photo. Where do you think this game is taking place?

2 What is your favorite Olympic event to watch? Why?

3 What do you think are some of the issues and problems with competitive sports?

The Ancient vs. the Modern Olympics

Before You Read

1 **Previewing the Topic** Work in groups. Look at the photos and pictures and read the questions below to compare the ancient and modern Olympics.

1. What do you see in the ancient pictures? What's in the modern photos?
2. What do the ancient and modern pictures have in common? (What similarities are there in the pictures?)
3. What is clearly different about the ancient and modern pictures? (What contrasts do you see?)

▼ Athletes competing in the ancient Olympics

► Athlete competing in the modern Olympics

2 **Predicting** Think and talk about possible answers to these questions. What will the readings say? You can make predictions. When you read "The Ancient Olympics" and "The Modern Olympics," look for the answers.

1. What events used to take place in the ancient Greek Olympics—during the opening ceremonies, the sports competitions, and the closing ceremonies? Which events are customary before, during, and at the end of the modern Olympics?

2. In which ways could girls and women take part in the original Olympic Games? How have they participated in the modern Games so far?

3. How did world politics affect the Olympic Games of the ancient Greek world? Since 1896, what effects have political conflicts had on the Olympics?

▲ The modern Olympics

The ancient Olympics ▶

3 Previewing Vocabulary Here are some vocabulary items from the first reading selection. Listen to the words. Put a check mark (✓) next to the words you don't know. Don't use a dictionary.

Nouns
- achievement
- altar
- ceremony
- chariot
- competition
- conflict
- coordination
- demonstrations
- organizations

- participants
- peacefulness
- promise
- representatives
- sacrifices
- sanctuary
- spectators
- statue
- trainer

Verbs
- award
- boycott
- cancel
- compete
- contribute
- participate
- re-create

Adjectives
- celebrated
- competitive
- extreme
- international
- original
- troubled

Read

4 Reading an Article Read the following article. Then read the explanations and do the activities that follow.

The Ancient vs. the Modern Olympics

A   In a world troubled by political **conflict**, the Olympic Games have symbolized peace and unity throughout their history. In the ancient Greek Olympics, youthful athletes honored the gods with **demonstrations** of their speed and **coordination**. Based on the highest ideals, the Olympic Games were offered in the spirit of peace, for the love of sport, and honest, fair   5
competition. Although the Olympics have changed over time, you might be surprised to learn that according to historians there are many similarities between the **original** Olympic Games and the modern ones.

Here are two articles to compare the Olympic competitions of past millennia with the widely celebrated Olympic Games of the 21st century.   10

The Olympic Events, Athens, Greece, the 4th Century A.D.

B   As the greatest of our national festivals comes to a close again, here are some of its highlights and history:
- Since 776 B.C., our summer Olympic Games have been held every four years at the sanctuary of our ruler Zeus on Mount Olympus.
- As usual, this year's Games began with the promise of fairness by athletes   15

and judges to Zeus. There was a ceremony before the statue and altar of the great god. There were contests for young boys. Participants and spectators met with old friends. There were speeches, poetry readings, tours, feasts, parades, and singing.

- Next came the **competitive** sports events: the pentathlon (five track and field events, including the discus throw, javelin throw, the long jump, running, and wrestling); boxing; the four-horse chariot race; horse racing; and an **extreme** combination of wrestling and boxing. Under a full moon, there were sacrifices to the King of the Gods.

- On the fifth and final day, prizes were awarded—wreaths made of a special olive tree branch from the sanctuary. Some winners received prizes worth money. There were more feasts for and by the winners. Then the competitors and spectators went home—mostly on foot through the mountains.

Women in the Olympic Games

C   Most of the athletes at this year's events were young men, of course. Even so, unmarried girls **competed** in foot races at the Festival of Hera (Zeus' wife). They were also spectators at the Festival of Zeus. The owner of the winning chariot team and the trainer of the winning horse in the races were female, too! On the other hand, married women were not allowed in the sanctuary of Zeus. They didn't want to be thrown off a cliff, so no one broke this rule.

The Politics of the Olympics

D   In my opinion, the most important **achievement** of the Olympic Games has been its peacefulness—not only at the Games, but in all of the Greek world. Of course, the actual events fill only five short days. Even so, during the three months before and after the competitions, there is an agreement to protect travelers, so there is usually no fighting between or among competing cities. Although there have been exceptions, in its long history of over a millennium, the Ancient Games have never been **canceled** for political reasons. In general, even during the times of major wars, the Games have **contributed** to the cause of peace for well over a thousand years.

www.ancientvsmodernolympics.com

HOME PAGE   MY ACCOUNT   HELP

The Olympic Events, Athens, Greece, August 29, 2004

A   As another wonderful worldwide Olympic festival comes to a close, here are some of its highlights and history:

- With a few exceptions, our modern Olympic Games have been held every four years in a different city around the world. This year, they again took place where they started—in Greece.

- As usual, this year's games began with the opening ceremony. Representatives of all athletes and judges made promises of fairness. For the first time in history, the Olympic flame had traveled to all continents before the Games. The opening ceremony ended with fireworks and the lighting of the Olympic Cauldron. 10

- For spectators and TV watchers, the most popular competitions were aquatics (swimming and diving), athletics (track and field), basketball, boxing, cycling, fencing, gymnastics, the modern pentathlon, soccer, volleyball, weightlifting, and wrestling. There were also 20 other sports, including the triathlon (swimming, biking, and running) and equestrian 15 (horse) events.

- Prizes were awarded after each event—the gold medal for the first place winner, silver for second place, and bronze for third. On the 17th and last day, the athletes got together for the closing ceremony. There were musical performances and speeches. The head of the International Olympic 20 Committee closed the 2004 Olympic Games.

Women in the Olympic Games

B   To this day, only about one-third of all Olympic competitors are female. Even so, the 2004 Olympics included the most female athletes ever. Women participated in events such as gymnastics, fencing, tae kwon do, basketball, beach volleyball, tennis, track and field, cycling, aquatics, soccer, hockey, 25 triathlon, and others. For the first time in history, women competed in the shot put—held at its original site in Olympia! However, there is still concern about the low number of female leaders in national and international competitive sports **organizations**.

The Politics of the Olympics

C   In my opinion, the most important achievement of these Olympic 30 Games was its peacefulness. In their 108-year history, the modern Olympics have been canceled three times because of world wars. Some countries have **boycotted** the Games for political reasons. Furthermore, the International Olympic Committee (IOC) has kept certain nations out of the Games because of their policies. There were terrorist attacks during the 1972 and 35 1996 Games. In contrast, in spite of the host organizers' and participants' worry, there was no violence during the 17 days of the 2004 Olympics. Despite worldwide problems, the representatives of 202 lands got along well. The Games contributed to the cause of peace.

D   As we have seen, the worldwide Olympic Games **re-created** at the end 40 of the 19th century have been different in many ways from the original Olympics of thousands of years ago. Even so, our modern competitions are more similar to the ancient ones than many people want to believe.

5 **Recognizing Reading Structure: Similarities and Differences**
The readings "The Ancient Olympics" and "The Modern Olympics" are two parallel articles, one after the other. The first article tells about the Olympic Games of the ancient Greek world. The second article gives information about the modern Olympic Games. Both articles, of approximately the same length, discuss the same subtopics.

Read the important ideas below from the reading. If the point is from the article on the Ancient Olympics, write *A* in the blank. If the point is from the article about the Modern Olympics, write *M* in the blank. Some ideas appear in both articles. Write *both* in the blank before those ideas.

1. __A__ The Olympics were always held on Mount Olympus in honor of Zeus—not at different cities in the world.

2. _both_ Some of the events of this year's Games were the opening ceremonies, the pentathlon, boxing, equestrian competitions, and the closing ceremonies.

3. _____ Many of the prizes awarded at the Games were symbolic. Wreaths honored some of the winners' achievements but didn't have monetary value.

4. _____ Most of the participants were young men. Married women couldn't participate in any of the sports or even watch them, but they could own and train horses.

5. _____ Although fewer women than men participated in the Olympic Games, there were both male and female teams in many of the sports. Olympic organizations included both sexes. Anyone could be a spectator—male and female, single and married.

6. _____ The Olympic Games were held every four years for over 1,000 years. There were no cancellations, boycotts, or acts of political terrorism.

6 **Understanding the Main Idea** Which of the following sentences best expresses the main idea, or point, of the reading "The Ancient vs. the Modern Olympics"? Circle letter *a*, *b*, or *c*. Can you tell a few facts from the reading to support that statement?

a. In contrast to the modern worldwide Olympic Games, the ancient Greek Olympics were purely noncompetitive demonstrations of speed and coordination; even so, they were often canceled because of political conflict and terrorism.

b. Both the ancient and the modern Olympic Games are known primarily for their problems: death for unmarried women, the violence of the sports events, cheating, doping, and so on; however, these beliefs about the competitions are largely myths.

c. The original ancient Greek Olympic Games were similar in many ways to the modern Olympic competitions in today's world.

Strategy

Using a Venn Diagram to Organize Supporting Details

A Venn diagram can help you organize the details of two different topics you are comparing and contrasting. By separating the details that describe each topic and identifying the details that describe both topics, you can see their similarities and differences more easily.

7 **Using a Venn Diagram to Organize Supporting Details** In each box are some details about the information in the two articles "The Ancient Olympics" and "The Modern Olympics." Some details are about the ancient Olympics, some are about the modern Olympics, and some are about both. Write the letters and/or the phrases of the details in the correct place in the Venn diagram.

The Olympic Events
A. take place every four summers
B. held at the sanctuary of Zeus on Mt. Olympus near Athens, Greece
C. held in various world cities
D. begin with promises of fairness by athletes and judges
E. include sacrifices in honor of Zeus as well as feasts
F. start with the lighting of the Olympic Cauldron as part of the opening ceremony
G. include some sports competitions = footraces, the pentathlon, equestrian events
H. include other events = four-horse chariot race, extreme wrestling, and boxing
I. include other events = aquatics, cycling, soccer, basketball, volleyball, gymnastics
J. offer prizes = olive tree wreaths
K. offer prizes = gold, silver, and bronze medals for 1st, 2nd, 3rd places

Ancient Olympic Games   Modern Olympic Games

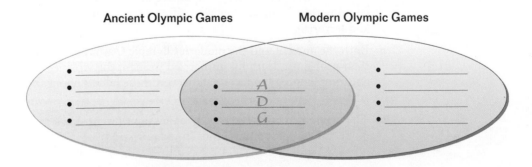

Women in the Olympic Games
L. more men than women participants
M. unmarried women only = in footraces and audience
N. women athletes in many sports
O. married women in sanctuary of Zeus were killed (thrown off a cliff)
P. small number of women in Olympic organizations is an issue

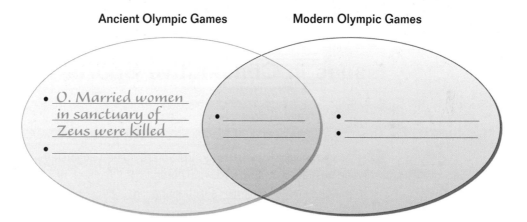

Ancient Olympic Games   **Modern Olympic Games**

- *O. Married women in sanctuary of Zeus were killed*
- _____

: _____
  _____

: _____
  _____

The Politics of the Olympics
Q. spirit of the Games = contribution to peace
R. three-month peace agreement among rival city-states to protect travelers to and from the Games
S. Olympics canceled because of hostilities during two world wars
T. sometimes political boycotts of the Olympics and terrorist attacks during them

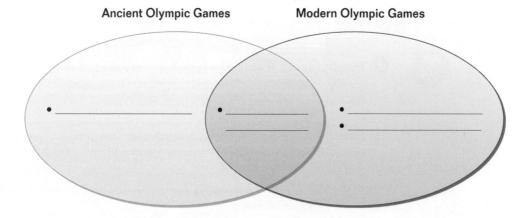

Ancient Olympic Games   **Modern Olympic Games**

- _____

: _____
  _____

: _____
  _____

8 **Discussing the Reading** In groups of three, talk about your answers to these questions. Then tell the class the most interesting information or ideas.

1. Before you read the article "The Ancient Olympics," did you have any images of or beliefs about ancient sports festivals like the Olympic Games in ancient Greece? If so, what were they? Have they changed? If so, how?

2. Have you ever been an Olympic competitor? Have you ever been a spectator at the modern Olympic Games? If so, when and where? If not, do you usually follow the summer or winter Olympics in the media? Why or why not?

PART 2 **Main Ideas and Details**

Issues in Competitive Sports

Before You Read

1 **Previewing Vocabulary** Below are some vocabulary items from the next reading. Listen to the words and phrases. Put a check mark (✓) next to the words you don't know. Don't use a dictionary.

Nouns
- bribery
- commercialism
- doping
- fans
- influence
- nationalism
- opposition
- patriotism
- pride
- purpose

- scandal
- sponsors
- sponsorship
- sports
- sportsmanship

Verbs
- clean up (their) act
- corrupt

- decrease
- disqualify
- expand
- influence
- preserve
- promote
- set (new) records
- solve
- televise

Adjectives
- banned
- dedicated
- dishonest
- intolerable
- nondiscriminatory
- performance-enhancing
- profitable

Read

2 **Recognizing Point of View** For every point of view about a topic, there is usually an opposing or contrasting opinion. These opposite views may be based on the same—and/or on different—facts and ideas.

Read the two letters on the following pages. They present two opposing points of view on controversial issues in competitive sports. Which letter supports competitive sports? Which letter doesn't? At the top of each letter, fill in the blank of the title, "The World Should _____ Sports Competition," with either *Promote* or *Stop*.

Issues in Competitive Sports in the World Today

The World Should _____ **Sports Competition**

Dear Editor,

A   The Olympic movement is representative of the principles and practices of all international sports competitions, but it has failed. The original ideals behind the Olympics have been **corrupted** and damaged. Here are some of the current problems and trends in competitive sports worldwide: 5

- Some of the most famous athletes in the world take and will continue to take **banned** drugs. A recent poll asked them, "If you knew you could get away with it, would you use performance-enhancing substances to increase your chance of winning?" Almost 95 percent said "yes." The second question was, "If you could take performance-enhancing drugs,   10 not get caught, win every contest for five years, but then die from the side effects of the substances, would you do it?" More than half answered "yes."

- Many observers have the same opinion: the majority of world records in recent decades were drug assisted. Advertisers, **fans**, and spectators want   15 athletes to set new records, so **opposition** to doping is only talk.

- Athletes and the idea of wholesome international competition have become less important than the interests of TV networks. Even the IOC (the International Olympic Committee), which makes billions from the big companies, has become uncomfortable with the amount of corporate   20 sponsorship at recent Olympic Games. Some players seem to be representing their corporate sponsors as much as their countries. Also, the TV networks make all the decisions about the use of air time. They televise activities that look good on the screen—like beach volleyball or snowboarding—instead of real sports that attract smaller audiences. Commercialism and the   25 mass media have damaged the original spirit and purpose of international sports competition.

- Bribery and scandal have always been part of competitive sports. Even in ancient history, Greek city-states fought over control of sports competitions; powerful officials influenced judges in their decisions. In   30 modern times, bribery has been a part of the selection of host cities for the **profitable** Olympics. Aren't international sports supposed to promote moral development, individual achievement, cooperative sportsmanship, and multicultural understanding? Instead, the patriotism of sports has often become nationalism—unhealthy group pride. Unfair judges have awarded   35 medals because of national pride rather than true athletic performance. This is not a healthy practice in the search for world peace. In conclusion, the situation of the modern Olympic Games and other sports competitions has become **intolerable**. Competitive sports are sending the wrong message to athletes and young people around the world. They should therefore be stopped. 40

Regards,
Sophia Martin

The World Should _____ **Sports Competition**

Dear Editor,

B   The Olympic movement, representative of the principles and practices 45 of all international sports competitions, has had a positive influence on individual people and societies around the world. Here are some of the current benefits of and trends in competitive **sports** worldwide:

• Doctors, laboratories, and sports officials are trying to **solve** the problem of illegal drug use by competitive athletes. In 1999, the IOC (the International 50 Olympic Committee) formed the World Anti-Doping Agency to prevent drug use in international competition. Each country has an agency to test its own athletes. Scientists are developing tests to discover new forms of doping. At the 2008 Summer Olympic Games, at least six athletes were **disqualified** for drug use. 55

• Drug testing is becoming common in competitive sports. This will continue to protect young people from the dangerous side effects of doping. The testing also contributes to the ideals of fair play and good sportsmanship.

• In order to survive, international sports organizations have become 60 more business-like. In the early and mid 20th century, the IOC—as well as national and local organizing committees—used to depend on dedicated staff members, volunteer workers, and local fund-raising. Their budgets were small. Commercial interests and money from TV networks have changed all that. Beginning in the mid-1980s, for example, huge 65 payments from corporate sponsors and the media have allowed the Olympic movement to **expand**. Scholarships, sports education programs, and direct financial aid to developing countries have helped spread the ideals of competitive sports. These ideals include improved health, development of personal character, and good sportsmanship throughout the world. 70

• Bribery and other kinds of scandal **decrease** spectators' interest in (and money from) sports competitions. The attention has forced dishonest officials to quit, and international organizations have been "cleaning up their act." Are stronger rules making athletes, coaches, judges, and fans change their attitude about international competitive sports? I hope so! 75 I want to see fair play and cooperation. And I want to see governments create more helpful, **nondiscriminatory** policies. Patriotism may become

a healthy emotion based on the pride of achievement and international understanding—a necessary development in the search for world peace.
- In conclusion, international sports competition—based on the ideals of the ancient and modern Olympic Games—are a positive force. They are sending a healthy message to athletes and young people around the world. We should preserve and promote competitive sports.

Sincerely,
Ali Badawi

80

85

After You Read

Strategy

Distinguishing Opinion from Fact

Most views about a topic include both facts and opinions as supporting details. How can you distinguish between the two?

- A fact is supported by evidence. It does not include personal feelings; it is objective. It can be proven—perhaps through historical data, scientific research, or statistics.
- An opinion is based on individual beliefs, emotions, or ideas. It may be based on fact but cannot be proven. It is a personal conclusion or judgment; it is subjective.

3 **Identifying Opinions and Facts** Identify each of the following items about competitive sports as an objective fact (*F*) or a subjective opinion (*O*). You may look back at the reading selection if necessary. Can you tell the reasons for your answers?

1. _____ In a recent poll, 95% of polled athletes said that if they wouldn't get caught, they would take performance-enhancing drugs to increase their chances of winning in competition.

2. _____ Advertisers, fans, and spectators don't oppose doping (the use of performance-enhancing drugs) because they like to see athletes set exciting new records.

3. _____ The purpose of drug testing and the formation of world and national anti-doping agencies is to prevent and/or to punish the use of banned substances in international competitions.

4. _____ More and more, the IOC and other competitive sports organizations are bringing in huge sums of money from commercial sources such as corporate sponsorships and the sale of broadcast rights to TV networks.

5. _____ Sports competitions should be financed by local fund-raising only; they should not be broadcast worldwide.

6. _____ Bribery and scandal—such as in the choice of host cities and the judging of events—have always been a part of competitive sports. So have nationalistic bias and patriotic pride.

7. _____ International sports competition is supposed to support and promote moral development, athletic achievement, team cooperation, and cultural understanding at local, national, and international levels.

8. _____ Olympics and other international sport competitions can and should be made more positive forces in the troubled modern world. It doesn't matter if they've succeeded or failed in the past.

Strategy

Summarizing Opinions

The letters in "Issues in Competitive Sports in the World Today" give reasons for and against the preservation and promotion of worldwide competitive sports as they are now. Here are some steps to follow to summarize letters of opinion like these:

- From the title, introduction, or conclusion of each letter, write a main-idea statement of the writer's point of view—the main point of his or her opinion.

- State the important supporting points for that viewpoint. If necessary, include connecting words or other transitions from Chapter 7 that explain the logic of the writer's conclusion.

- Do you think the writer "made the case" for his or her opinion? Tell why or why not.

4 Summarizing Opinions Work in small groups of an even number of participants—four or six. Half of each group cooperates in writing a summary of the letter "The World Should Stop Sports Competition." The other half writes a summary of the opposite viewpoint—"The World Should Promote Sports Competition." Each group reads or tells its summary to the other.

Choose the two most convincing points of view. All group participants work together to rearrange, change, and/or add supporting detail (arguments) to the summary of the most convincing points of view. Then they can present their arguments and conclusion to the whole class.

5 Discussing the Reading Talk about your answers to these questions.

1. How important are competitive sports in the world today—especially in worldwide festivals? Why do you think they are important?

2. Suppose you are on an international, national, or local sports committee. How would you change the rules, practices, customs, and/or attitudes connected with competitive sports? For what purposes would you make these changes?

6 Talking It Over People often debate ideas, expressing opposing points of view. Below are some statements about current issues in worldwide competitive sports. First, match each statement in Column A with its opposite (contrasting) opinion in Column B. Write the letters on the lines.

Then work in groups of four. For each pair of statements, two people choose one side. The other two people choose the other side. With your partner prepare all the possible reasons you can think of for your point of view. Your "opponent" or "opposing team" will compile the opposite or contrasting reasoning. Then tell your classmates your opinions.

After you debate your issue, class members can vote on the "winning team."

Column A:
Statements, Opinions, Viewpoints

1. _____ Performance-enhancing drugs should be banned from sports. Athletes found using them should be punished.

2. _____ Whether it is pride for a city or a country, patriotism has a negative influence in the world. People should support everyone rather than just one nation.

3. _____ Bribery, corruption, and scandal are elements of sports competitions and other areas of life. They have existed since ancient times and will continue to exist in the future.

4. _____ Women and men should be equally represented in all areas of competitive sports. There should be equality in money, corporate sponsorship, and media air time.

5. _____ Politics should be like sports contests. Politics should have judges and be based on rules, penalties, competition, and winning.

Column B:
Opposing Statements, Opinions, Viewpoints

a. With stronger rules and media involvement, we can stop bribery and corruption. This is important for competitive sports as well as politics.

b. Equality between the sexes is impossible in sports. Male and female competitors have always had different abilities. Fans, corporate sponsorship, and media will always support male athletes more than females.

c. Athletes should be allowed to take supplements and other substances to improve their athletic ability. They shouldn't be punished.

d. Politics ought to be based on cooperation rather than competition. Politics shouldn't be anything like competitive sports.

e. The idea of pride toward all humans instead of any one nation just doesn't work. Societies are based on different principles and ideals, so patriotism toward one nation is important.

Strategy

Understanding Prefixes

In addition to the negative prefixes *dis-*, *il-*, *im-*, *in-*, *non-*, and *un-*, there are other common syllables that change the meaning of base words when they are added to the beginning. Here are some of them—with their general meanings and examples.

Prefix	General Meaning	Examples
com-, *con-*, *co-*, *cor-*	with; together	compassion, convenient, co-worker, corporation
de-	down or away from	decrease, decline, detach
ex-, *e-*	out of, away from	exit, expand, emit
inter-	between; among	interview, intermission, Internet
pre-	before, in advance of, earlier	prepare, prefix, prepaid, precede
pro-	for, favoring, supporting	promotion, progress, propel
re-	again, back	repairs, repeat, re-created

1 **Understanding Prefixes: Matching** Paying attention to the underlined prefix and other word parts, match the vocabulary items and their parts of speech in Column A with their possible explanations in Column B.

Column A

1. __C__ con**tribute** (verb)
2. _____ **pre**dictions (noun)
3. _____ **con**flict (noun)
4. _____ **com**pete (verb)
5. _____ **co**ordination (noun)
6. _____ **pro**fessional (noun)
7. _____ **inter**national (adj.)
8. _____ **cor**rupt (adj.)
9. _____ **ex**treme (adj.)
10. _____ **re**wards (noun)

Column B

a. the farthest possible; very great or intense

b. prizes given for winning or other behaviors

c. to give to something other people are also giving to

d. a person who has special education or training

e. a disagreement

f. involving two or more countries

g. dishonest; willing to lie, cheat, or steal

h. organized activity of muscle groups in athletics

i. to go against in order to win

j. acts of telling the future

Reviewing Prefixes

Below is a review list of common word beginnings with their general meanings. In the paragraphs that follow, you can use the prefixes as clues to unfamiliar words—and you can look up words in the dictionary.

Prefixes	Approximate Meanings	Prefixes	Approximate Meanings
a-, ab-	away from	*intro-*	inward
a-, ad-, ap-	to	*mis-*	wrong
con-, com-, co-, col-, cor-	with; together	*non-*	not
de-	from, away	*ob-*	against
dif-, dis-	apart; not	*pre-*	before
e-, ex-	out (of); former	*pro-*	for, on behalf of
in-	into; very; not	*re-*	again
inter-	between	*uni-*	one; single

2 **Understanding Prefixes** Within each pair of parentheses ( ), circle the vocabulary item that best fits the meaning of the context.

1. A sport (consists / contributes) of a physical activity for the purpose of (procreation / recreation) and/or (competition / petition). Many people participate or (compete / repeat) in sports to (achieve / deceive) excellence or to develop a skill.

2. Archaeologists have uncovered examples of prehistoric cave art that show activity (resembling / assembling) sports from over 30,000 years ago. Some (objects / interjects) and structures suggest that Chinese people took part in gymnastics (events / prevents) as early as 4000 B.C. Activities like swimming and fishing (evolved / involved) into regulated sports with rules in ancient Egypt. Other sports (excluded / included) javelin throwing, high jump, and wrestling. Ancient Persian sports were (connected / corrected) to combat skills. In fact, military culture (inversely / universally) prevailed in sports in those

days. The situation wasn't much (different / indifferent) in ancient Greece. In (addition / edition) to traditional sports, the Greeks (deduced / introduced) chariot and other races—including marathon (delays / relays).

3. The Industrial Revolution and mass (deduction / production) of the 18th and 19th centuries greatly changed the lives of ordinary people. People were provided with (decreased / increased) leisure time, which (disabled / enabled) them to play or (observe / preserve) team sports as spectators. Sports became (confessional / professional), which made them even more popular. So did the (advent / invent) of mass media.

Strategy

Understanding Prefixes, Stems, and Suffixes
To review, a *suffix* (word ending) often indicates the part of speech of a word. A *prefix* (word beginning) may change the meaning of the base word or *stem* (the main part of a longer word). With knowledge of these three elements, readers may be able to figure out new or difficult vocabulary, especially long words with several parts.

3 Practicing Prefixes, Stems, and Suffixes In the following paragraphs, use your knowledge of word parts to choose the best and most appropriate missing vocabulary items. Choose from the words in the box before each paragraph.

commonly (adverb)	environmentally (adverb)	professional (adjective)
describes (verb)	individual (adjective)	recreation (noun)
development (noun)	invention (noun)	transportation (noun)

1. *Cycling* is a word that _____describes_____ the riding of bicycles not only for _____ and fun, but also as a _____ sport. It has a number of benefits both to the _____ person and society in general. It is healthy _____ (to and from work) as well as an _____ -friendly means of exercise. The activity probably began in the early 1800s, with the _____ and _____ of the earliest bikes. These were _____ made of wood and had three wheels. The modern bicycle was first produced in 1892.

concept (noun)	event (noun)	prevent (verb)
constructed (verb)	involves (verb)	promote (verb)
different (adjective)	prevails (verb)	renowned (adjective)

2. Since the beginning of the 20th century, the bicycle has evolved enormously with the _____ of cycling as a sport and the demands of _____ kinds of terrain (ground). Probably, the most _____ (famous) cycling _____ in history is the Tour de France, which _____ cyclists from around the world riding over many types of land to the center of Paris. Also, governments have tried to _____ cycling as a healthy alternative to cars. Bike lanes have been _____ and lockers have been provided to _____ the theft of bicyclists' belongings. In fact, in some countries a "cycling culture" _____ .

④ **Identifying Antonyms** Read the vocabulary words in Column A. Choose the word in Column B that has the opposite meaning from the vocabulary word.

Column A

1. __f__ corrupt
2. _____ disqualify
3. _____ expand
4. _____ banned
5. _____ opposition
6. _____ fans
7. _____ intolerable
8. _____ profitable
9. _____ solve, answer
10. _____ boycott
11. _____ cancel
12. _____ competitive

Column B

a. support
b. losing money
c. contract, make smaller
d. schedule
e. athletes
f. honest
g. cooperative
h. create a problem
i. allowed
j. acceptable
k. buy, purchase
l. qualify

⑤ **Focusing on High-Frequency Words** Read the paragraph on page 228 and fill in each blank with a word from the box.

changed	conflict	offered	speed
competition	history	original	

In a world troubled by political _____, the Olympic Games
have symbolized peace and unity throughout their _____.
1   2
In the ancient Greek Olympics, youthful athletes honored the gods with
demonstrations of their _____ and coordination. Based on the
3
highest ideals, the Olympic Games were _____ in the spirit of
4
peace, for the love of sport, and honest, fair _____. Although
5
the Olympics have _____ over time, you might be surprised
6
to learn that according to historians there are many similarities between the
_____ Olympic Games and the modern ones.
7

6 **Making Connections** Do an Internet search about a sport, a team, or an
athlete that you are interested in. Type in the name of the sport, person, or team,
and then another word like *biography* or *facts*.

Take notes on what you learn in the outline below. Do you think your sport, person,
or team is worth following or participating in? Try to convince your class of your
point of view.

Example:

David Beckham biography

Topic: _____

What you learned: _____

_____

_____

_____

Your point of view about the topic and why: _____

_____

_____

_____

FOCUS

Taking Notes and Recognizing Contrasts in Reading Passages

The two readings in Part 2 of this chapter ("Issues in Competitive Sports in the World Today") showed opposing points of view in two separate letters. Sometimes opposing viewpoints appear within a single reading on the TOEFL® iBT. If you recognize this point-by-point approach, you can take helpful notes.

You are allowed to take notes during the TOEFL® iBT. Each reading in the reading section stays on the screen until you decide to move to the next reading or until the time limit (20 minutes) has expired. Because you can look back at the reading as you answer questions, you do not have to take notes about most things, but any contrasts should be put into a list. This will help you see the structure of a reading, understand the flow of ideas, and answer some questions about contrasts.

If a TOEFL® iBT reading shows point-by-point contrasts, divide part of your notepaper (provided by the test supervisors) into two columns. Use the left column for points made on one side of the argument, and use the right-hand column for points on the other. Try to arrange them so points that are in direct contrast appear next to each other, as in the example below for "Issues in Competitive Sports in the World Today."

Competitive Sports Today

Pro	Con
programs to stop illegal drug use	use of illegal drugs

Practicing Taking Notes About Contrasts Read the following passage about street sports. Take notes about contrasts, using the two-column style described above. Then using only your notes, answer the questions that follow.

Street Sports and the Olympics

A   Most cultures have at least one popular street sport—a game that children or adults play informally whenever they can get enough players together. Typically, even the poorest members of society can play a street sport because it involves very little equipment. It also involves very little planning or organization.

B   In the United States, for example, basketball is probably the most commonly played street sport. Since it requires only a basket, a paved surface, and a basketball, it can be played in nearly any city park or home driveway. In Canada and parts of the U.S., the everyday sport is ice hockey, played in winter with ice skates on a frozen pond and in summer with in-line skates in a parking lot. In most of the world, soccer is the informal sport of choice. Even easier to organize than street basketball, it requires only a ball and a wide-open space. In Thailand, Malaysia, and Vietnam, a game called *sepak takraw* is played by children and adults in nearly every town or village. It involves kicking a simple wicker ball over a head-high net, like volleyball played with the feet.

C   Street sports are great for neighborhood games, but are they suitable for international competition? Fans of any given street sport would like to see it in the Olympic Games. Other people may say the Olympics should keep it out. Typical objections are that the street sport is not really a sport, or it is too local, or the Olympics simply have enough events already.

D   The controversy is less about basketball, ice hockey, or soccer than it is about other street sports. Basketball, no longer a mostly North American game, has been an Olympic sport since 1936. Soccer (officially called football) was the first team sport to become a regular Olympic event (1908). Ice hockey has been part of the Winter Games ever since the league's establishment in 1924.

E   Sports like *sepak takraw* are another story. Those who love this game hoped to see it added to the Olympic line-up in 2012. Its athleticism is obvious, *sepak takraw*'s supporters say. As an Asian sport, it can provide some balance to the Olympics' European and North American events. It is as well organized and popular as any other sport, according to its fans. Those who would keep the game out of the Olympics argue mostly that it is simply too local. Few people outside one region play it. Although there are *sepak takraw* associations in Canada, Australia, and elsewhere, most of them are very small. Olympic medals in *sepak takraw*, its opponents say, would simply be gifts to a few Southeast Asian nations.

F   A different kind of controversy surrounds such "extreme" street sports as skateboarding. Its proponents say that it is one of the few real sports played by actual amateurs. (The modern Olympics began as an event for nonprofessional athletes.) According to skateboarders, it is a true sport of the people, unlike synchronized swimming or ballroom dancing (both Olympic events). It is also far more athletic. And its supporters claim that it is kept out of the Olympics simply because skateboarders do not look very "Olympic." They favor odd hairstyles, often behave recklessly, and try not to look like traditional Olympic athletes. This is a complaint voiced by players of many sports—if you look too poor, you cannot enter the rich man's Olympics.

G   On the other side, Olympic purists argue that it is very fair to keep scruffy looks and wild behavior out of the Games. The Olympic Games are the visible part of a movement, they say, to encourage peace and civility around the world. Athletes who do not live by Olympic ideals do not belong. Furthermore, skateboarding's opponents claim it is not a sport. It doesn't have a well-established network of associations around the world. It has few rules, and skateboarders have few lower-level international tournaments. Skateboarders argue that they are very well organized. They point out that the somewhat-related sport of snowboarding has made a fine addition to the Winter Games. Its addition to the winter line-up has not damaged the Olympic spirit, they say, but has updated it.

H   As badly as *sepak takraw* players or skateboarders think they are treated, players of several other street sports feel they have a stronger complaint. Rugby, American football, and cricket, for example, are immensely popular in the nations that play them. They are also quite accessible as street sports. They represent long traditions among the common people, their supporters say. Rugby and cricket fans feel especially hurt because these sports were once Olympic events but were dropped to make room for other sports.

1. Which of the following best expresses the main idea of the passage?
   - (A) Street sports make good Olympic sports because they are played by nonprofessionals.
   - (B) Once a street sport enters the Olympics, it loses popularity among common people.
   - (C) Olympic officials are biased against sports that are played by ordinary people.
   - (D) Controversy surrounds the hopes for some street sports to become Olympic sports.

2. Which of the following is NOT mentioned in the passage as a street sport?
   - (A) soccer
   - (B) volleyball
   - (C) skateboarding
   - (D) cricket

3. According to Paragraphs B and D, what do basketball, ice hockey, and soccer have in common?

   (A) They are all North American street sports.

   (B) They have strong positions as Olympic sports.

   (C) Their supporters are trying to get them accepted as new Olympic sports.

   (D) There is disagreement about whether they should be Olympic sports.

4. Which of the following is an argument against *sepak takraw* as an Olympic sport, according to Paragraph E?

   (A) It is not international enough.

   (B) It goes against Olympic ideals.

   (C) It is not very athletic.

   (D) It is not a sport.

5. According to Paragraphs F and G, skateboarders believe that Olympic officials keep them out because of their unusual looks and wild behavior. Which argument do skateboarding's opponents make in response?

   (A) that there is no prejudice against skateboarders because of their looks and behavior

   (B) that several Olympic sports already allow people with unusual looks and behavior

   (C) that skateboarders' looks and behavior would lead to fighting at the Games

   (D) that it is OK to keep certain unusual looks and behaviors out of the Games

6. Which of the following sports was once part of the Olympic Games, but was then dropped?

   (A) baseball

   (B) soccer

   (C) rugby

   (D) American football

Self-Assessment Log

Read the lists below. Check (✓) the strategies and vocabulary that you learned in this chapter. Look through the chapter or ask your instructor about the strategies and words that you do not understand.

Reading and Vocabulary-Building Strategies

☐ Recognizing reading structure: similarities and differences
☐ Understanding the main idea
☐ Using a Venn diagram to organize supporting details
☐ Recognizing point of view
☐ Distinguishing opinion from fact
☐ Summarizing opinions
☐ Understanding prefixes, stems, and suffixes
☐ Identifying antonyms

Target Vocabulary

Nouns	Verbs	Adjectives
achievement*	boycott	banned
competition*	cancel	competitive
conflict*	compete*	extreme*
coordination	contribute*	intolerable
demonstrations	corrupt	nondiscriminatory
fans	decrease	original*
opposition*	disqualify	profitable*
organizations*	expand	
sports*	re-create	
	solve	

* These words are among the 2,000 most frequently used words in English.

Vocabulary Index

*These words are among the 2,000 most-frequently used words in English.

informal
infrastructure
intentional
interact
involved
keep going
level*
location*
low-income
monitor
motivation
neighborhoods
network*
observe
observers
organize*
organization*
participate
physical*
reality*
real-life
recognize*
relatively
resources*
responsibilities*
retirement
risk*
rural*
sensors
sites*
socially acceptable
spiritual
steps*
structured
suburban
suburbs
technology*
tend (to)*
therefore*
transportation
urban*
virtual
wireless

Chapter 5

adequate
ancient*
architects
attached
beat

branches*
camp/camper
centuries*
civilizations
clay
construct
control*
descendents
develop*
discover*
durable
entertain
feed
fill in
flat*
forefathers
form*
frames/framing
generations*
global
guide
hardened
homeless
impress
independent*
invention
mansions
manufacturing
necessity
obey
obligation
permanent*
prehistoric
produce
property*
protection*
punish/punishment
range from… to
reside
sacrifice
shelter
slaves
society*
spoil
temporary
tools*
trend*
wealthy
weapons*
youngsters

Chapter 6

agree*
amazing
annoyed
architecture
attention*
civilization
clear*
contradict
contradiction
convincingly
customer*
describe*
develop*
enthusiastic
excellent*
experience*
greet
ignoring*
invent
knowing
legacy
local*
loudly
media*
medicine
opposing
pain*
patiently
pleasant
politely
proud
rude
rudely
scientific*
social*
societies*
soft*
successful*
terrible*
tourist

Chapter 7

accurate
characteristics*
claims*
combination*
correct
cure
damage*

*These words are among the 2,000 most-frequently used words in English.

decisions*
disease*
dishonest
elderly*
engineering*
environment*
famous*
genes
genetic
improve*
increase*
inhabitants
length*
longevity
long-lived
moderate
oppose
patients*
population*
prevent*
proven
purpose*
solve
sour
streams
structure*
unpolluted
valid

Chapter 8

addicted
addiction
adulthood
adults*
advantage*
aural
behavior*
bloody*
boring
computerized
concentrate*
dissatisfied
elderly*
emotional
envious
envy
exciting
hospitals*
immoral

improve*
investigate*
media*
natural*
nursing
personalities
practice*
programming*
provide*
reality*
relationship*
replace*
scares
scary
shadowy
stars*
suspenseful
unlimited
viewers
violence*
visual media

Chapter 9

aggressive
arrange*
arranged*
discouraged
discuss*
enthusiastically
feet
fortunately
generations*
guy
inches
interview
match*
mates
optimistic
perfect*
popular*
reply*
socks
speedy*
spouses
worried*

Chapter 10

achievement*
banned
boycott
cancel
compete*
competition*
competitive
conflict*
contribute*
coordination
corrupt
decrease
demonstrations
disqualify
expand
extreme*
fans
international*
intolerable
nondiscriminatory
opposition*
organizations*
original*
profitable*
re-create
solve
sports*

*These words are among the 2,000 most-frequently used words in English.

Skills Index